Campaign Finance Law

Campaign Finance Law

A Comparative Constitutional Analysis Between the US, the UK and Greece

Orestis Omran

eleven

Published, sold and distributed by Eleven
P.O. Box 85576
2508 CG The Hague
The Netherlands
Tel.: +31 70 33 070 33
Fax: +31 70 33 070 30
e-mail: sales@elevenpub.nl
www.elevenpub.com

Sold and distributed in USA and Canada
Independent Publishers Group
814 N. Franklin Street
Chicago, IL 60610
USA
Order Placement: (800) 888-4741
Fax: (312) 337-5985
orders@ipgbook.com
www.ipgbook.com

Eleven is an imprint of Boom uitgevers Den Haag.

ISBN 978-94-6236-219-2
ISBN 978-90-8974-889-8 (E-book)

Table of Contents

Chapter 1 Introduction

1.1 Campaign Finance: The Topic and Its History

It is often said that 'Money is the mother's milk of politics'.[1] This may be conceived of as an explanation not only of the *modus operandi* of the modern campaign finance systems around the world, but also of their very own existence.[2] The influence of big money and special interests in the public policy of the governments of established and new democracies alike, along with the increasing concentration of wealth in fewer parties' and candidates' hands, which may be accompanied by government deregulation, has recently led to a heated debate about the role and operation of modern campaign finance systems.[3]

1.1.1 The Topic: A Definition

Political campaign finance regulation ('campaign finance regulation') may be generally understood as the set of rules, the objective of which is to limit the influence of money on politics,[4] and that regulate the direct and indirect financing of the election campaigns of political parties and candidates alike. An election campaign may in turn be understood as the series of operations designed to bring about the prevailing of a party in an election or the election of a specific candidate to office.

Campaign finance regulation answers questions such as the following: Who can donate money to a political party or candidate for office? How much money can each donor donate? How much money of its own can a party or candidate spend to get elected? What are the formalities that need to be complied with in order to make or receive a legitimate donation? The answers to these questions are given respectively by one of the campaign finance norms, which have been developed over the years to restrict the undue influence of big money in politics: contribution limits, total expenditure limits, prohibition of contributions and expenditures by persons and entities whose participation in the election process presents sufficient potential for corruption, transparency and other reporting obligations are the fundamental campaign finance norms.

1 'Now is the Time for All Good Men', *TIME* (New York, 5 January 1968) 44.
2 Herbert E. Alexander, 'Money and Politics: Rethinking a Conceptual Framework', in Herbert E. Alexander (ed), *Comparative Political Finance in the 1980s* (CUP 1989) 10-12.
3 Justin Fisher and Todd A. Eisenstadt, 'What is to be done' (2004) 10 Party Politics 619, 619.
4 Craig C. Donsanto and Nancy L. Simmons, *Federal Prosecution of Election Offenses*, (7th rev. edn, William S. Hein & Co 2007) 134.

1.1.2 The History

The United States

The historical roots of campaign finance regulation can be traced back to the United States ('U.S.') in the mid 19th century. The first systematic efforts to regulate the financing of political campaigns by law date back to 1867, when Congress passed a law that prohibited federal officers from requesting political contributions in assistance of their campaigns from Navy Yard workers.[5] In 1907, in light of embarrassing accusations that he had promised a French ambassadorship to a senator from New York in exchange for $200,000 in big business campaign donations,[6] then President Theodore Roosevelt, in his State of the Union address, was the first to propose what was essentially a public campaign finance system.[7] The Tillman Act,[8] which was enacted soon after, prohibited corporations and national banks from contributing money directly to presidential or congressional campaigns. The law, which only applied to general elections, was widely flouted through loopholes. It was the first law to attempt to regulate federal campaigns, however there were very few instances when it was actually enforced.

The rest of 20th century was characterized by a number of efforts to regulate federal campaign financing in the United States. The Federal Corrupt Practices Act (1910)[9] and

5 In fact, the first failed attempt to regulate campaign finance came in 1837, when Congressman John Bell of Tennessee, a member of the Whig Party, introduced a bill prohibiting assessments meaning '[A]ny pay or advance by a federal officer toward the election of any public functionary, whether of the general or State Government'. Congress, however, did not vote on it. Robert E. Mutch, 'The First Federal Campaign Finance Bills', in Paula Baker (ed.), *Money and Politic$* (The Pennsylvania State University Press 2002) 35.

6 Kate Pickert, 'Campaign Financing: A brief history' *TIME* (30 June 2008) http://content.time.com/time/nation/article/0,8599,1819288,00.html last accessed 29 October 2019.

7 President Theodore Roosevelt said that 'The need for collecting large campaign funds would vanish if Congress provided ... an appropriation ample enough to meet the necessity for thorough organization and machinery, which requires a large expenditure of money', adding that candidates who took public funds should be required to limit donation amounts and publicly disclose their receipts, ibid.

8 34 Stat. 864.

9 2 U.S.C 431 (36 Stat. 822); this is considered as the first disclosure law; it required House candidates to disclose campaign spending and the source of all campaign contributions.

its various amendments,[10] the Public Utilities Holding Act (1935),[11] the Hatch Act (1939),[12] the Smith Conally Act (1943),[13] and the Taft-Hartley Act (1947)[14] were examples of such attempts. Nevertheless, these laws proved to be inefficient, resulting in a need for a radical reform that would tackle all outstanding issues. In 1971, Congress passed the Federal Election Campaign Act ('FECA'),[15] which repealed the Federal Corrupt Practices Act of 1910[16] and provided for full reporting of campaign contributions and expenditures, but also limited spending on media advertisements by candidates. Congress then amended the FECA in response to the scandals of the Watergate era.[17] The most important goals of the amendment were the implementation of contribution and expenditure limits for congressional and presidential elections, the completion of the partial public financing system for presidential elections and the establishment of the Federal Election Commission ('FEC') as an independent agency to police election practices.[18]

Two years later in its landmark campaign finance decision *Buckley v. Valeo*,[19] the Supreme Court of the U.S. ('SCOTUS') held that the provisions of FECA limiting individual contributions to campaigns were constitutional, despite First Amendment objections; at the same time, while both the partial public finance system for presidential elections and the disclosure requirements were upheld, limitations on expenditures did not pass constitutional muster on First Amendments grounds. *Buckley*

---

10 The Federal Corrupt Practices Act was amended a year later, in 1911, to require also Senate candidates to adhere to certain disclosure rules. In 1925, a further amendment by Congress imposed a total ban on any corporation contribution to a federal campaign, a strict disclosure requirement for all donations greater than $50 and an overall spending limit of $25,000. The amended law was the primary campaign finance instrument under U.S. law, but it remained largely unenforced or bypassed. President Lyndon Johnson described it as more of a loophole than of law. See: Lyndon Johnson, *Statement by the President Upon Signing the Foreign Investors Tax Act and the Presidential Election Fund Act*, 13 November 1966, www.presidency.ucsb.edu/documents/statement-the-president-upon-signing-the-foreign-investors-tax-act-and-the-presidential last accessed 18 October 2019.

11 15 U.S.C. §79; the Public Utilities Holding Act prohibited utilities companies from making contributions to federal campaigns.

12 53 Stat. 1147; the Hatch Act provided for a total ban on contributions to candidates for federal office by employees of the federal government. These employees were also prohibited from publicly expressing political views or participating anyhow in election campaigns.

13 50a U.S.C. § 1501; The Smith Connally Act banned labor unions from contributing to federal campaigns. The historical importance of this ban is considerable: To circumvent the prohibition, labor unions established in 1944 the first political action committees which are considered as the predecessor of future Political Action Committees ('PACs'), an institution that influenced decisively modern U.S. campaign finance legislation and jurisprudence.

14 29 U.S.C. § 141; The Taft-Hartley Act imposed additional prohibitions on federal contributions by unions, banks and corporations.

15 2 U.S.C. § 431 (86 Stat. 3).

16 Supra n 10.

17 Jason B. Frasco, 'Full Public Funding: An effective and legally viable model for campaign finance reform in the states' (2007) 92 Cornell L. Rev. 733, 737.

18 Ibid.

19 *Buckley v. Valeo*, 424 U.S. 1 (1976) (*per curiam*).

has ever since been the cornerstone of the campaign finance framework in the United States.[20] In 2002, Congress passed the Bipartisan Campaign Reform Act ('BCRA')[21] which attempted to limit the influence of political money by banning 'soft money' contributions to party organizations and restricting the ability of corporations to fund electioneering communications. 'Soft money' refers to funds given to parties for purposes other than supporting candidates for federal office and thus remained outside the scope of the FECA.[22] This is essentially the latest fundamental instrument that addressed campaign finance in the U.S. Campaign finance law has been ever since judge-made to a great extent.

The SCOTUS in the *Citizens United* case[23] ruled that the government may not, under the First Amendment, suppress political speech on the basis of the speaker's corporate identity[24] and that the provision of the Act which barred independent corporate expenditures for electioneering communications violated the First Amendment.[25] The most recent example of SCOTUS' jurisprudence that seems to substantially affect the campaign finance landscape in the U.S. is *McCutcheon v. FEC*,[26] which ruled that aggregate contribution limits do not survive First Amendment scrutiny - partially overruling *Buckley*.[27]

Europe

In Europe, the evolution of campaign finance law is more recent. Campaign finance regulation did not exist until three decades ago in many European Union ('E.U.') jurisdictions, and only recently the Committee of Ministers of the Council of Europe recognized that it is '[C]onvinced that raising public awareness on the issues of

20 J. Robert Abraham, 'Saving Buckley: Creating a Stable Campaign Finance Framework' (2010) 110 Colum. L. Rev. 1078.

21 116 Stat. 81 *thru* 116 Stat. 116.

22 See Chapter 3, Section 3.2.1

23 *Citizens United v. FEC*, 558 U.S. 310 (2010).

24 With this decision, the Supreme Court overruled *Austin v. Michigan Chamber of Commerce*, 494 U.S. 652 (1990). In the majority decision, Justice Anthony Kennedy said: '*We now conclude that independent expenditures, including those made by corporations, do not give rise to corruption or the appearance of corruption.*'

25 Overruling *McConnell v. FEC*, 540 U.S. 93 (2003).

26 McCutcheon v. Federal Election Commission, 572 U.S. ___ (2014), docket no 12-536.

27 The Court held that, because aggregate limits restricting how much money a donor may contribute to candidates for federal office, political parties, and political action committees do not further the government's interest in preventing quid pro quo corruption or the appearance of such corruption, while at the same time seriously restricting participation in the democratic process, they are invalid under the First Amendment. The limit had been a total of $48,600 every two years for all federal candidates and an aggregate of $74,600 to political parties and committees. In comments before reading his dissenting opinion on the bench, Justice Stephen G. Breyer (joined by Justice Ginsburg, Justice Sotomayor and Justice Kagan) stated that: 'If *Citizens United* opened a door, today's decision we fear will open a *floodgate*'.

prevention and fight against corruption in the field of funding of political parties is essential to the good functioning of democratic institutions.'[28] Nevertheless, the legal developments on the campaign finance sphere in most E.U. jurisdictions have been modestly slow and definitely slower than in the U.S. This different pace is due to a number of structural and institutional reasons, which this book will touch upon in more detail in subsequent chapters.

France

Until relatively recently, regulating campaign financing was clearly not one of the top priorities of the French legislature, although reforms had been discussed.[29] It was only in 1988[30] that the executive and legislature, under the pressure of numerous scandals started to issue laws and decrees relating to the funding of political parties and election campaigns.[31] French campaign finance law is characterized by strict regulations which include substantial limitations in contributions and expenditure, a total ban of corporate contributions to political parties and candidates along with direct[32] and indirect[33] public financing.

Germany

In Germany, a structured public campaign finance system securing public funds for all major parties has existed since 1958.[34] The constitutional justifications of the system are thought to be linked with the division of powers under the German Constitution of 1949. The German system is characterized by the dominant institutional role of parties. There are no limits on the amounts that individuals or corporations may contribute and the regulation regime relies almost completely on disclosure rules, with many restrictions regarding the origin of contributions (for instance, donations from public entities, local councils and charitable organizations are traditionally prohibited).[35] Campaign finance

28 Quoted in Magnus Öhman and Hani Zainulbhai, *Political Finance Regulation: The Global Experience* (International Foundation for Electoral Systems 2009) 17.

29 For a comprehensive analysis of French campaign finance law, see the relevant section on the website of the Library of the Congress www.loc.gov/law/help/campaign-finance/france.php last accessed 18 October 2019.

30 Loi 88-227 du 11 mars 1988 relative à la transparence financière de la vie politique, J.O., 12 Mar. 1988, p. 3290.

31 Véronique Pujas and Martin Rhodes, 'Party Finance and Political Scandal in Italy, Spain, and France' (1999) 22 West Eur. Politics 41.

32 Reimbursement of 50% of the campaign expenditure permitted by the law. For total expenditure limits, see Loi 90-55 du 15 janvier 1990 relative à la limitation des dépenses électorales et à la clarification du financement des activités, J.O., 16 Jan. 1990, 639.

33 For example, free access to public television and radio for political advertisements is provided during the election period.

34 All parties that have obtained 0.5 percent of the vote in the latest national or European election, or one percent in the latest state election in one of the German states, are granted public funding.

35 Thomas Grant, *Lobbying, Government Relations and Campaign Finance Worldwide* (Oceana Publications 2005) 127.

law and accountability requirements focus on the party, not the individual candidate, due to the mixed member proportional representation election system.[36] Parties annually receive public funds according to the number of votes received in the latest European, federal and state election as well as proportionately to the income they derive from member fees and donations.[37]

The United Kingdom

In the United Kingdom ('U.K.'), the first law that dealt with campaign finance issues was the Corrupt and Illegal Practices Prevention Act 1883. Together with the Election Petitions and Corrupt Practices Act 1868 and the Ballot Act 1872, this Act establishes the Statutory Foundations of the pre-2000 party political funding and campaign finance in the U.K.[38] The 1883 Act placed a rather burdensome limit on election expenditure at the constituency level, which if exceeded – or if 'expenditure returns' were improperly filed – could lead even to the voiding of an election result.[39] Nevertheless, the legislation was characterized by a considerable gap: The expenditure limits could be circumvented if incurred by a third party on behalf of a candidate. The loophole was closed by the Representation of the People Act 1918, which prohibited third parties from incurring expenses above a very low limit[40] with a view of achieving the election of a candidate in office, without the consent of the candidate.[41] This Act however did not manage to close another loophole, namely the application of expenditure limits only at the constituency (local) level and not at a national level. As early as 1880, the legislature could not have predicted the shift from local to national campaigning and the importance that the latter were to gain in elections for government. It took a few decades and the intervention of the judiciary in *R v. Tronoh Mines Ltd*[42] to address the ineffectiveness of expenditure limits at the constituency level by ruling that the limits were not applicable to expenditure incurred to support one party generally at all constituencies; the limits were to the contrary imposed only to expenditure incurred to support a specific candidate at a particular constituency.

The rest of the 20th century came without any serious legislative effort to regulate electoral campaign financing other than the 1983 Representation of the People Act, which, in line with pre-existing legislation, provided for strict expenditure limits. The

36 For a detailed analysis of the proportional representation system see Jacques De Ville and F. Chohan-Khota, 'What Is a System of Proportional Representation' (1996) 113 S. Afr. Law J. 400.

37 Grant T. (n 35) 128-129.

38 Ghalleigh Navraj Singh, 'Expenditure, Donations and Public Funding under the United Kingdom's Political Parties, Elections and Referendums Act 2000 - And Beyond?', in KD Ewing and Samuel Issacharoff (eds), *Party Funding and Campaign Financing in International Perspective* (Hart Publishing 2006) 35.

39 Ibid. 36-37.

40 Roughly the equivalent of GBP 5 in 1983 prices, which was also the amount set by subsection 75 (1) under the Representation of the People Act 1983 as amended by the Representation of the People Act 1985.

41 Singh (n 38) 37.

42 *R v. Tronoh Mines Ltd* [1951] 1 All ER 697.

1990s were characterized by broader public discontent about the absence of a standalone robust campaign finance regulatory system which resulted in the establishment in 1994 of the Committee on Standards in Public Life (originally known as 'the Nolan Committee' from Lord Nolan, who was its first Chairman) to advise the Prime Minister on ethical standards of public life; the committee, however, was not allowed to touch upon party finances. In 1997, the public was stunned when hearing about potential *quid pro quo* campaign donations[43] and demanded from the legislature the passing of legislation adequate to introduce more transparency in the funding of both political parties and candidates and establish an effective campaign finance regulatory system. The expansion of the terms of reference of the Nolan Committee to cover political parties financing and its subsequent reports led eventually to the adoption of a new law, the Political Parties, Elections and Referendums Act 2000 ('PPERA')[44] that changed completely campaign finance regulation in the U.K. to such an extent that scholars have adopted a division between pre-PPERA and post-PPERA framework when analyzing the relevant aspects of U.K. campaign finance.[45]

The PPERA introduced massive reforms in literally every aspect of campaign finance regulation in the U.K.: Strict disclosure and reporting requirements for political parties and individual candidates for office, limiting the list of permitted donors, expenditure caps for parties at the national level and the establishment of the Electoral Commission as the body to ensure rigid enforcement of the new provisions.[46] The PPERA, as amended, is until today the core instrument defining U.K. campaign finance law.

Central, Eastern and Southern Europe

In Central, Eastern and Southern Europe, the history of campaign finance laws is more recent and is closely linked to institutional changes of greater magnitude that also defined their recent constitutional history. In Greece, for example, the military dictatorship that ruled the country between 1967 and 1974 defined the country's modern democratic history. The 1975 Constitution that sealed the transition to democracy included specific provisions on the institutional role of parties[47] in the political system as well as the conditions for their public and private financing, the relevant transparency requirements and the enforcement mechanisms.[48] The Constitution left it up to the

43 See the Formula One scandal in November 1997, where Tony Blair's government's announcement that Formula One would be exempt from a ban on sponsorship by tobacco companies was deemed as a return for Bernie Ecclestone's – leading figure in the racing world – donation of GBP 1,000,000 to the Labour Party. For a detailed analysis see: Alan Grant, 'Party and Election Finance in Britain and America: A Comparative Analysis' (2005) 58 Parliam. Aff. 71.

44 Political Parties, Elections and Referendums Act 2000 (c. 41).

45 For the relevant division and a full analysis of the pre-PPERA system, see KD Ewing, *The Funding of Political Parties in Britain* (CUP 1987).

46 Grant A. (n 43) 77.

47 See Article 29 para 1 of the 1975 Greek Constitution.

48 See Article 29 para 2 of the 1975 Greek Constitution, amended in 2001 and as such until today.

parliamentary legislature to determine the specifics of the new system, while it established discretion of the legislator to provide for public financing of the political parties, which became an *expressis verbis* right of the political parties to claim public financing after the 2001 Constitutional Revision .[49]

Law 1443/1984 was the first to execute the constitutional mandate for a campaign finance law. It introduced what was essentially a public campaign finance system in the country, determining the terms and conditions of the disbursement of public funds in favor of political parties, introducing also certain transparency requirements such as mandatory audits and book keeping.[50] Law 1443/1984 played an important role in the distribution of public funds during the particularly politically turbulent period between 1989 and 1990, which was characterized by consecutive elections (three elections between June 1989 and April 1990) due to the inability to form a stable governmental majority.

Nevertheless, Law 1443/1984 was deemed as only partially dealing with the issue of campaign financing and was definitely insufficient in securing the necessary transparency at a period when the public demanded legislative action against phenomena of severe corruption in the public sphere. Law 2429/1996 came to replace the previous unsatisfactory framework by introducing a number of novelties such as the distinction between regular and election public funding,[51] explicit prohibitions during the pre-election period, maximum expenditure and contribution limits at both the party and the candidate level and the establishment of a bipartisan committee[52] that would enforce the law, in particular with regard to reporting and other disclosure requirements.

The current legislative framework consists of Law 3023/2002,[53] which was introduced only a few years later to cover loopholes of Law 2429, which was considered a relatively successful law. The new provisions clarify further the conditions for the receipt of regular and election public funding by political parties, regulate areas of campaign finance such as the free airtime during election periods for political parties,[54] introduce strict donation limits, regulate other forms of indirect public funding such as public space for pre-electoral gatherings and advertising,[55] refer to the disclosure of the parties accounts to

49 Αθανάσιος Γ. Ξηρός, *Ζητήματα Δικαίου των Πολιτικών Κομμάτων* (Αντ. Ν. Σάκκουλας 2010) 291.

50 See Article 1 to 7 of Law 1443/1984 (Officially: Financial Support of Political Parties and Other Provisions), ΦΕΚ Α΄ 73, 1984 (that is #73 of Volume 1 of the Official Journal of the Government of 1984).

51 Already in Article 1, para 2 of Law 2429/1996 (Officially: Political Parties Financing - Disclosure and Monitoring of Political Parties' Finances and Candidates to Parliament - Asset Declaration of Political and Civil Functionaries, Mass Media and Press Owners and Other Categories of Persons, and Other Provisions), ΦΕΚ Α΄ 155, 1996.

52 Ibid. Articles 19 and 33.

53 Law 3023/2002 (Officially: Political Parties Financing by the State. Revenues and Expenses, Publicity, Disclosure and Monitoring of Political Parties' Finances and Candidates to the Parliament), ΦΕΚ Α΄ 146, 2002.

54 These issues had been regulated by special laws until then, complicating the overall framework, and allowing for various circumventions increasing public distrust.

55 See Law 3023/2002, Articles 9-14.

ensure the provisions of adequate information to the public[56] and establish the Control Commission as the enforcement agency of the legislation.[57]

In Spain, where democracy was restored a little bit later than in Greece, in 1978 (after the death of the dictator Franco, who had ruled the country for almost forty years), it is surprising that the pre-constitution law of 21/ 1976, the first organized effort to regulate campaign financing, is still valid, as amended, until today.[58] The law provided for reimbursement of electoral expenses under certain conditions. Amended in 1978,[59] 1985,[60] 1987,[61] and 2002,[62] the law provides today extensive coverage of a number of campaign finance issues creating what is essentially a public campaign finance system.

The history of campaign finance regulation is even more recent in the former Communist countries of Central and Eastern Europe. These countries adopted liberal regulations that were a natural response to the former communist system,[63] but also because they constitute laboratories of institutional experimentation in comparison to the wealthier democracies of Western Europe which introduced regulations in order to generate important institutional or behavioral instruments to restrain the excessive influence of money on politics.[64] In the beginning of the 1990s, direct public subsidies for political parties had already become a dominant feature of most democracies, being used in 78 percent of Central Eastern European countries.[65] For most of the post communist countries, public funding of parties and candidates (either in the form of reimbursement of electoral expenditures, or annual subventions) has been the only effort to control the sources of political money and decrease the influence of private interests in politics.[66] Indirect public funding includes free airtime during election periods.[67] Countries, the legislation of which does not provide for some kind of public

56 Ibid. Articles 15-20.
57 Ibid. Article 21.
58 Grant T. (n 35) 452-453.
59 By Ley 39/1978 and Ley 54/1978.
60 By Ley Organica 5/1985.
61 By Ley Organica 7/1987.
62 By Ley Organica 1/2003.
63 Jānis Ikstens, Daniel Smilov and Marcin Walecki, 'Campaign Finance in Central and Eastern Europe: Lessons Learned and Challenges Ahead' (International Foundation for Election Systems 2002) 9.
64 Jānis Ikstens, Daniel Smilov and Marcin Walecki, 'Party and Campaign Funding in Eastern Europe: A Study of 18 Member Countries of the ACEEEO' (Paper Presented at the ACEEEO Annual Conference 'Transparent Election Campaigns in the 21st Century' held in Brijuni, Croatia, 2001) 13.
65 Ibid. 6.
66 Ibid.
67 However, only Bosnia-Herzegovina and Slovakia completely ban paid political advertisements. See ibid.; also Ikstens, Smilov & Walecki 2002 (n 61) 12.

campaign finance, for example Latvia, Moldova and Ukraine,[68] have a much higher index of 'buying of legislative votes'.[69]

1.2 Fundamental Rationales of Campaign Finance Regulation

There are two fundamental rationales of campaign finance regulation that are usually cited by modern jurisprudence and scholarship:[70] i) Tackling political corruption; ii) Promoting equality in its various forms. On the one hand, it may be considered that the *dictum* of *Buckley*, often repeated by the SCOTUS, pursuant to which '[P]reventing corruption or the appearance of corruption are the only legitimate and compelling government interests thus far identified for restricting campaign finances'[71] adequately describes the fundamental choices of many campaign finance systems in the world. Corruption, perceived of as the misuse of public office for private gain,[72] has been closely associated with elections for the central government and other local *officia* in modern democracies. Paying off the voters to get elected or buying the vote by promising favors linked to the *officium* sought after the election has been identified as a common institutional problem of many democratic systems and its prevention thereof has been identified at least by the SCOTUS as sufficient to restrict the constitutionally established freedom of speech.[73] On the other hand, equality is placed on the background of many national campaign finance systems. There, the legislature strives to establish a level playing field between candidates for office by eliminating or at least restricting the advantage that certain candidates' strong financial capabilities, access to donors and the media might give them in the political race. Equality may also lie at the basis of the limits on donations to political candidates by individuals provided by law: wealthy citizens should not be able to influence the outcome of an election more than other less wealthy

---

68 For an overview of the campaign finance system in Ukraine see Oleh Protsyk, 'Campaign and Party Finance in Ukraine: Dilemmas of Regulation in the Context of Weakly Institutionalized Political and Legal Systems' (International Foundation for Election Systems 2002).

69 See *Anti-corruption in Transition: A Contribution to the Policy Debate* (World Bank 2000).

70 David Strauss, 'Corruption, Equality and Campaign Finance Reform' (1994) 94 Colum. L.Rev. 1369.

71 As outlined in *FEC v. National Conservative Political Action Committee*, 470 U.S. 496-497 (1985).

72 Definition of corruption given by the World Bank. Other definitions given include the following: '[A]n illegal payment to a public agent to obtain a benefit that may or may not be deserved in the absence of pay offs', see Susan Rose-Ackerman, 'When Is Corruption Harmful?', in Arnold J. Heidenheimer and Michael Johnston (eds), *Political Corruption: Concepts & Contexts* (3rd edn, Routledge 2017) 353, or '[T]he sale by government officials of government property for private gain', see Andrei Schleifer and Robert W. Vishny, 'Corruption' (1993) 108 Q. J. Econ. 599. The definition of corruption is further examined in Chapter 2.

73 The Court in *Buckley* ruled that: '[T]he concept that government may restrict the speech of some elements of our society in order to enhance the relative voice of others is wholly foreign to the First Amendment. . .', *Buckley* (n 19) 48-49. See also J. Skelly Wright, 'Money and the Pollution of Politics: Is the First Amendment an Obstacle to Political Equality?' (1982) 82 Colum. L. Rev. 609.

citizens. Of course this opens the discussion about the relationship between equality and freedom of speech.[74]

Other constitutional principles may also play a role when structuring campaign finance regulation. Transparency is certainly one of those. In a democracy, the public has a vested interest in having access to the financial data of political candidates, the names of donors and the amounts of donations that such candidates may receive; this is because they need to select their representatives in full knowledge of their financial resources and of the undue influence that such resources may play on their decision making, if elected. Democratic inclusion is also a principle that modern democracies aim to safeguard.[75] All citizens shall feel useful for the democratic system; exclusions from office or from supporting any representative because of someone's limited financial resources or connections harm one of the very essences of a democracy: the unlimited constituent power of the people.[76]

All these are analyzed in detail in Chapter 2 and will be revisited in other Chapters when looking at the particulars of the country specific case studies.

1.2.1 Scope of the Present Project

This project aims to answer the question what principles and objectives of campaign finance regulation can be identified. What are the common and different constitutional approaches in achieving these principles and objectives?

This aim is pursued through a comparative analysis and criticism of the constitutional aspects of current campaign finance legislation in the United States, the United Kingdom and Greece. By using those three *prima facie* different country specific case studies,[77] I aim at identifying the common and different constitutional approaches in establishing a level playing field amongst political parties and candidates alike or fighting political corruption via the establishment and operation of campaign finance systems.

By identifying the role played by supreme courts in leveling the ground in elections for office or preventing political corruption in the different constitutional cultures of the three country specific case studies and the constitutional principles these courts used in their reasoning, and by discussing direct and indirect public funding of political

74 For a comprehensive analysis of this relationship in campaign finance see Jean A. Luckowski and James J. Lopach, 'Freedom versus Equality in Campaign Finance Reform' (2002) 93 The Social Studies 124.

75 See the interesting questions posed, admittedly from a U.S. perspective, by David T. Canon, 'The Representation of Racial Interests in the U.S. Congress', in Christina Wolbrecht and Rodney E. Hero (eds), *The Politics of Democratic Inclusion* (Temple University Press 2005) 303-304.

76 Wilhelm Hasbach, 'The Essence of Democracy' (1915) 9 Am. Political Sci. Rev. 50.

77 Despite certain similarities, the three countries differ significantly not only in terms of historical and constitutional origins of their campaign finance systems but also on other important issues, such as the organization of the government, the competences of their fundamental institutions and the role of public and private funds in elections.

campaigns versus private campaign financing, in conjunction with the efficiency of campaign finance enforcement and supervisory mechanisms, this project will outline the different priorities and choices of the legislature when shaping campaign finance regulation in each jurisdiction and demonstrate explanations of such priorities and options, with a view of drawing some more universal conclusions about modern campaign finance regulation. The analysis of supreme courts' case-law[78] shall offer valuable insight into the judiciary's effort to level the ground in elections for office or prevent political corruption in the different constitutional cultures of the three country specific case studies and the constitutional principles these courts used in their reasoning. For what is after all a constitutional law discourse, case law (or lack thereof) is going to be the prime research material to determine the interaction of the regulatory with the wider constitutional framework and its principles, as supreme courts are in an institutionally unique position to determine the exact content of such principles, often both abstract and vague.

1.2.2 Research Questions

Through the use of three different country specific case studies, this project aims at answering the question what principles and objectives of campaign finance regulation can be identified, and what the common and different constitutional approaches in achieving these principles and objectives are in the three selected jurisdictions.

Prior to proceeding with a more substantive analysis of constitutional principles per jurisdiction, **Chapter 2** engages in analyzing those principles that are recognized as lying behind the various segments of campaign finance regulatory frameworks. This provides the reader with an understanding of the institutional context within which regulation takes place. A closer systematic look into political equality and corruption as the fundamental rationales of campaign finance regulation - and their interplay with freedom of speech - together with a comprehensive analysis of ancillary, yet important, principles such as transparency and democratic inclusion shall complete the theoretical background of this study. **Chapter 2** will also provide more insight into the country selection exercise and demonstrate how the specific choice of jurisdictions vis-à-vis the specific theoretical background serves the purpose of answering this study's central research question. A broader attempt is also made to establish a novel typology of campaign finance systems based on legal and factual elements. Such typology helps to better understand the different choices of the regulatory frameworks under examination

78 Supreme courts' judgments are useful because they demonstrate the very constitutional principles to which this or the other choice of the legislature should correspond and based on which they undergo judicial review. In some countries, the most radical campaign finance breakthroughs that lead to partial or complete reform were based on relevant Supreme Courts judgments.

and adds an additional perspective to the relationship between the rather abstract constitutional principles of the main research question with the realities of campaign financing.

By an in-depth analysis of legislation and jurisprudence in each jurisdiction, four issues, the discussion of which help answering the central research question, are addressed.

First comes the role of public and private campaign finance norms in eliminating political corruption. **Chapter 3**, focusing on the campaign finance regulatory system of the U.S. at the federal level, includes a systematic analysis of the jurisprudence of the SCOTUS and reveals the central role that corruption plays in the judicial review - and legislation - in the U.S.

Second, the importance of the right to equality for the adoption and revision of legislation targeted at establishing a level playing field for political parties and candidates is assessed. Campaign finance regulation is often thought to aim at establishing a level playing field between candidates and parties in the elections. However, certain restrictions, especially those imposing a cap on the total expenditure during campaigns, may *ab initio* violate the constitutionally established right of freedom of speech, while others, such as the provision of free air time only to certain political parties before general elections, may violate the constitutional right of equality. These concerns will become more evident in **Chapters 4 and 5**, which address the legislation and jurisprudence in the U.K. and Greece respectively. The effort to uphold the constitutionally established principle of equality is evident in both jurisdictions' regulatory frameworks; however, the way such a principle is viewed by Courts and regulatory authorities, especially when it interplays with corruption[79] or the freedom of speech, shall help us draw conclusions about the broader role of equality in campaign finance.

Third is the role of campaign finance control mechanisms, which is examined in order to determine how national campaign finance legislation in the three jurisdictions achieves compliance and how they contribute to realizing the underlying rationales and principles. This theme deals with the supervisory and enforcement system that each examined national campaign finance legislation provides to achieve compliance. The respective country studies in **Chapters 3, 4 and 5** analyze the concerned supervisory mechanisms with a particular focus on their structure, the breadth of their competence and the links they may have with the legislative or the executive branch and how such links influence their effectiveness.

For each of the three jurisdictions, the effectiveness of tackling political corruption is analyzed using the Third Evaluation Round of the Group of States against Corruption of

79 See Strauss 1994 (n 70) 1371-1375, where he argues that political corruption is in fact a derivative problem, which would have been resolved, were the problem of inequality solved first.

the Council of Europe ('GRECO') on a per country basis in **Chapters 3, 4 and 5**, bearing always in mind the assessment of the value of its evaluations at the end of **Chapter 2**.

The ability of control authorities to trace and prosecute breaches of campaign finance legislation is thought to be directly linked with the principle of transparency whose establishment and enforcement enhances trust showed by the citizenry to modern democracies. This is related to the fourth and broader issue of the future of campaign finance: Shall campaign finance reform on both the regulatory and the enforcement side become a means of establishing a better democracy?

Chapter 6 engages in a comparative assessment of the three campaign finance regulatory systems. This will help understand the different approaches to the regulation of all three branches of power in each jurisdiction, and will thus contribute to answering the main research question, namely what the common and different constitutional approaches are in achieving the respective principles and objectives of the three selected jurisdictions, while providing a broader perspective to the relevant judicial or legislative balancing exercise. Finally, **Chapter 7** will include concluding remarks while opening the discussion about the identification of universal Dos and Do-Nots for campaign finance regulation.

1.3 Choice of Jurisdictions and Research Techniques

In trying to identify the key institutional concepts related to campaign finance regulation prior to laying the foundations for a comparative project, facts and data from various countries were reviewed including from the U.S., Canada, Germany, France, Spain, Brazil and the former Communist countries of Central and Eastern Europe. Such analysis is essential when dealing with the global dimension of campaign finance regulation. However, as already mentioned, this project focuses on three specific jurisdictions, namely the U.S., the U.K. and Greece. Obviously, going at any reasonable depth into the intricacies of campaign finance regulation to produce some comparative value necessitated a considerable reduction of the subject jurisdictions, in this case down to only three. Below, the main reasons behind the specific country selection shall be explained.

The author's intention was for the choice of jurisdictions to be two pronged. First, all jurisdictions needed to present a minimum set of characteristics that would allow research objectivity, thoroughness and data reliability within the specific topic. Second, the regulatory framework of each jurisdiction needed to reflect some of the major institutional principles analyzed in **Chapter 2**, which would help answer the main research question of this study.

The first prerequisite was for such jurisdiction to present existing and functional democratic institutions. As election campaigning and its financing thereof are inextricably linked with the democratic process, choosing to study the relevant regulation in a country where such a process is highly problematical, or even practically non-existent, would result in a travesty of the research proportional to the travesty of democratic institutions in such a jurisdiction. The democratic institutions in the country to be examined did not have to be amongst the strongest or the oldest (although a certain period of stable democratic governance was deemed helpful, allowing for better conclusions after the dust had settled), nor did they have to be the most extensive; for comparative purposes, it would be best if at least in some of the jurisdictions to be examined that was not actually the case. Variety helps comparison. The second prerequisite was for the countries selected to present a depth of campaign finance regulation, institutional history and jurisprudence – not necessarily with a proportional division between such elements – to allow for a reliable comparative assessment to take place.

As already briefly mentioned and is further analyzed in **Chapter 3**, the U.S. has if not the longest and richest, then certainly one amongst the longest and richest histories in campaign finance regulation and related litigation and jurisprudence. The speed with which this country's democratic institutions emerged and developed in the 19th century went hand in hand with a flourishing economy, highlighting more than ever the relationship between money and power. Such relationship is even today debated in the context of the presidential democracy that is thought to affect the entire planet. Regulation in the U.S. came relatively late; nevertheless, it was one of the first relevant regulatory frameworks in the world. For that reason alone, the U.S. would make a very good example and could serve as the yardstick for the other jurisdictions. However, as one becomes engaged in studying U.S. constitutional law, and not just campaign finance regulation, one cannot help but notice a very strong sense of exceptionalism permeating it; perhaps this is not something restricted in constitutional law, but exceptionalism in this specific field is certainly the case. It was, therefore, somehow unavoidable, if not *per se* pursued, to use the U.S. as one of this study's selections for comparison, to test the outer boundaries of this specific field of law.

At a first level of analysis, it would be interesting to compare the U.S. with another common law jurisdiction, although of a different background, to test this historical and constitutional exceptionalism. The U.K. emerged as the best candidate, as its position within the European Union (Brexit being unheard of at the time the present study was contemplated) and the Council of Europe meant that, not only was its legal system under influence from civil law jurisdictions, but that the jurisdiction of the European Court of Human Rights (and to a lesser extent the European Court of Justice) over cases brought before the courts of law of the U.K. could offer further insight into the interaction of a common law system with a majority of civil law judges. Moreover, the focus of the U.K. on principles such as equality, transparency and inclusion, as opposed to the corruption-centered U.S. approach, offered good comparative grounds for an analysis of the institutional choices of yet a common law legislature.

There remained, however, the need for a third jurisdiction to test against the other two. Greece was perceived to be a very good candidate: it is a civil law jurisdiction (and in fact highly influenced by the German legal system), with a relatively short, yet long enough, stable democracy, and a record in the various corruption indices not as good as that of either the U.S. or the U.K., fulfilling the role of a jurisdiction with not so old, strong or extensive institutions. Moreover, the Greek legislature approach seems to be focused extensively on the establishment of a level playing field amongst political parties and candidates, while its judiciary has engaged in a balancing exercise of applicable principles such as freedom of speech. That is another good reason for choosing Greece, as its example could comparatively fit the perspective form which this study deals with campaign finance. Last, but not least, the author, having Greek as his mother tongue and a background in Greek law, would be able to research deeper than for example if the case study chosen was that of another EU jurisdiction with a similar background.[80]

To achieve the comparative assessment, a complete review of the available legislation, literature, scholarship and jurisprudence was conducted. All the available scientific documents on campaign finance and its constitutional repercussions, various research papers and publications, case reports, legislation and treaties, international soft law as well as all the available statistical data were consulted in this study. In this regard, accessing legal databases on the Internet has been very useful and contributed to a systematic review. Apart from the qualitative techniques described above, a study on quantitative information was conducted, where available. More specifically, statistical data analysis was used, tailored to the needs of this study in order to make useful conclusions regarding the operation of campaign finance at a universal level.

1.4 ACADEMIC AND SOCIAL RELEVANCE

Although there is seemingly lots of scholarship addressing many of the issues which this project aims at examining, there is currently rather limited scholarship on the interplay between campaign finance regulation and certain constitutional principles, let alone a

80 This is not a negligible advantage, as the analysis of GRECO reports on Greece in Chapter 5 will demonstrate; their authors failed in many cases to overcome the language barrier and penetrate into the legal details of several of the provisions they were evaluating.

comparative study in the constitutional sphere as the one suggested by the present study.[81]

Dealing with an issue that lies within the fundamentals of the operation of modern democracies, namely the financing of political parties and candidates, the final product of the suggested research, which is summarized in **Chapter 7**, will contain a systematic and comparative overview of three different though representative campaign finance systems and provide valuable conclusions of a universal character to constitutional law scholars and students with regard to the constitutional aspect of public and private campaign finance norms. A thorough analysis of the results of judicial review will seek to address some so far unanswered questions, including the identification of the factors that influence the legislature and the courts of each jurisdiction in making a choice between reducing corruption, establishing a level playing field between candidates and parties and protecting free speech when drafting or reviewing campaign finance regulation; these results of the examination of each of the three countries will be compared in **Chapter 6** to reach valuable conclusions in **Chapter 7**.

In addition, existing public and private campaign finance norms will be tested in order to assess – to the extent possible – whether the imposition of restrictions or limitations on private contributions manages to prevent corruption or the appearance of corruption in the pre and post electoral process. Moreover, there is limited analysis in the current scholarship about the importance of the operation of supervisory bodies in the establishment of a level playing field between political parties and candidates alike and the prevention or elimination of corruption amongst the political personnel,[82] and the examination and comparison of the competent bodies of the three jurisdictions will be of considerable value on its own.

In addition, the current research project examines three facets of high social relevance vis-à-vis campaign finance: equality, democratic inclusion and institutional corruption.

First, the study looks at the normative value of equality in political campaigning and identifies how supreme courts and the legislature – in at least two of the jurisdictions of focus – strive to provide equal opportunities to political candidates and voters to be

---

81 Comparative Constitutional Law manuals due to the broad characters of the topics they need to cover, do not address the issue of campaign finance in great extent or address the issue in brief and in the context of other topics such as that of political parties. See for example: Richard H. Pildes, 'Political Parties and Constitutionalism', in Tom Ginsburg and Rosalind Dixon, *Comparative Constitutional Law* (Edward Elgar 2010) 254-264.

82 Current scholarship usually focuses on the general functions of these bodies and with issues relevant to the appointment of their members, e.g. partisan appointments, however few go as overall as making the link between their decisions and their effects in eliminating corruption in politics.

elected and affect the outcome of elections respectively. Moreover, it will focus on all three countries, using specific examples and shedding light on the caveats that hamper the democratic organization of societies. For example, social injustice, as reflected in the lack of, or inadequate, representation in democratic institutions,[83] is a pressing social problem that merits analysis in the present study. Certain social classes are practically excluded from democratic participation, which defeats the whole essence of democracy and relates to instances of institutional corruption. Both equality and democratic inclusion are naturally reflective of social importance, and their significance in framing the constitutional framework of campaign finance regulation in each of the three jurisdictions will be assessed.

Further, the corrupting influence of big money in politics is, indubitably, a severe pathogeny of modern democratic states. Institutional corruption, generally perceived of as the misuse of public power for private gain[84] – under which political corruption would certainly fall – and private corruption as the misuse of any entrusted power for the same purpose,[85] are just the two sides of the same coin. By addressing illegitimate campaign contributions and other corrupt practices during elections, this project will deal directly with the universal fight against corruption, contributing to the elimination of *quid pro quo* political corruption. Ultimately, the project aspires to approach a provide some basic guidelines for a sustainable regulatory reform that will achieve better democratic governance at the macro-institutional level, and will tackle corruption at the micro-social one.

When all is said and done, campaign finance considerably influences who will win an election, since empirical evidence suggests a strong correlation between party donation and chances of winning.[86] It is imperative to explore this, yet undiscovered, topic of

83 For a conceptual analysis of democracy and its links to social injustice, see Robin Luckham, Anne Marie Goetz and Mary Kaldor, 'Democratic Institutions and Politics in Context of Inequality, Poverty and Conflict' (1998) Institute of Development Studies Working Paper 104 https://opendocs.ids.ac.uk/opendocs/bitstream/handle/20.500.12413/3434/Wp104.pdf?sequence=1&isAllowed=y last accessed 18 October 2019.

84 See Lawrence Lessig, 'Foreword: 'Institutional Corruption' Defined' (2013) 41 J. Law Med. Ethics, where the author argues that institutional corruption is manifest when there is a systemic and strategic influence which is legal, or even currently ethical, that undermines the institution's effectiveness by diverting it from its purpose or weakening its ability to achieve its purpose, including, to the extent relevant to its purpose, weakening either the public's trust in that institution or the institution's inherent trustworthiness.

85 See Council Framework Decision 2003/568/JHA of 22 July 2003by the Council of the EU on combating corruption in the private sector.

86 See Wesley Lowery, '91% of the time the better-financed candidate wins. Don't act surprised' *The Washington Post* (Washington, D.C., April 4, 2014), and the chart included therein. In the U.S. over the last twenty years (since 2000) success in the House of Representatives and Senate elections went as a rule to candidates who overspent their opponents at almost 85% of the cases; in the 2006 Senate election the win rate of better-financed candidates was 'only' 72.7%, while in the 2004 House election it peaked at 97.5%. The win rate of better-financed candidates in the 2018 elections was 82.9% for the Senate and 88.8% for the House of Representatives, Center for Responsive Politics, 'Did Money Win?', OpenSecrets.org www.opensecrets.org/elections-overview/did-money-win last accessed 3 March 2019.

scholarly debate and pave the path of regulatory reforms towards transparency, openness and accountability. The value of the project rests in its wide scope, its original methodological input, and its practical interaction with societal concerns. It is a topic that exhibits high social relevance with perhaps the most pressing issue globally, that being the very essence of modern democracy.

Chapter 2 The Constitutional Framework of Campaign Finance Regulation: Fundamental Principles

Before examining campaign finance regulation in the three jurisdictions concerned in this project, it is important to lay the groundwork necessary for such a task. Certain fundamental concepts and principles, which have served (or may serve) as the rationale of such regulation and thus shaped the institutional framework, within which the discussion takes place, are briefly explored. The examined principles have been the stated objectives of campaign finance regulation or have been proposed to serve as such; a basic grasp of them is thus necessary to better understand the choices made by the legislative, executive and judicial branches of the three jurisdictions. Furthermore, a classification of the campaign finance regulatory systems on the basis of the source of the funds aims at the same target, namely achieving a better understanding of the issues to be discussed in the following Chapters, while at the same time helping to gather some further insight into the choice of jurisdictions, already discussed in Chapter 1.

2.1 Identifying the Rationales: A Primer

As already mentioned in Chapter 1, the U.S. has a very rich history in campaign finance regulation. Even though its relevant jurisprudence has some unique characteristics, due to its extensive background, it may serve as a starter for identifying the institutional principles acknowledged behind campaign finance regulation. In its seminal decision in the *Buckley v. Valeo* case,[1] the SCOTUS was the first supreme court of law to enter the discussion about the rationales of campaign finance regulation. It concluded that preventing corruption or the appearance of corruption is a legitimate and compelling government interest for restricting campaign finance,[2] while restricting the speech of some elements of society in order to enhance the relative voice of others is not.[3] Although one may not agree with the Court's conclusion of what constitutes a legitimate government interest and what not, the decision has nonetheless identified two major rationales of campaign finance regulation, namely (the prevention of)

1 *Buckley v. Valeo*, 424 U.S. 1 (1976).
2 *FEC v. National Conservative Political Action Committee*, 470 U.S. 496-497 (1985).
3 *Buckley v. Valeo*, 424 U.S. 48-49 (1976).

corruption and equality,[4] although it did not accept the latter as a basis for limiting freedom of speech. Before exploring such regulation with all its legislative and judicial *minutiae* any further, it is worth examining these two concepts in some detail, as they are not easy to define (especially corruption). We shall also proceed with analyzing some other important concepts, such as public trust, political inclusion, freedom of speech, and transparency, whose interplay with campaign finance regulation has been legislatively and judicially identified in many jurisdictions.

2.1.1 Political Corruption

Political corruption, besides benefitting the few in expense of the many, tends to hamper economic growth, distort due process, preempt basic rights and undermine the legitimacy of the state.[5] This wide spectrum of negative ramifications together with the many incidents of politicians being accused or found guilty of corruption around the world is enough to justify the fight against corruption as one of the fundamental reasons behind campaign finance regulation.

2.1.1.1 A Proper Definition

What is really corruption, then? There is a tendency amongst researchers and anti-corruption campaigners to choose a definition that suits their specific purpose.[6] Choosing a definition without any bias seems an almost impossible task. A broad definition is not an answer to such a conundrum: The broader a definition is, the more aspects of social life it encompasses. Transparency International used to define corruption as 'the misuse of offices and institutions for private gain', although its anti-corruption activities appear to conform to a rather narrower definition, not concerning itself with most private and even some public institutions (as for example the church); perhaps this is why the definition was at some point altered to 'the misuse of entrusted power for private gain'.[7] Indeed, such a broad definition could leave institutions such as civic societies, other voluntary pro bono associations and clubs or the church administration within its scope; this is something that would not serve the purposes of the present project. The definition of corruption by the World Bank, which defines a corrupt practice as the offering, giving, receiving or soliciting, directly or indirectly,

4 Robert C. Post, *Citizens Divided: Campaign Finance Reform and the Constitution* (Harvard University Press 2014) 47.

5 United Nations, 'UN Guide for Anti-Corruption Policies' (United Nations Office on Drugs and Crime 2003) 25-26.

6 Oskar Kurer, 'Definitions of Corruption', in Paul M. Haywood (ed), *Routledge Handbook of Political Corruption* (Routledge 2014) 30.

7 Transparency International, 'What Is Corruption?' www.transparency.org/what-is-corruption last accessed 28 November 2019.

anything of value to influence improperly the actions of another party',[8] can be said to suffer from a similar broad spectrum. At the same time, an additional requirement for an adequate definition for the purposes of a discourse such as the present one is for it to conform to common usage; otherwise, it may well become pointless. Therefore, in order to avoid the risk of falling into irrelevance by formulating a very specific definition, corruption can be described as *the abuse of public office for private gain*, a definition that is (i) functional for the purpose of this discourse and (ii) conforms substantially to common usage, being one of the most widely used ones;[9] in this respect, the considerable similarity of the newer definition of Transparency International ('the misuse of entrusted power for private gain') should be noted. Of course, as any definition of corruption,[10] it may be argued that it falls in certain respects short of its objective, or that it can be interpreted in a way that excludes or includes certain social behavior that ought to have been left in or out of its bounds respectively. It is no wonder that no consensus on an exact definition of corruption can be reached,[11] the issue often being bypassed instead of being resolved.[12] This should not, however, hamper the current effort, which is to demonstrate the nexus between campaign finance regulation and political corruption, the former being one of the tools to combat the latter in modern democracies.

2.1.1.2 Syndromes of Corruption

The Corruption Perception Index of Transparency International is one the indices used to compare corruption levels in various states; emphasizing traditional corruption techniques, on which Western countries tend to have better control, it tends to favor these countries over the rest of the world.[13] Rank-ordering different states, one after another, in the same index, effectively defines the problem of corruption as the same all over the world.[14] This may well fail to address the complex and often contrasting underlying causes of corruption in each country and the qualitative differences of each case.[15] This is why the view of different patterns/classes (or 'syndromes') of corruption, grouped into categories broad enough as to preserve important commonalities, yet specific enough as to expose the contrasts amongst the different conditions shaping

---

8 This is the definition given at the official website of the World Bank under corruption, World Bank, 'What is Fraud and Corruption', https://www.worldbank.org/en/about/unit/integrity-vice-presidency/What-can-the-World-Bank-Groups-INT-investigate, last accessed on 27 May 2021.

9 Kurer (n 6) 31.

10 Ibid. 30. Indeed, the entire article is a very insightful discourse about the extreme difficulty of formulating an accurate definition of corruption, explaining as well as challenging various proposed criteria and emphasizing some of the dichotomies involved, as for example between the public and the private sector or legal and illegal activities.

11 Michael Johnston, *Syndromes of Corrution: Wealth, Power, and Democracy* (CUP 2005) 10-11.

12 Ibid. 18.

13 Charles Funderbunk, 'Political Corruption: Causes and Consequences' in Charles Funderbunk (ed), *Political Corruption in Comparative Perspective: Sources, Status and Prospects* (Ashgate 2012) 11.

14 Johnston (n 11) 17.

15 Ibid.

corruption worldwide, is gaining increasing acceptance.[16] Of course, such a grouping cannot encompass and exhaust all possible combinations of forms of corruption; it represents nevertheless an accurate enough simplification for the purpose of the present work. It is no coincidence that the definition of corruption adopted above, namely *the abuse of public office for private gain*, is not very different from the one put forward by Michael Johnston, who pioneered the concept of syndromes of corruption. Johnston defined corruption as *the abuse of public roles or resources for private benefit.*[17]

According to the syndromes of corruption approach, states are classified into one of four categories according to a combination of their political and economic participation and institutions.[18] The four categories based on the characteristics corruption has in each country are the following:[19]

a) *Influence markets* corruption: characteristic of advanced market democracies, this type of political corruption usually consists of attempts of private institutions to gain access to and influence within the policy making procedures and state institutions; here politicians often act as middlemen.
b) *Elite Cartel* corruption: in market economies where institutions are somewhat weaker, networks of national elites (political, economic, bureaucratic etc.) share benefits and use corrupt incentives and exchanges to protect their position.
c) *Oligarch and Clan* corruption: where political and economic liberalization are combined with weak institutions and weak public-private boundaries, contending elites and their supporters wrestle over potential profits, while any opposition to the oligarchy finds itself often neutralized by it.
d) *Official Mogul* corruption: in states where institutions are very weak and political competition limited, but economic opportunities are rapidly expanding, powerful state officials and politicians, operating often with relative impunity, use their influence to enrich themselves, in the most extreme cases turning the state into a kleptocracy, along the lines of Mobutu's Zaire.[20]

The above categories are broad enough to include multiple cases each, while at the same time they present clearly defined borders that allow most cases to easily find their place in one of them. As such, when trying to take a comparative view of political corruption in more than one country and, considering the central role of corruption as a rationale for campaign finance regulation, campaign, these four categories prove to be a useful and

16 For example by Funderbunk (n 13) 11-12. The term 'syndromes' of corruption has been pioneered in the eponymous book *Syndromes of Corrution: Wealth, Power, and Democracy* by Johnston (n 11).

17 Johnston (n 11) 12.

18 Ibid. 3; furthermore, the first and second chapters of this book address issues of determining the balance between these parameters.

19 The listing follows the succinct summary of the categories' characteristics by Funderbunk (n 13) 11-12.

20 For the case of Mobutu's Zaire see for example Soren Ambrose, *Social Movements and the Politics of Debt Cancellation* (2005) 6 Chin. J. Int. Law 267, 277; as well as Funderbunk (n 13) 7-9.

valuable tool, especially when deciding on the jurisdictions to include in the present study.

2.1.2 *Equality*

Equality is a rather broad concept; in its core lays the tenet that individuals (and groups) should be accorded the same status, rights and opportunities. For the purposes of campaign finance regulation, what is important is political equality. Political equality refers to the extent to which the citizens of a state have an equal voice on governmental decisions. It is the usual approach in democracies to accord each citizen equal recognition as an individual member of the political system.[21] Equal consideration of the preferences and interests of each citizen is what democracy is all about.[22] From this general precept stem principles such as one person/one vote, equality before the law and freedom of expression.[23] Indeed, the one person/one vote principle exemplifies commitment to political equality.[24] Political equality and self-government go hand-in-hand. If persons are equal, no one has an inherent right of dominating others.[25] The only way anyone can relinquish this equality and liberty is by voluntarily uniting in a body politic under majority rule.[26] Equality lays at the foundation of democracy and it may seem paradoxical that furthering it does not appear to be a legitimate and compelling government concern in campaign finance regulation according to the view taken by the majority of the SCOTUS in its case law.

A common counterargument to calls for restricting the role of money in election campaigning is that citizens do not differ only in the amount of money they possess, but also in other assets that may be of value to a political campaign, such as celebrity or free time, yet no one suggests that such assets should be regulated.[27] The argument appears logically coherent and persuasive, yet while it would seem convincing to the SCOTUS, neither it, nor other arguments in the same vein and in support of the same approach to campaign finance regulation (of a more *laissez faire* attitude), have impressed the judiciary of many other jurisdictions that dealt with campaign finance regulation questions. Perhaps it is not the concept of equality in general that stands in

---

21 John Baker, Kathleen Lynch, Sara Cantillon and Judy Walsh, *Equality: From Theory to Action* (2nd edition, Routledge 2009) 96.

22 Sidney Verba, 'Political Equality: What Is It? Why Do We Need It?' (2001) Review Paper for Russell Sage Foundation, 2 www.russellsage.org/sites/all/files/u4/Verba.pdf last accessed 27 October 2019.

23 Ibid.

24 Cass R. Sunstein, 'Political Equality and Unintended Consequences' (1994) 94 Colum. L. Rev. 1390, 1392.

25 J. Skelly Wright, 'Money and the Pollution of Politics: Is the First Amendment an Obstacle to Political Equality?' 82 (1982) Colum. L. Rev. 609, 626.

26 John Locke, '2nd Treatise of Government' Chapter viii §95, in John Locke, *Two Treatises of Government and a Letter Concerning Toleration* (Yale University Press 2003) 141-142.

27 David Strauss, 'Corruption, Equality and Campaign Finance Reform' (1994) 94 Colum. L.Rev. 1369, 1384.

the way, but how it is approached in each *forum*: different approaches based on preconceived notions and the specific conditions of each country may lead to conceptions that, while attempting to be as workable as possible within the larger framework, leave room to the possibility of abuse.[28]

When one examines issues of campaign finance regulation, it is useful to keep in mind the complications inherent in the formulation of specific conceptions of widely used and approved principles. Even solutions that are greatly favored by proponents of equality, such as campaign contribution limits, may not always be what they seem; it may well be that they are structured in a way that, in fact, impedes equality. In some rare cases limits are not absolute but linked to the income of the contributor; in Brazil, for example, corporations can contribute up to 2% of their turnover and individual citizens up to 10% of their income,[29] decreasing absolute equality, at least amongst contributors. In this regard, one could argue that such limits actually result in making contributors unequal before the law,[30] as in addition to failing to curb the influx of money into campaigning, they also formalize the inherent economic inequality of contributors.

Therefore, even if the admirable aspiration to promote equality in the context of campaign finance regulation is not as clear-cut as one would assume, what happens when such regulation infringes upon freedom of speech, for example?

2.1.3 Freedom of Speech

Another constitutional principle closely linked with political equality is the freedom of speech. In ancient Athens *isegoria* (ἰσηγορία) and *parrhesia* (παρρησία), the equal right of all citizens to address the assembly and the right to speak freely before it respectively, were two of the fundamental pillars of the Athenian democracy.[31] Indeed, *isegoria* may have been more cherished by the citizens of Athens than *isonomia* (ἰσονομία), or equality before the law.[32] The term 'freedom of expression' is often used synonymously with

28 For example, the facts of the *Bowman v. the United Kingdom* case before the European Court of Human Rights, *Bowman v. the United Kingdom* ECHR 1998-I 175, the specifics of which will be further elaborated upon in Chapter 4, may be interpreted as such a legislative abuse, induced by the aspiration to promote political equality, to the detriment of freedom of speech.

29 Organization for Economic Co-operation and Development, *Money in Politics: Sound Political Competition and Trust in Government* (2013) Organization for Economic Co-operation and Development Background Paper, 27.

30 Ibid.

31 Nadia Urbinati, 'Free Speech as the Citizen's Right', commentary in Robert C. Post, *Citizens Divided: Campaign Finance Reform and the Constitution* (Harvard University Press 2014) 133.

32 Ibid. n 2, 233, quoting Mogens Herman Hansen, *The Athenian Democracy in the Age of Demosthenes* (Oklahoma University Press 1999) 83-84. It should be noted, however, that the meaning given by Hansen in 81-85 to *isonomia* is not the same as that suggested from the literal translation of the word and differs from the meaning the word has in modern Greek or English (as isonomy), having more to do with equal political rights than equality before the law.

freedom of speech, but it is, practically, a wider concept, as it includes any act of seeking, receiving, and imparting information or ideas. The freedom of expression is recognized as a human right in the Universal Declaration of Human Rights under Article 19,[33] as well as in the International Covenant of Civil and Political Rights.[34] In the three jurisdictions under examination, it is protected by the Constitutions of the U.S. and of Greece, as discussed in the relevant Chapters, while Article 10 of the European Convention of Human Rights is binding on the U.K. and Greece. In the context of campaign finance regulation, and especially in that of U.S. federal jurisprudence as further elaborated upon in Chapter 3, one is sometimes confronted with the paradox of the narrower concept of freedom of speech within election campaigning being perceived as in conflict with the wider concept of freedom of expression during the elections; the former freedom of the electoral body is balanced with the latter freedom of contributors and disbursers of funds.

Freedom of speech and campaign finance regulation has a strange relationship. Restricting campaign contributions and expenditures is of course a restriction on the freedom of speech of the persons who contribute or disburse such funds. On the other hand, one of the rationales of campaign finance regulation is, as already noted, to facilitate the expression of persons considered disadvantaged in the political field. In fact, the regulation aims at leveling the playing field between candidates and parties who have uneven financial resources, to the extent this is possible. This is done in two ways: (i) positively, by attributing means to the least financially able candidates and parties to communicate their political message; (ii) negatively, by limiting the use of the resources of the stronger financially parties and candidates. This relationship, where the state must act very carefully in order to strike the necessary balance between the freedom of expression of two entirely different groups, reflects the relevant careful balancing required by campaign finance regulation in general. And although the SCOTUS concluded that restricting the speech of some elements of the society in order to enhance the relative voice of others is not a compelling government interest justifying restrictions of the freedom of speech,[35] this is not necessarily the case in other

33 Article 19 of the Universal Declaration of Human Rights has as follows: 'Everyone has the right to freedom of opinion and expression; this right includes freedom to hold opinions without interference and to seek, receive and impart information and ideas through any media and regardless of frontiers.'

34 Article 19 of the *Covenant of Civil and Political Rights* has as follows: '1. Everyone shall have the right to hold opinions without interference. 2. Everyone shall have the right to freedom of expression; this right shall include freedom to seek, receive and impart information and ideas of all kinds, regardless of frontiers, either orally, in writing or in print, in the form of art, or through any other media of his choice. 3. The exercise of the rights provided for in paragraph 2 of this article carries with it special duties and responsibilities. It may therefore be subject to certain restrictions, but these shall only be such as are provided by law and are necessary: (a) For respect of the rights or reputations of others; (b) For the protection of national security or of public order (*ordre public*), or of public health or morals.'

35 See Chapter 1 n 73.

jurisdictions. In Canada, for example, the Supreme Court has upheld the stringent restrictions imposed on all campaign contributions and expenditures by Canadian law, noting that the egalitarian model adopted by that country's legislature is an essential component of the democratic society.[36] Furthermore, campaign finance legislation in Canada with said stringent restrictions is considered to legitimately aim at strengthening public trust in the political and electoral process and enhancing fairness and transparency,[37] as will be analyzed right below.

2.1.4 Legitimacy and Public Trust

Intricately linked with corruption is the institutional principle of legitimacy.[38] Legitimacy refers to a regime's actual display of commitment to major structural features that are sufficient, in combination, to make morally supportable that regime's demands on citizens for a regular and consistent submission to its output of political acts, regardless of their agreement with the policy behind, or even the justice of, each act.[39]

It should be noted, however, that in the context of the present analysis the term is used to specifically refer to the legitimacy of the western democratic state and its institutions in the eyes of its citizens.

Legitimacy is above all a matter of public trust, since the lack of the latter tends to delegitimize any regime, democratic or not. And trust is a delicate plant.[40] One could get useful insights about the relationship between legitimacy and the electoral process, part of which is campaign finance, in Lawrence Lessig's book *Republic, Lost*; he argues there, that elections should function so as to make the government dependent on its people.[41] By substituting the more American-oriented term 'republic' in Lessig's analysis with representative democracy, which he admits to be its meaning,[42] we arrive at some more widely applicable principle, which lies outside the context of U.S. politics as well. As elections are about the people exercising control over their elected representatives, they should collect and set out the people's views of the representatives and the latter's actions. And the representatives should be answerable to the people alone.[43] Therefore, campaign finance should be regulated to keep representatives accountable to the people, not to the

36 *Harper v. Canada*, 1 SCR 827, 2004 SCC 33 § 62.

37 Janet L. Hiebert, 'Elections, Democracy and Free Speech: More at Stake than an Unfettered Right to Advertise' in KD Ewing and Samuel Issacharoff (eds), *Party Funding and Campaign Financing in International Perspective* (Hart Publishing 2006) 276.

38 *Buckley v. Valeo*, 424 U.S. 27 (1976).

39 Frank Michelman, 'Legitimacy, Strict Scrutiny, and the Case against the Supreme Court' in Robert C. Post, *Citizens Divided: Campaign Finance Reform and the Constitution* (Harvard University Press 2014) 116.

40 OECD 2013 (n 29) 18.

41 Lawrence Lessig, *Republic, Lost: How Money Corrupts Congress – and a Plan to Stop It* (Twelve 2011) 95.

42 Ibid. 127.

43 Ibid. 128.

funders of election campaigns, in the sense that elected officials need to respond for their actions and omissions to the people that elected through the normal democratic procedures rather than serve the interests of their funders. As there is a gap between the people and the funders, unregulated contributions or unrestricted independent expenditures would undermine basic democratic principles.[44] This approach to the rationale of campaign finance regulation is often called the 'anti-distortion principle' and has been accepted by the SCOTUS in its reasoning in the *Austin* case.[45]

Legitimacy is closely related not only to corruption, but to freedom of speech as well. The people should be confident that the election process will culminate in the selection of representatives that are responsive to public opinion. If not, then the link between freedom of speech and democratic government is broken.[46] If the people do not trust that their elected representatives attend to public opinion, freedom of expression to participate in the public discourse misses its very purpose. There is no reason to try to influence public discourse by expressing one's views, if these views are going to be completely ignored by elected officials, although the election process does not have to be such as to result in the election of persons acting as the delegates (as opposed to trustees) of the people; it only has to generate public trust to the responsiveness of the elected to the people's opinions.[47]

Public confidence in the electoral process encourages the citizens to participate in the democratic process,[48] not only by actual voting in the elections, but also by more active involvement in the political discourse that formulates public opinion. In this regard, the integrity of the electoral process is a unique kind of value, because it depends on what the people actually believe, and therefore is not dissimilar to the right of freedom of speech to the extent it protects public discourse.[49] Such unique characteristic of the integrity of the electoral process is the reason why its evaluation is to a certain extent necessarily political in its nature:[50] the electoral process is the means by which people decide on what they think is good and bad for them and building confidence in its legitimacy renders that subsequently a very political process The importance of the people's perception of the actions of their elected representatives can be best illustrated by an example, mentioned in an Organization for Economic Co-Operation and Development Background Paper.[51] In October of 2013 the German Christian Democratic Party of Chancellor Angela Merkel received a contribution of €690,000 from three of the owners of the automobile company BMW. In the very same week the Christian Democratic Party received the donation, the

44 Ibid. 232-233.
45 *Austin v. Michigan Chamber of Commerce*, 494 U.S. 652 (1990).
46 Post (n 4) 60.
47 Ibid. 61.
48 Ibid. 87-88.
49 Ibid. 88 and n 196.
50 Ibid. 88-89.
51 OECD 2013 (n 29) 18.

German government used its powerful position in the European Commission to block European Union efforts for tougher carbon-dioxide emissions targets, greatly favoring BMW, the high-end car fleet of which has a considerably higher emissions output compared to much of its European competition. Despite the legality of the contribution and its immediate disclosure, there was considerable public outcry, leaving the German government in a tight spot and its conduct widely questioned. Had the German chancellor acted the same way without her party receiving any contribution, it would have been easy to explain the government's decision as having been motivated by the importance of the car industry for the German economy. The public might well have not expected anything different from a government which has always been (or was perceived to have been) close to national economic interests. The main basis of outcry was the perception by the public of the government putting party considerations before all others, an aggravating circumstance being perhaps the close temporal link between those two events that left the impression of a *quid pro quo* relationship between them. This example elucidates vividly how important the perception of the representatives' actions by the people is, especially if one considers how this is the kind of perceived as improper behavior which subverts the public trust in the democratic process.

2.1.5 Transparency

Transparency has a complicated relationship with the other identified rationales of campaign finance regulation. Disclosure requirements in campaign finance are a useful tool to fight political corruption and to enhance public trust; at the same time, they hardly infringe on the right of freedom of speech the way limits on campaign contributions and expenses do. Moreover, besides their role in furthering the goals of each campaign finance regulation regime, disclosure requirements also help monitor regulatory compliance with the applicable framework.[52] Without disclosure, monitoring compliance with the regulatory regime is, in fact, crippled.[53]

Disclosure promotes not only transparency, but accountability as well.[54] Due to its wide applicability across the spectrum of campaign finance, and its relatively light footprint, transparency appears to be one of the least controversial weapons in the arsenal of regulators. The only tension that may arise with extensive reporting requirements is with privacy rights and applicable legislation.[55] It is not mere

52 Organization for Security and Co-operation in Europe, *Handbook for the Observation of Campaign Finance* (Organization for Security and Co-operation in Europe–Office for Democratic Institutions and Human Rights 2015) 20.

53 OECD 2013 (n 29) 36.

54 OSCE (n 52) 20-21.

55 Ibid. 41-42.

coincidence that disclosure requirements are a common ground in most regulatory systems,[56] with Switzerland being the only Organization for Economic Co-Operation and Development country, for which a GRECO report was prepared, having not adopted any reporting requirements.[57]

The above positive aspects of transparency in campaign finance should not set aside the inherent weaknesses of disclosure requirements, especially when trying to implement them. Imperfect monitoring may result in serious regulatory breaches by parties and candidates that are less well organized, advised or funded; in contrast, parties and candidates better resourced, as well as their s, are in a better position to seek and obtain professional advice, enabling them to structure their financing in such a way as to avoid effective disclosure, or proceed with compliant reporting.[58] Indeed, the variety and ingenuity of methods to bypass disclosure requirements in various jurisdictions is as great as the variety of the specific rules to be bypassed: contributions through intermediaries or by proxy, piecemeal donations in the absence of aggregate limits, interest-free or fictitious loans that are never repaid, are just a few that international experience has brought to light. Increased regulation is not necessarily the solution in such cases, as stricter rules often lead to more loopholes in the system, thus undermining the legitimacy of the election process.[59] Furthermore, disclosure without quantitative limitations and *vice versa* may turn out to be simply ineffective, when for example the recipients of controversial contributions decide to accept them nevertheless accepting thus the political cost thereof.[60]

2.1.6 Inclusion

Considering how important campaign finance regulation is, one could easily reach the conclusion that money in politics is a curse for democracy. This is not true, at least partially. Money is a boon as well as a bane for the democratic process. Despite the common negative perception of the role of money in politics due to its obvious role in

---

56 Magnus Ohman, *Political Finance Regulations Across the World: An Overview of the International IDEA Database* (International Institute for Democracy and Electoral Assistance 2012) 38. According to it, in 88% of the countries for which data is available, there is some form of disclosure requirement. More specifically, in 82 countries there is a reporting obligation for both political parties and candidates, in 44 only for political parties, in 10 only for candidates and in 19 there is no reporting obligation whatsoever, ibid. 39.

57 OECD 2013 (n 29) 38.

58 Graeme Orr, 'Political Finance Law in Australia' in KD Ewing and Samuel Issacharoff (eds), *Party Funding and Campaign Financing in International Perspective* (Hart Publishing 2006) 118.

59 Akiko Ejima, 'Transparency and Disclosure in Japanese Political Reform' in KD Ewing and Samuel Issacharoff (eds), *Party Funding and Campaign Financing in International Perspective* (Hart Publishing 2006) 150.

60 KD Ewing, 'The Disclosure of Political Donations in Britain' in KD Ewing and Samuel Issacharoff (eds), *Party Funding and Campaign Financing in International Perspective* (Hart Publishing 2006) 62-68, describes a variety of controversial donations on the U.K. political scene.

political corruption, it also has an enabling and empowering role. Giving money is along with giving time one of the practically available channels of actual political participation available to the citizen, and – if one were to accept Robert Nozick's libertarian argument about the relationship between money and time[61] – a more valuable one, since money is not as easily attainable as time.[62] Moreover, money allows candidates and parties with new ideas to communicate more effectively with voters and challenge the traditional political elites and the existing status quo.[63] This illustrates the need for a balanced regulatory approach, as regulation can bias political competition, either setting incentives for new competitors or helping to consolidate existing parties.[64] Money can be a factor of inclusion as much as of exclusion in politics. The availability of money to political parties enables them to recruit political personnel from less privileged social backgrounds, who would not be able to finance their political engagement by personal means. It is not just that their means are more limited, but that they have also more limited access to networks of potentials that could help alleviate the lack of funds.[65] Therefore, money enables political personnel of low and middle class background to afford their participation in the election process, even without the extensive personal resources of their more wealthy colleagues, and thus protects political office from becoming solely the social and economic elites' privilege.

Campaign finance regulation has also an additional role in promoting inclusion, which bears a great resemblance to the role of public trust, already addressed above. A fairer and less dominated by special interests political landscape helps promote the inclusion of all voters' groups which for various reasons have become marginalized and sidelined in the democratic process. The reasons of such marginalization may vary, including amongst others social, economic, racial and others. Marginalization can lead to political alienation[66] and further decrease public trust and political engagement, as political marginalization of a group smothers its political articulation and results in its political alienation.[67] Political alienation is practically the lack of public trust in conjunction with the absence of political interest.[68]

---

61 Robert Nozick, *Anarchy, State and Utopia* (Basic Books 1974) 165. Robert Nozick argument is that taxing one's money could be as unacceptable as taxing one's leisure (which would constitute forced labor).

62 Ibid. To gain time one has to simply do nothing, which is not the case when one chooses goods over leisure.

63 OECD 2013 (n 29) 3.

64 Ibid.

65 Patrick Flavin, 'Campaign Finance Laws, Policy Outcomes, and Political Equality in the American States' (2015) 68 Political Res. Q. 77, 80.

66 Maria Oskarson, 'Social and Political Marginalization in Hard Times' (2010) Paper prepared for the 2010 American Political Science Association (APSA) annual meeting in Washington D.C., USA September 2-5, 2010, and Swedish Political Science Meeting in Gothenburg, September 30 to October 2, 2010, 3; https://papers.ssrn.com/sol3/papers.cfm?abstract_id=1643161, last accessed 26 May 2021.

67 Ibid.

68 Ibid. 8-9.

As the political involvement of citizens is a prerequisite for democracy,[69] one can gain insight from a new perspective on the role of money and its regulation in election campaigns as well as its importance. Regulation should strive to keep out special interests, while at the same time allowing the flow of adequate funds to facilitate the political articulation of marginalized groups: this is a task, the difficulty of which might help explain many controversial aspects of campaign finance and that the analysis of the SCOTUS' case law on the subject in the next Chapter demonstrates.

2.3 TYPOLOGY

2.3.1 *Functional Placement*

At the outset, the three jurisdictions under examination, seen together, seemed to be rightly placed on the three spots of a hypothetical linear campaign finance depiction. On the one end, the corruption-focused U.S. with a sophisticated framework to regulate but not excessively restrict the role of money in politics; on the other end stands Greece with a heavily focused on public financing system that seems though to have failed to tackle the flow of illegitimate funding in politics, lowering considerably the levels of public trust in such a system. And right in the middle, the U.K. with a 'mixed' approach, regulating both public and private funding – which are found proportionately in practice – and with a commitment to disclosure that enhances public trust and inclusion.

The above functional approach to the selection of the jurisdictions, which this study focuses on, matches closely the typology of campaign finance systems chosen by the author, as will be further analyzed below. The correspondence of each jurisdiction with a specific campaign finance system category enhanced their representative character and further validated their selection.

2.3.2 *Types of Campaign Finance and Its Regulation*

Regulatory intervention of states in the field of campaign finance has been eloquently described as 'the legislature's judgement regarding the proper balance between political liberty and political equality'.[70] The most typical campaign finance regulatory measures are contribution and expenditure limits, along with disclosure requirements, which not only serve the purpose of transparency, but also facilitate the monitoring and

69 Ibid. 7.

70 Kathleen Hunker, 'Elections across the Pond: Comparing Campaign Finance Regimes in the United States and United Kingdom' (2013) 36 Harv. J. Law Public Policy 1099, 1101.

enforcement of such limits.[71] Contribution limits are regarded as a way of reducing undue political influence of the provider of an economic facility, while expenditure limits aim at establishing equality of opportunities between the diverse political forces.[72]

Campaign finance has been traditionally distinguished into private and public, based on a major criterion: the sources of the economic contributions to political parties and candidates. Private campaign finance stems from private individuals and legal entities, while public campaign finance consists in contributions provided by the state. Both categories of finance include monetary as well as in kind contributions. The recipients of public or private campaign finance can be either political parties or individual candidates. The majority of countries, at least in the northern hemisphere, have adopted a mixed system under which not only public, but also private campaign finance is being regulated.[73]

Public, as well as private, campaign finance can be further distinguished into direct and indirect. In public campaign finance, the former refers to monetary subsidies which are provided by the state, while the latter concerns the provision of free of charge services, such as access to public media for electoral purposes, use of state-owned venues for campaigning purposes and free postage. The provision of public campaign finance is usually conditioned on criteria such as the parliamentary representation or achievement of a minimum percentage of electoral success. The same applies *mutatis mutandis* to private campaign finance, but such typology is further complicated because, in addition to fundraising activities, donations made by private entities, loans granted or facilities made available to candidates or political parties, free provision of services or access to the media as well as the use of the candidates' own resources,[74] there is also the factor of independent expenses in favor or against candidates.

The *ratio* behind the public campaign finance regulation can be traced in (i) the elimination of the influence to political parties by the various interest groups and wealthy donors; (ii) the promotion of political pluralism and (iii) the establishment of a level playing field among the competing political forces.[75] On the other hand, the provision and regulation of private campaign finance aims at securing equal access to the political arena for small and new political parties and candidates that most of times do not qualify for the eligibility criteria of public campaign finance.[76]

71 OSCE (n 52) 20.

72 Ibid. 31-32.

73 Ibid. 18.

74 Ibid. 18-19.

75 Ibid. 30-31; Neil Malhotra, 'The Impact of Public Financing on Electoral Competition: Evidence from Arizona and Maine' (2008) 8 State Politics Policy Q. 263-264.

76 OSCE (n 52) 33.

It may be argued that every state aiming at ensuring political stability and independence of candidates is responsible for providing at least some economic resources in pursuing this goal.[77] Furthermore, public campaign finance can shield political parties from 'interested money' provided by donors in exchange for a private favor and ultimately reduce phenomena of political corruption. This type of finance can also be conditioned upon the parties (i) introducing structural reforms to ensure their internal and external democratic operation; (ii) adopting gender equality or other positive discrimination norms to ensure broader popular representation in politics; and (iii) operating under expenditure transparency and accountability procedures.[78] Public campaign financing is also thought to help political parties to correspond to the high costs of campaigning, which can be a tough deed, especially in developing countries.[79]

On the other hand, private campaign finance strengthens the relationship between political parties and the voters. It can be argued that it also fosters participatory democracy, by engaging citizens in politics and encouraging them to actively involve themselves in other ways than simply exercising their right to vote. Moreover, private campaign finance opens the political arena to the public and transforms political parties into *fora* where voters' opinion can be freely expressed. If political parties were exclusively financed by the state, they could become indifferent to their voters and consequently public opinion would become neglected. On top of that, due to the fact that public campaign finance is in principle distributed based on electoral success, private finance can be used to counterbalance this inequality and to support smaller parties or new political initiatives.[80] Finally, private funding constitutes a voluntary expression of the voters' political preference,[81] and for this reason it is discharged from the common criticism against public campaign finance, namely that it deprives public money from covering more vital needs of the citizens.[82]

As already observed, the majority of modern democracies regulate both public and private campaign finance in the context of their relevant national regulatory systems; this results in modern campaign finance systems not falling necessarily and exclusively and strictly under a certain type – public or private – but rather including features from both categories, being, in fact 'mixed' systems. In this regard, the old school absolute distinction between public and private campaign finance systems may not be realistic, accurate or pertinent anymore.

---

77 Administration and Cost of Elections (ACE) Electoral Knowledge Network, 'The ACE Encyclopaedia: Parties and Candidates' (2013) 31 http://aceproject.org/ace-en/pdf/pc/view last accessed 22 October 2019.

78 OSCE (n 52) 19.

79 ACE Electoral Knowledge Network (n 76) 31-32.

80 OSCE (n 50) 33.

81 This means that through private funding, voters provide their money to the political party or the candidate that they consider as the best competent to represent their interest. A common accusation against public funding is that it distributes tax-payers' money to parties that they do not support in reality.

82 OSCE (n 50) 19; ACE Electoral Knowledge Network (n 76) 30-31.

For the purposes of the present analysis, we shall distinguish the campaign finance systems into three categories depending on (a) the analogy between the public and private campaign finance norms they present (**the regulatory criterion**) and (b) the actual source of the political system's financing (**the financing criterion**): (i) public campaign finance systems with certain private campaign finance elements, where public finance of elections plays a predominant role in the operation of the system and that is reflected on the regulation as well. Greece is a good example for this category; (ii) private campaign finance systems with certain public campaign finance elements, where private financing of elections plays a predominant role in the operation of politics while the legal framework focuses predominantly on regulating the influence of such private funds. The U.S. conforms to this category; (iii) true 'mixed' systems where there is a relative balance between public and private campaign finance norms, and such proportion is inherent in regulation. The U.K. may well be considered to operate such a 'mixed' campaign finance system.

As mentioned, the above typology not only seems to be reflective of the regulatory and factual realities of campaign finance but also serves the specific country selection in this study. The above recollection of the typology and the categorization of each jurisdiction shall help the reader understand the different choices of the legislature and the judiciary in each country, as explained in the next Chapters, while also assisting the project's comparative goal.

2.4 GRECO: A Most Useful Tool

It is fortunate that all three countries under examination (the U.S., the U.K. and Greece) are members of the Group of States against Corruption (GRECO), which was established by the Council of Europe in 1999.[83] It is also fortunate that the pieces of legislation regulating campaign finance in those three countries (the FECA[84] as amended by the BCRA,[85] the PPERA[86] and Law 3023/2002)[87] have been enacted before and thus all predate the Third Round of Evaluation, launched by GRECO on 1 January 2007, which had as one of its two themes the transparency of Party Funding with reference to the Recommendation of the Committee of Ministers to member states on common rules against corruption in the funding of political parties and electoral campaigns. The

83 Although GRECO was established by the Council of Europe, membership is not limited to its members only. Belarus is member of GRECO without being a member of the Council of Europe and the same applies for the U.S., which is the other (and only non-European) member of GRECO but not of the Council of Europe. Council of Europe, 'What is GRECO' www.coe.int/en/web/greco/about-greco/what-is-greco last accessed on 29 October 2019.

84 See Chapter 1 n 15.

85 See Chapter 1 n 21.

86 See Chapter 1 n 44.

87 See Chapter 1 n 53.

timing is very fortunate indeed, because it allows insight into not only the findings and recommendations of GRECO, but also the three states' legislative reaction to them, further facilitating a substantive comparative analysis of campaign finance regulation in the three jurisdictions in relation to their targeting and ability to tackle corruption. GRECO's Third Round of Evaluation as a systematic campaign finance research project on a per jurisdiction basis is unique and it uses precisely that ability of the different campaign finance systems to battle political corruption to provide recommendations to Member States for improvements in their respective campaign finance systems; that perspective is used in providing our country specific analysis to follow, but also in identifying the institutional framework within which each country specific regulation operates.

It should be noted here that GRECO's evaluations of campaign finance in the three jurisdictions, although quite helpful as they attempt and often succeed to highlight crucial aspects of each regulatory regime and the challenges it faces, are not as useful for directly comparing the different paradigms, for reason to be explained in Chapter 6, but which at present can be summed up as lacking in systematic cohesion. These assessments are very valuable, however, not only because they are the only such tool, but also because they illustrate the different perspectives adopted by GRECO in each of the three cases as well as the perception of each regime by an outside observer with all the preconceived notions and bias that this may entail, providing fascinating insight into the interaction of the national regulatory mechanisms with supranational institutional impulses, as GRECO's evaluations contain specific suggestions and are followed by newer assessments of compliance with such suggestions.

Chapter 3 Campaign Finance Regulation in the U.S.

3.1 Historical Background, Main Characteristics and Constitutional Aspects

3.1.1 The Roots of Campaign Finance Regulation in the U.S.

As already mentioned in Chapter 1, the roots of U.S. campaign finance regulation can be traced back to the 19th century. Most attempts, however, to regulate campaign finance were rather fragmentary, being included within the framework of other bills and addressing very specific facets of campaign finance. For example, the – often quoted as being the first relevant attempt – prohibition of requesting political contributions to candidates for office from navy yard workers of 1867 was included in the Naval Appropriations Bill of that year. The same prohibition was later extended to all government workers under the Civil Service Reform Act of 1883,[1] also known as the Pendleton Act. Similar examples include the Tillman Act of 1907[2] prohibiting contributions by corporations and national banks to any election to any political office; the Public Utilities Holding Act of 1935,[3] prohibiting contributions to federal campaigns by utility companies; the Hatch Act of 1939[4] (An Act to Prevent Pernicious Political Activities) banning contributions to candidates for federal office by employees of the federal government; the Smith-Connally (Anti-Strike) Act of 1943,[5] formally the War Labor Disputes Act, banning labor unions from contributing to federal campaigns; and the Taft-Hartley Act of 1947[6] (Labor Management Relations Act), limiting spending by unions in federal elections, restricting direct contributions by corporations and interstate banks, and barring them all from making independent expenditures in support of or in opposition to federal candidates. On the other hand, the main legislative attempt to regulate campaign finance, the Federal Corrupt Practices Act (FCPA) of 1910, as amended in 1911 and 1925, was far from perfect,[7] even without considering that the SCOTUS struck down the provisions of the 1911 amendment extending the act's

1 Ch 27, 22 Stat 403.
2 See Chapter 1 n 8.
3 See Chapter 1 n 11.
4 See Chapter 1 n 12.
5 See Chapter 1 n 13.
6 See Chapter 1 n 14.
7 See Chapter 1 n 9 for a pertinent remark by President Lyndon Johnson.

requirements to primary elections[8] as being outside Congress's authority to regulate elections and remaining within the authority of the states. This law, which formed the nucleus of the wider regulatory framework formed by the other aforementioned Acts, failed to provide for the establishment of a regulatory authority which would monitor the compliance with the financial disclosure requirements of the Act; it also set few - if any actual - penalties for different types of incompliance, and most importantly, especially after the 1925 amendment, left enforcement up to Congress,[9] which, however, rarely took any action in this respect.

The first time the role played by corporate money in elections came to the foreground was in the beginning of the 20th century. In this context, and taking advantage of a 1905 investigation into a life insurance scandal that kicked off the first scandal-reform cycle[10] (not unlike the one after Watergate), election campaign reformers managed to pass the already mentioned Tillman Act,[11] named after the Democrat Senator from South Carolina Benjamin R. 'Pitchfork Ben' Tillman, who belonged to the Southern Democrats, and was known in relation of Jim Crow Laws that sought to disenfranchise the black populace of the southern states and to enforce racial segregation.[12] Relying on the U.S. Congress's authority to regulate interstate commerce, the original proposal sought to ban all contributions to any election campaign (including state and local ones) by any corporation engaged in foreign or interstate commerce, effectively banning all but the smallest corporations from contributing to any election;[13] the end result was considerably weaker, however, the final text adopted providing: '[T]hat it shall be unlawful for any national bank, or any corporation organized by authority of any laws of Congress, to make a money contribution in connection with any election to any political office. It shall also be unlawful for any corporation whatever to make a money contribution in connection with any election at which Presidential and Vice-Presidential electors or a Representative in Congress is to be voted for or any election by any State legislature of a United States Senator.';[14] thus it excluded from its scope the vast majority of corporations, incorporated under state law, and was limited to the handful of corporate entities created by congressional charter (like the Federal Reserve Bank for example).

While the provisions of the act were in practice unenforceable in the absence of a competent regulating body and of any disclosure requirements, the act was important nonetheless, remaining in force to this day,[15] and stands out. It answered the questions

8 *Newberry v. U.S.*, 256 U.S. 232 (1921).

9 In an (ill- or well-advised, depending on the sought after final results) attempt by the legislators, one would venture the guess, to bypass some of the constraints that could be placed by the judiciary, as demonstrated in the *Newberry* decision.

10 Robert E. Mutch, *Buying the Vote: A History of Campaign Finance Reform* (OUP 2014) 33.

11 See Chapter 1 n 8.

12 Mutch 2014 (n 10) 48.

13 Ibid.

14 34 Stat 864.

15 52 U.S.C. § 30118.

posed by the rise of the big corporations to the idea of democracy by stating that corporations are not citizens and do not have the political rights of citizens,[16] such as the right to contribute to election campaigning. This formal statement of democratic principle in an Act of Congress remained uncontested for more than half a century, right up to the post-Watergate reforms; one could venture the guess, however, that this may have been due to the act's unenforceability and the ease with which it was being circumvented by corporations, using their directors for making unregulated personal contributions subsequently reimbursed by increased bonuses.[17]

The Tillman Act was further enhanced by the Taft-Hartley Act of 1947[18] (Labor Management Relations Act), limiting spending by unions in federal elections, restricting direct contributions by corporations and interstate banks and barring them all from making independent expenditures in support of or in opposition to federal candidates. From a wider perspective, this act could be considered as the vehicle of a new conservative attack against labor unions by the U.S. Congress, after Republicans won its control for the first time since the Hoover administration (1929-1933),[19] as it aimed at extending the restrictions imposed by the Tillman Act on corporations to labor unions as well. Similarly to the aforementioned act, its effective enforcement was hampered by the lack of a dedicated competent authority. This weakness would remain a common denominator of all campaign finance legislation.

3.1.2 *The Origins of the Current Legal Framework: The Federal Election Campaign Act*

Due to the serious limitations of the framework set out by the FCPA and its amendments, its replacement by the Federal Election Campaign Act (FECA) of 1971[20] was a natural enough development, notwithstanding the fact that the latter was in essence mainly a revision and recodification of the former act.[21] The new Act required disclosure of all contributors or lenders of $100 or more, restricted campaign spending by a candidate or his immediate family members from personal funds and limited media advertising expenditures according to demographic limits. The watershed event the Watergate scandal proved to be, however, revealed all kind of abuses connected to the campaign financing system and uncovered the extensive corruption of the Committee to Re-Elect the President (CRP, but usually referred to by the acronym CREEP). The CRP used a

16 Mutch 2014 (n 10) 50.
17 Ibid. 87.
18 See Chapter 1 n 14. It remains in force to this day.
19 Mutch 2014 (n 10) 107.
20 2 U.S.C. § 30101, actually enacted on February 2 of 1972, despite its title.
21 Mutch 2014 (n 10) 130.

slush (black) fund to finance its illegal and criminal activities.[22] In the wake of the Watergate affair came the 1974 Amendment to the FECA,[23] which fundamentally changed and radically expanded the scope of the act, being an amendment in name only.[24]

The revisions to the FECA included contribution limitations (by individuals or groups to federal candidates, by individuals or groups to non-candidate political organizations or committees, and by political committees to federal candidates), aggregate contribution limitations within an election cycle[25] by individuals to federal candidates, individual expenditure limitations for individuals or groups, and campaign expenditure limitations for federal candidates. Furthermore, public funding for presidential elections was provided for and the disclosure requirements were increased. Last, but certainly not least, a new agency was created, the Federal Election Commission (FEC), with the exclusive authority – amongst others – to enforce the limitations and prohibitions on contributions and expenditures, investigate and prosecute violations, and administer the reporting system for campaign finance disclosure as well as the presidential funding system.

3.2 THE ROLE OF THE U.S. SUPREME COURT: SHAPING CAMPAIGN FINANCE REGULATION

The role of the SCOTUS in campaign finance regulation in the U.S. cannot be stressed enough. All legislative attempts to regulate campaign finance, whether state or federal, when challenged, are almost always bound to come eventually before it. It would not be an exaggeration to claim that the SCOTUS shapes campaign finance regulation in the U.S. because of its powers of constitutional review and of final authoritative interpretation of for all relevant legislation passed at the state or federal level. Any analysis of U.S. campaign finance law would not be complete without a thorough review of the Supreme Court's jurisprudence. The latter's reach, though, becomes truly international when looking into the concepts of freedom of speech and equality as the normative standards for regulating campaign finance with a view to combating political corruption, despite the various national approaches that may be encountered because of the different constitutional traditions and realities in each jurisdiction, as will be

22 Ronal Collins and David Skover, *When Money Speaks: The McCutcheon Decision, Campaign Finance Laws and the First Amendment* (Top Five Books LLC 2014), 17 and 47-48.

23 Federal Election Campaign Act Amendments, 88 Stat 1263.

24 Collins and Skover (n 22) 48; Mutch 2014 (n 10) 137.

25 The federal election cycles in the U.S. are two years for the members of the House of Representatives, six years for the members of the Senate with elections to elect one-third of them staggered every two years, and four years for the President, Thomas Grant, *Lobbying, Government Relations and Campaign Finance Worldwide* (Oceana Publications 2005) 560.

demonstrated in the next Chapter in the discussion of the Court's jurisprudence by the House of Lords.

Nevertheless, because of the way the composition of the SCOTUS is determined (its Chief Justice and its eight Associate Justices are nominated by the President and confirmed by the Senate), much has been said about its political orientation and the latter's effects on its decisions.[26] Certainly, many of its more recent decisions on campaign finance rest on marginal majorities and tend to reveal a division amongst its members based on a dichotomy between the so called conservatives and reformers judges. This should not detract, however, from its important role and the more than adequate way it performs its duties. Whatever one feels about the political background of its decisions – often provoked by the socially controversial nature of the issues under review – the Court's institutional foundations remain strong and should be perceived as such. Considering its vast case law, the overview of some of the most pertinent campaign finance cases above, can offer only a short but far from perfect glimpse of the major trends of its jurisprudence regarding campaign finance regulation in the U.S. It demonstrates, though, the major rationales the Court adopts when trying to answer this or the other campaign finance question and the overall approach taken by the U.S. system to any illegitimate campaign financing perceived as hampering the democratic institutions in the country.

3.2.1 The Foundations

Buckley v. Valeo (1976)

The 1974 revisions of the FECA caused the formation of a coalition of conservatives and liberals, who viewed it as circumscribing political speech, led by Conservative Party of New York Senator James Buckley, Democratic former Senator of Minnesota and presidential candidate Eugene McCarthy and New York Civil Liberties Union executive director Ira Glasser, and set on challenging the 1974 Amendment to the FECA in federal court.[27] The coalition filed suit in the U.S. District Court for the District of Columbia on January 2, 1972, one day after the 1974 Amendment to the FECA came into force, putting first on the list of defendants the name of the at the time Secretary of the Senate Francis Valeo, and arguing that the contribution and expenditure limitations along with the disclosure requirements violated the First Amendment[28] rights of the citizens, based on

26 See for example Richard A. Posner, *The Federal Judiciary: Strengths and Weaknesses* (Harvard University Press 2017) 86-87.

27 Collins and Skover (n 22) 49-50; Mutch 2014 (n 10) 140.

28 The text of the First Amendment to the U.S. Constitution has as follows: 'Congress shall make no law respecting an establishment of religion, or prohibiting the free exercise thereof; or abridging the freedom of speech, or of the press; or the right of the people peaceably to assemble, and to petition the government for a redress of grievances.'

the premise that money constituted free speech and association in the context of the federal election campaigns.[29]

As the FECA explicitly provided for an expedited special review process of any constitutional challenge, the *Buckley v. Valeo* case quickly climbed the stairs of justice and, after a short stop at the U.S. Court of Appeals for the District of Columbia,[30] reached the SCOTUS within a year. The Court, being also under pressure to decide the case before the 1976 presidential election session, delivered its decision[31] on January 30, 1976, only 81 days after hearing the oral arguments of the parties, in a 294-page tome of surprising length and complexity.[32]

Its judgment was Solomon-like in that, while it affirmed the constitutionality of the contribution limitations – both base and aggregate – as well as the disclosure requirements and the presidential campaign public funding system, it struck down all spending restrictions, thus endorsing (partly) the plaintiffs' argument that money constituted free speech, at least in respect of campaign expenditures by candidates themselves or by third parties on the latter's behalf.[33] One could venture the guess that the objective of this contribution-expenditure dichotomy was to reach a delicate compromise[34] and to strike a balance between campaign finance regulation and more liberal concerns. If, however, the SCOTUS aimed to please everybody, it seems that it failed to do so, in light of the considerable criticism its decision attracted.[35]

The contribution-expenditure dichotomy could perhaps be more easily understood as the result of the dichotomy between the two different theories of First Amendment value the Court applied in the *Buckley v. Valeo* case, such theories being in considerable tension between each other.[36] On the one hand, in justifying its upholding the contribution limitations of the law, the SCOTUS advanced arguments consistent with a volitional approach to money in the context of campaign finance: the source of First Amendment value of contributions was accepted to be the volitional impulse of the spender, the voluntary dedication of money to an expressive purpose.[37] On the other hand, the

---

29 Collins and Skover (n 21) 50-51.

30 Which, it should be noted, upheld the constitutionality of all but one of the amendment's provisions, Collins and Skover (n 21) 50-51; Mutch 2014 (n 10) 140. The decision of the U.S. Court of Appeals for the District of Columbia itself: *Buckley v. Valeo*, 519 F.2d 821 (D.C. Cir. 1975).

31 *Buckley v. Valeo*, 424 U.S. 1-294 (1976).

32 Collins and Skover (n 21) 51 and 57.

33 It is notable, however, that nowhere in its decision does the Court straightforwardly equate speech and money, Monica Youn, 'First Amendment Fault Lines and the *Citizens United* Decision' (2011) 5 Harv. L. & Pol'y Rev. 135, 141.

34 The term Metternichean has also been used to describe the delicate character of such a compromise, Collins and Skover (n 21) 63.

35 Ibid., also, Ronald Dworkin, 'The Decision that Threatens Democracy' *NYRB* (New York, 13 May 2010); Youn (n 33) 138.

36 This argument is based on and further (and more extensively) elaborated upon in Monica Youn's masterful article 'First Amendment Fault Lines and the *Citizens United* Decision', Youn (n 33), mainly 138-143.

37 Ibid. 138-140.

arguments made against spending limits were based on a 'commodity-like' rationale regarding such expenses: the source of First Amendment value of expenditures is the market and that value can be quantified externally through market measures and not such subjective measures as volition or intensity.[38] In the first case, the expressive value of a contribution is exhausted when the transfer of funds between contributor and recipient is completed, since it ceases to express anything of the spender's intent, while in the latter the expressive value of money remains regardless of how many hands it passes through, as long as any transactions conform to the overall design of the spender.[39] Thus the value of contributions from a First Amendment point of view is lower in relation to that of expenses, and it is considered constitutionally acceptable to limit the former, but not the latter.

Whatever the SCOTUS's motives and the rationale in deciding the *Buckley v. Valeo* case were, its decision shaped the landscape of campaign finance for the next decades and has been the cornerstone of campaign finance regulation analysis, even at an international level. As a direct result of the Court's ruling, there was a new Amendment to the FECA in 1976,[40] so that the law would conform to it.[41] Another amendment followed in 1979,[42] which along with a series of relevant advisory opinions of the FEC, led to the creation of a campaign finance framework based on the distinction between 'hard' and 'soft' money.[43] In U.S. campaign finance context, 'hard money' refers to the funds given directly to candidates for federal office (or parties in order to support candidates for federal office) and is strictly regulated according to the provisions of the FECA, while 'soft money' refers to funds given to parties for purposes other than supporting candidates for federal office and is thus outside the scope of the FECA.

In the wake of the *Buckley* decision, there has been considerable interaction between the legislative, executive and judicial branches of the federal government in respect of federal campaign finance regulation, with initiatives by the U.S. Congress and the FEC (an independent agency, the members of which are appointed by the President of the U.S. by and with the advice of the Senate according to the 1976 amendment to the FECA)[44] being challenged before the federal courts, and the legal framework amended as appropriate according to the decisions of the federal judiciary (in all – the noteworthy – cases the SCOTUS). To these should be added challenges to state legislation which, if

38 Ibid. 141-143.

39 Ibid. 140 and 142.

40 Federal Election Campaign Act Amendments, 90 Stat 475.

41 Besides striking all expenditure limits, the *Buckley* decision had also found the appointment scheme of the FEC unconstitutional and Congress modified it as well.

42 Federal Election Campaign Act Amendments of 1979, 98 Stat 1339. Between the Amendments of 1976 and 1979 there has been also a minor one in 1977, An act to amend the Federal Election Campaign Act of 1971 to extend the authorization of appropriations contained in such Act, 91 Stat 1110.

43 Collins and Skover (n 21) 69-70; Mutch 2014 (n 10) 163, n 1 (the note itself on 293-294).

44 2 U.S.C. 437c(a)(l).

accepted, could affect federal legislation as well. The most important of the relevant case law is discussed in the following paragraphs.

3.2.2 Evolution

First National Bank of Boston v. Bellotti (1978)

The SCOTUS in *Buckley v. Valeo* had not squarely addressed the status of corporate spending for political campaign advocacy and it was this area where the Court's jurisprudence evolved in novel ways,[45] reflecting the importance of what can rightly be assumed to be the most vital constitutional issue in campaign finance regulation in the U.S. Chronologically, the first one amongst the important decisions concerning campaign finance before the SCOTUS after the *Buckley v. Valeo* case, and also the first one where the issue of corporate spending was raised, was its decision in the *First National Bank of Boston v. Bellotti* case (Francis Bellotti being at the time the Attorney General of the Commonwealth of Massachusetts).[46] The case concerned a constitutional challenge to a state statute passed by the Commonwealth of Massachusetts in 1976, disallowing the use of corporate funds for making any direct or indirect expenditure to influence the vote on any question submitted to the voters, other than one materially affecting the property, business or assets of the corporation.[47] Although it did not concern a direct challenge against federal campaign finance regulation, the case is worth mentioning because, if the challengers' argument about the participation of corporations in political discourse was accepted, it would overturn series of legislation, including the Taft-Hartley Act of 1947 and going back all the way to the Tillman Act 1907. The case was also important because it touched upon the issue of corporate First Amendment rights. The Supreme Judicial Court of Massachusetts had already unanimously rejected the challengers' argument that corporations had, via the Fourteenth Amendment, free speech right coextensive with the First Amendment rights of natural persons.[48] The SCOTUS reached its decision striking down the Massachusetts statute by sidestepping the main question – whether corporations have a First Amendment right to be heard – and, by some sleight of hand, replacing it with the question of whether the public has a First Amendment right to hear corporate speech: to the latter question it answered emphatically in the affirmative: 'If the speakers here were not corporations, no one would suggest that the State could silence their proposed speech … The inherent worth of the speech in terms of its capacity for informing the public does not depend upon the identity of its source, whether corporation, association, union, or individual.'[49] Thus the Court struck down the

45 Collins and Skover (n 21) 66.
46 *First National Bank of Boston v. Bellotti*, 435 U.S. 765 (1978).
47 Ibid. 768.
48 *First National Bank of Boston v. Attorney General*, 359 N.E.2d 1262 (Mass. 1977).
49 *First National Bank of Boston v. Bellotti*, 435 U.S. 777 (1978).

Massachusetts statute, while avoiding according corporations the same free-speech rights as those accorded to natural persons. The decision of the SCOTUS represented a major shift in First Amendment Doctrine,[50] as well as a high-water mark of the commodity rationale discussed earlier,[51] although it carefully avoided according corporations the same free-speech rights as those accorded to individuals.

Generally, at least for the first three decades after its *Buckley* decision, the SCOTUS did not deviate from the course set in 1976, upholding the main points of that decision - and the distinction between contributions and expenditures as well as the dichotomy between the volitional and commodity approach to First Amendment value attached to them - and expanding on and qualifying various aspects of it.

California Medical Association v. FEC (1981)

In the *California Medical Association v. FEC* case[52] the SCOTUS upheld the constitutionality of the FECA's $5,000 limitation on contributions to political action committees, reasoning that

> [T]he 'speech by proxy' that CMA seeks to achieve through its contributions to CALPAC is not the sort of political advocacy that this Court in *Buckley* found entitled to full First Amendment protection,[53]

thus accepting that the transfer of the funds to the recipient exhausted the volitional impulse of the spender[54] as well as the First Amendment value of the funds in question.

FEC v. National Conservative Political Action Committee (1985)

Similarly, in the *FEC v. National Conservative Political Action Committee*[55] the SCOTUS followed the *Buckley* rationale and struck the $1,000 limit imposed on expenditures by independent (not authorized by the candidate to do so) political action committees in support of presidential candidates having elected public financing[56] within the framework of the Presidential Election Campaign Fund Act of 1966,[57] reasoning that government regulation of expenditures violates the First Amendment and invoking the

---

50 Mutch 2014 (n 10) 153.

51 Youn (n 33) 145-146.

52 *California Medical Association v. FEC*, 453 U.S. 182 (1981).

53 Ibid. 196. CMA stands for California Medical Association, while CALPAC is the California Medical Association *Political Action Committee, the multicandidate political action committee formed by the CMA and intended recipient of the above the $5,000 limit contributions.*

54 Youn (n 32) 147.

55 *FEC v. National Conservative Political Action Committee*, 470 U.S. 480 (1985).

56 26 U.S.C. § 9012(f).

57 26 U.S.C. § 6096.

volitional approach.[58] Perhaps the most important contribution of this decision is a dictum by the Court, according to which 'preventing corruption or the appearance of corruption are the only legitimate and compelling government interests thus far identified for restricting campaign finances';[59] this dictum has been extensively and repeatedly quoted as epitomizing the Court's position *vis à vis* corruption and shall be further examined later on.

FEC v. Massachusetts Citizens for Life, Inc. (1986)

Concerning the major issue before the SCOTUS, namely the use of corporate funds in campaign finance, there were two more cases of importance in the '80s. The first was *FEC v. Massachusetts Citizens for Life, Inc.*[60] The appellee concerned was a voluntary association that had been incorporated as a nonprofit, non-stock corporation, and which had used treasury funds to make an independent expenditure in the 1978 midterm elections. As the money used came directly from its treasury and not from a Political Action Committee, the FEC had charged it with violating the Tillman Act.[61] By distinguishing between for-profit and nonprofit corporations, the Court affirmed the decision of the U.S. Court of Appeals for the First Circuit[62] as, in the majority's opinion, the reason behind the prohibition on the use of corporate funds for elections was the risk of the unfair advantage of disproportional representation of substantial accumulations of capital amassed in the 'economic marketplace' in the 'political marketplace',[63] which could not apply in the case of nonprofit corporations, if two additional conditions were met: a) they were organized solely to spend on ideological issues and express candidate advocacy (and not to contribute to candidates) and b) were not funded by corporations or labor unions. This elaborate reasoning was criticized in the dissenting opinion written by the Chief Justice and joined by three more Justices, as being of a 'basically legislative character'.[64] The Chief Justice's criticism notwithstanding, *FEC v. Massachusetts Citizens for Life, Inc.* seemed to avoid any of the implications of the *First National Bank of Boston v. Bellotti* decision about the First Amendment rights of corporations and to keep the restrictions on corporate

58 See, however, Monica Youn's argument in Youn (n 33) 147-149, on how the SCOTUS, starting with its decision on *FEC v. National Conservative Political Action Committee*, turned the application of the volitional rationale on its head, as the Court had 'arrived at an approach that treated contributions and expenditures as mirror-image opposites – political contributions would be treated as proxy speech, whose First Amendment value was nonmonetizable, liquid, and intransitive, while political expenditures by individuals and political organizations would be treated as monetizable, organizationally rooted, and transitive'.

59 *FEC v. National Conservative Political Action Committee*, 470 U.S. 496-497 (1985).

60 *FEC v. Massachusetts Citizens for Life, Inc.*, 479 U.S. 238 (1986).

61 Mutch 2014 (n 10) 156.

62 *FEC v. Massachusetts Citizens for Life, Inc.*, 769 F.2d 13 (1st Cir. 1985).

63 *FEC v. Massachusetts Citizens for Life, Inc.*, 479 U.S. 257-258 (1986).

64 Ibid. 271.

expenditures on the road paved by *Buckley v. Valeo*, while expanding the anticorruption rationale of the latter, as the 'unfair advantage' argument advanced to justify government regulation went beyond the narrow definition of corruption in *Buckley* and was considerably wider than the content of the anticorruption rationale accepted in *Bellotti*.[65]

Austin v. Michigan Chamber of Commerce (1990)

The second case of importance was *Austin v. Michigan Chamber of Commerce*[66] which concerned a state statute, the Michigan Campaign Finance Act, barring all corporations (excluding media corporations) from spending corporate funds for candidate or issue advocacy. Although the appellee had an active and well-funded Political Action Committee, it wanted to use funds from its treasury for independent expenditures.[67] In *Austin*, were involved all the dichotomies of previous cases of campaign finance: contributions/expenditures, for-profit/nonprofit corporations, individuals/corporations.[68] The main challenge to the statute, however, involved whether funds from for-profit corporations' treasuries could finance expenditures in candidate elections.[69] In the end, the SCOTUS reversed the decision of the U.S. Court of Appeals for the Sixth Circuit[70] – and partially Buckley, as we shall see below – and upheld the constitutionality of the state statute, arguing that since the membership of the appellee – though itself a non-profit corporation – comprised three-quarters of for-profit corporations '[I]t could ... serve as a conduit for corporate political spending'.[71]

The majority's decision rested on what was called a 'different type of corruption in the political arena: the corrosive and distorting effects of immense aggregations of wealth that are accumulated with the help of the corporate form and that have little or no correlation to the public's support for the corporation's political ideas.'[72] The Court adopted a more extensive and systemic understanding of corruption in relation to elections, where money had the potential not only to corrupt certain individuals (the candidates), but – more importantly – to undermine the integrity of the whole electoral process. The reasoning the Court followed, known as the anti-distortion rationale, is in reality an equality rationale;[73] such a rationale had been rejected in *Buckley* (about expenditures limits) and was not to be accepted again in future decisions. In both cases, however, there was the hint of importing the volitional rationale into the expenditures area: restrictions on

65 Mutch 2014 (n 10) 157.

66 *Austin v. Michigan Chamber of Commerce*, 494 U.S. 652 (1990). Richard Austin was the Michigan Secretary of State from 1971 to 1995.

67 Mutch 2014 (n 10) 157.

68 Ibid. 158. Behind the contributions/expenditures dichotomy hid also the volitional/commodity approach dichotomy.

69 Ibid.

70 856 F.2d 783 (6th Cir. 1988).

71 *Austin v. Michigan Chamber of Commerce*, 494 U.S. 664 (1990).

72 Ibid. 660.

73 Mutch 2014 (n 10) 157-158.

political expenditures lacking a volitional nexus, such as expenditures from corporate treasuries (which according to its reasoning in the *Buckley* case, as outlined above, did not express the volitional impulse of the spender), would pass constitutional muster.[74] The definition of the aspect of corruption which concerned the Court is, as a definition, highly conditional, because it depends on the method of accumulation of wealth and the relationship to public support, but it is grounded in a basic intuition that there must be some kind of equality in political access.[75] In its decision, the SCOTUS did not want to suggest that such equality shall be absolute, but rather that where political speech approaches a state of no proportionality ('little or no correlation'), it ceases to be political, protected speech, and that inequality has the potential to transform public speech into non-public, corrupt speech.[76]

3.2.3 *The Challenge of Soft Money*

Soft money, as mentioned, came to prominence with the Amendment to the FECA of 1979.[77] Over the next two decades, the use of soft money to bypass the restrictions of the FECA increased exponentially: during the 1996 presidential election, for example, parties raised more than three times more soft money than in the 1992 election,[78] while in 2000 about half the money spent by the parties, around half a billion USD, was soft money.[79] An attempt by the Bush administration in 1989 to ban soft money failed, as the Democratic-controlled Congress did not pass the bill, while a similar ban proposed by the Clinton administration never even came to a vote.[80] Using soft money for party-building activities (voter registration drives, polling, administrative expenses and the like) was perfectly legal and freed up hard money, which was then funneled into federal election campaigns regulated by the FECA.[81] Furthermore, national parties took advantage of variations in state laws regarding state and local elections campaign finance, by raising for example soft money in states where expenditures from corporate

---

74 Youn (n 33) 149.

75 Zephyr Teachout, 'The Anti-Corruption Principle' (2009) 94 Cornell L. Rev. 341, 393.

76 Ibid.

77 Supra n 39 and n 40.

78 Mutch 2014 (n 10) 163.

79 Stephen Breyer, *Active Liberty: Interpreting our Democratic Constitution* (Alfred A. Knopf 2006), 44, quoting from the record developed in *McConnell v. FEC.*

80 Mutch 2014 (n 10) 163.

81 Collins and Skover (n 21) 70. The *Buckley* decision mentioned the distinction between issue and express advocacy *arguendo* only to underline that 'the exacting interpretation of the statutory language necessary to avoid unconstitutional vagueness' facilitates 'circumvention by those seeking to exert improper influence upon a candidate or officeholder', *Buckley v. Valeo*, 424 U.S. 45 (1976), and found all restrictions on independent expenditures unconstitutional.

treasuries were allowed, and then transferring it to states where they were not; as long as the money had not been actually raised there, it was legal.[82] Additionally, the use of a loophole concerning issue-advocacy, namely expenditure to advocate for positions on certain important political issues instead of directly vouching for the specific candidate who had taken that position, created first by the *Buckley v. Valeo* decision and later broadened by *FEC v. Massachusetts Citizens for Life, Inc.* decision, also increased, and began to seriously undermine the FECA.

Expenditures for ads avoiding certain magic words such as 'vote for' or 'vote against', but addressing party or candidate specific political issues could escape all the legal prohibitions, limits and reporting requirements based on a very narrow reading of what really constituted 'express advocacy'.[83] This kind of increasing circumvention of FECA regulation combined with reports of questionable fundraising practices in President Clinton's re-election campaign (White House coffee chats, Lincoln Room sleepovers, rumors of foreign money)[84] resulted in a massive surge in the reform movement. This surge stirred the Congress into action and thus resulted in the Bipartisan Campaign Reform Act of 2002[85] (BCRA, also known as McCain-Feingold Act[86] from its senatorial sponsors, although the bill that became actually law was the similar Shays-Meehan Bill from the House of Representatives[87]), which amended the FECA.[88]

The BCRA aimed mainly at addressing the two major issues of soft money and the issue-advocacy loophole. Title I of the Act was about banning the use of soft money by parties and candidates; Title II was about eliminating the 'express advocacy' loophole by outlawing all broadcast, cable or satellite communications (lumped together under the term 'electioneering communications') financed with corporate or labor union funds and referring to a clearly identified candidate within 30 days of a primary or 60 days of a general election.

McConnell v. FEC (2003)

Almost immediately the new law was challenged by Republican Senator Mitch McConnell, who filed suit against the FEC. The regulation of soft money was

82 Such a scheme was first used by the Republican National Committee during the 1980 presidential election, Mutch 2014 (n 10) 163.

83 Collins and Skover (n 21) 72.

84 Ibid. 164. The rumors were about money channeled by China through Chinese-American businessmen.

85 116 Stat. 81.

86 S. 27 - 107th Congress (2001-2002).

87 H.R. 380 - 107th Congress (2001-2002).

88 Since the Amendment to the FECA of 1979 allowing soft money, supra n 42, and before the BCRA, there have been two minor ones, one in 1980 contained in an appropriations bill for the FECA (An act to authorize appropriations for the Federal Election Commission for fiscal year 1981, 94 Stat. 398) and one in 1995 (An act to amend the Federal Election Campaign Act of 1971 to improve the electoral process by permitting electronic filing and preservation of Federal Election Commission reports, and for other purposes, 109 Stat. 791).

challenged as violating free speech and association rights, the due-process clauses of the Fifth[89] and the Fourteenth[90] Amendments to the U.S. Constitution (by singling out political parties or discriminatory treatment) and the structure of federalism in the core of the constitutional scheme (by reaching into the realm of soft money, that is funds raised legitimately under state laws), while regulation of 'electioneering communications' was challenged as directly contravening the constitutional doctrine based on the distinction between contributions and expenditures established in *Buckley*.[91] The SCOTUS's decision in *McConnell v. FEC*[92] was very long and complex, with eight separate opinions, including two dissenting and three partially concurring and partially dissenting ones. The majority's decision refused to apply strict scrutiny review (the highest standard of judicial review), upheld the constitutionality of Titles I and II (the main axes of the BCRA) and, from the volitional/commodity rationale viewpoint, kept the First Amendment value of corporate expenditures relatively marginal, by avoiding to afford more protection to corporate free speech.[93] The Court stayed the course taken by it in *Buckley* and *Austin* and upheld the constitutionality of most of the relevant sections.[94] One could argue that this decision actually allowed more leeway to campaign finance regulation, since it recognized the functional meaninglessness of the 'magic-words' (such as 'Elect John Smith' or 'Vote Against Jane Doe') requirement from *Buckley* in establishing a clear distinction between electioneering speech and true issue ads. All ads and communications that identified a specific candidate within 30 days of a primary or 60 days of a general election were banned, regardless of whether they explicitly called for voting for or against the candidate.[95]

89 The text of the Fifth Amendment to the U.S. Constitution has as follows: 'No person shall be held to answer for a capital, or otherwise infamous crime, unless on a presentment or indictment of a Grand Jury, except in cases arising in the land or naval forces, or in the Militia, when in actual service in time of War or public danger; nor shall any person be subject for the same offence to be twice put in jeopardy of life or limb; nor shall be compelled in any criminal case to be a witness against himself, nor be deprived of life, liberty, or property, without due process of law; nor shall private property be taken for public use, without just compensation.'

90 The text of the relevant section of the Fourteenth Amendment to the U.S. Constitution reads as follows: 'All persons born or naturalized in the United States, and subject to the jurisdiction thereof, are citizens of the United States and of the State wherein they reside. No State shall make or enforce any law which shall abridge the privileges or immunities of citizens of the United States; nor shall any State deprive any person of life, liberty, or property, without due process of law; nor deny to any person within its jurisdiction the equal protection of the laws.'

91 Collins and Skover (n 21) 74-75.

92 *McConnell v. FEC*, 540 U.S. 93 (2003).

93 Youn (n 33) 152.

94 The sole exception being section 213 of the BCRA, which required political parties to make a choice between using limited coordinated expenditures or unlimited independent expenditures to support their nominees, *McConnell v. FEC*, 540 U.S. 213-219 (2003).

95 As the majority's decision remarked, 'campaign professionals testified that the most effective campaign ads, like the most effective commercials for products such as Coca-Cola, should, and did, avoid the use of the magic words', *McConnell v. FEC*, 540 U.S. 127 (2003).

FEC v. Wisconsin Right to Life, Inc (2003)
The increased leeway was shortly cut back with SCOTUS's decision in *FEC v. Wisconsin Right to Life, Inc.*[96] The case was about a nonprofit corporation planning to spend funds from its treasury for issue advocacy in the period before elections during which, according to the BCRA, no electioneering communications funded by corporate or union treasuries were allowed. The appellee, which although a non-profit corporation did not qualify for the exception established in *FEC v. Massachusetts Citizens for Life, Inc.*, since it accepted contributions from business corporations, argued that the proposed ads, asking voters to contact specific Senators and urge them to oppose any filibuster in the Senate's consideration of federal judicial nominations, addressed a current issue pending in Congress and did not advocate the election or defeat of a candidate; as such, the government had no compelling interest in prohibiting them from airing even during the election session. The matter had been further complicated, because by the time the ads were run, the Senate had already voted on the filibuster and had broken for a summer recess, raising the question of whether it was possible to have issue advocacy without an issue, which the FEC answered in the negative, finding the ads illegal under the BCRA as express advocacy.[97] It was an as-applied challenge,[98] and the majority took advantage of it in order to create a major exception to the BCRA's Title II provisions, severely diluting the precedential force of *McConnell*, without however expressly overruling it,[99] as its decision concluded that, unless an ad could not reasonably be interpreted as anything other than urging the support or defeat of a candidate, it was eligible for an 'as applied' exception to the BCRA limits on issue ads prior to an election.

3.2.4 The Fundamental Shift

Citizens United v. FEC (2010)
The gradually changing approach by the SCOTUS to the use of corporate money in the context of election campaign finance culminated in the *Citizens United v. FEC* decision,[100] where a turning point in its jurisprudence was reached. The case concerned a film produced by the nonprofit organization Citizens United and titled *Hilary: The Movie*; a feature-length attack against Senator Hilary Clinton, comprising a mix of news clips and negative comments by a list of commentators. Citizens United had distributed the film in DVD form and in theatres and wanted to make it available as a free download on cable television as well as to run broadcast advertisements promoting it, using its

96 *FEC v. Wisconsin Right to Life, Inc.*, 551 U.S. 449 (2007).
97 Mutch 2014 (n 10) 175.
98 Ibid.
99 Collins and Skover (n 21) 88.
100 *Citizens United v. FEC*, 558 U.S. 310 (2010).

treasury funds.[101] As this would take place within 30 days of the 2008 primary elections, Citizens United was prohibited from financing it because (i) the message was classified as an 'electioneering communication' and (ii) it was launched by a corporate group which, although nonprofit, was partly funded by for-profit corporate treasuries.[102]

The lawsuit of Citizens United was initially an as-applied challenge[103] to the restrictions on corporate express advocacy (those contained in Title II of the BCRA, which have survived facial challenge in *McConnell*). The SCOTUS heard oral arguments on 24 March 2009, but on 29 June (the last day of the 2009 term), in an unexpected move, requested reargument on whether its precedents in *Austin* and *McConnell* should be overturned and whether the restrictions on corporate expenditures should be held facially unconstitutional. The scope and potential consequences of the case now vastly expanded; reargument was heard on 9 September 2009.

The decision overturned *Austin* and *McConnell* and shattered any balance between the volitional and the commodity rationales, which until then had treated contributions as having a First Amendment value that could be deemed as non-monetizable, liquid and intransitive, and expenditures as possessing a First Amendment value which would be to the contrary monetizable, organizationally rooted and transitive.[104] The Court claimed that it could not resolve the case on narrower grounds, since despite *Hilary: The Movie* carefully avoiding to appear as expressly advocating Hilary Clinton's defeat, it could not be deemed to be doing anything else but that. Then it struck the provisions of the BCRA about the ban of 'electioneering communications' financed with corporate or labor union funds within 30 days of a primary or 60 days of a general election, as being identity-discriminatory under the First Amendment, because it constrained the rights of the speaker based on its corporate identity.[105] It also overturned *Austin* and the part of *McConnell* resting on *Austin* precedent, rejecting the anti-distortion argument, namely the conviction of the Court at that time about the existence of a compelling governmental interest in limiting political speech by corporations to prevent the corrosive and distorting effects of immense aggregations of wealth that are accumulated with the help of the corporate form and that have little or no correlation to the public's support for the corporation's political ideas. The *Citizens United v. FEC* decision attracted accusations of judicial imperialism and non-judicious activism, which were present in the criticism of

101 Mutch 2014 (n 10) 176; Youn (n 33) 154.

102 Collins and Skover (n 19) 95.

103 An as-applied challenge of the constitutionality of a statute alleges that only a particular application of a statute is unconstitutional (in this case, Citizens United claimed that the amount of corporate funds it received was too small to trigger the prohibition regarding corporate expenditures).

104 Youn (n 33) 153.

105 It should be noted, however, that nowhere in the decision is it stated that corporate expenditures represent an expression of the political opinions of corporations, ibid. 158.

the dissenting minority.[106] Although contributions were not at issue in *Citizens United*, the decision also raised the succinct question: 'Can *Buckley*'s contribution/expenditures rationale long survive if one half of the doctrine - contributions - is predicated on hierarchical distinctions based on spender volition, while the other half of the doctrine - expenditures - expressly forbids any such inquiry and deems any hierarchical treatment constitutionally suspect?'[107]

McCutcheon v. FEC (2014)

The answer to this question was not late in coming in the *McCutcheon v. FEC* decision.[108] This case concerned a challenge against the constitutionality of the aggregate limits imposed by the FECA on contributions made by individuals during an election cycle. The SCOTUS's decision found that the aggregate limits abridged unnecessarily the contributor's expressive and associational freedoms, and thus struck them down, partially overturning the *Buckley* precedent in respect of the cap on total contributions, while not examining - and thus retaining - base contribution limits as being outside the scope of the challenge's narrow limits. The notion that the federal state could limit the aggregate amount that could be contributed by a specific donor during an election cycle (respecting the cap placed on donations to individual candidates, which was left in peace, as it had not been challenged by the appellants) was found unconstitutional. 'In assessing the First Amendment interests at stake, the proper focus is on an individual's right to engage in political speech, not a collective conception of the public good.'[109] The contributions/expenditures dichotomy, first invented in *Buckley* almost 40 years prior to the *McCutcheon* and upheld ever since, was seriously weakened - if not outright demolished - in this decision. The integrity of the entire campaign finance legal framework was undermined, with the danger of it collapsing altogether being now visible.

Moreover, the *McCutcheon* decision put the last nail in the coffin of any First Amendment-sanctioned concept of systemic political corruption.[110] The SCOTUS had ever since *Buckley* been concerned not only about *quid pro quo* corruption, but the appearance of systemic corruption 'stemming from public awareness of the opportunities for abuse inherent in a regime of large individual financial contributions' as well.[111] Its view of corruption was at its broadest in *Austin*, where the Court espoused a more systemic understanding of the potential of 'immense aggregations of wealth that are

106 Collins and Skover (n 21) 109.

107 Youn (n 33).

108 McCutcheon v. Federal Election Commission, 572 U.S. ___ (2014), docket no 12-536.

109 From the syllabus of *McCutcheon v. FEC* slip decision, 3. The plurality's opinion written by the Chief Justice referred to the 'generalized conception of the public good', see *McCutcheon v. FEC* slip decision, Chief Justice's Roberts opinion, 17.

110 Collins and Skover (n 21) 160.

111 *Buckley v. Valeo*, 424 U.S. 1, 27 (1976).

accumulated with the help of the corporate form'.[112] And it did not considerably modify its view in *McConnell*, remaining concerned about the erosion of public confidence through the appearance of corruption.[113] The *McCutcheon* decision, however, rejected the notion of campaign finance regulation as a means to combat institutional (systemic) corruption.[114]

3.2.5. *Major Constitutional Issues in the Supreme Court's Jurisprudence*

The history of campaign finance regulation in the U.S. is a long one, going back to the second half of the 19th century and is, counting since an 1867 prohibition of requesting political contributions from navy yard workers included in the Naval Appropriations Bill of that year, more than 150 years old. This long history has generated a varied and wide in scope political and constitutional discourse, centered – from a legal point of view – on the jurisprudence of the SCOTUS. Over that long period, the Court's jurisprudence had the opportunity to address plenty of issues that had arisen from the application of various campaign finance rules. The main issue, especially during the last half century after the landmark decision of *Buckley v. Valeo*,[115] concerned the right of free speech as expressed through election contributions and expenditures, and its interaction with legitimate concerns of the government that may lead to its restriction.

The SCOTUS has examined in depth the issue of free speech from the scope of campaign finance and has formulated a doctrine of what kind of regulation is permissible and what is not. According to it, 'preventing corruption or the appearance of corruption are the only legitimate and compelling government interests thus far identified for restricting campaign finances',[116] whereas 'the concept that government may restrict the speech of some elements of our society in order to enhance the relative voice of others is wholly foreign to the First Amendment'.[117] So, it would seem that the SCOTUS has ruled that corruption is a legitimate government concern (or the only legitimate, if one does not pay attention to the qualifying 'thus far identified' remark in the aforementioned and widely quoted *dictum* of the *FEC v. National Conservative Political Action Committee* decision; it has to be admitted, however, that almost forty-five years later no other similar legitimate government concern has been identified by the Court) relevant to the restriction of free speech by campaign finance regulation, whereas inequality can never be such a concern. Or maybe it can?

---

112 The anti-distortion rationale, see supra n 72-74.

113 Collins and Skover (n 21) 76.

114 *McCutcheon v. FEC* slip decision 18-19 of Chief Justice's Roberts opinion.

115 *Buckley v. Valeo*, 424 U.S. (1976).

116 *FEC v. National Conservative Political Action Committee*, 470 U.S. 496-497 (1985).

117 *Buckley v. Valeo*, 424 U.S. 48-49 (1976), reiterated also in other decisions of the SCOTUS, amongst which *First National Bank of Boston v. Bellotti*, 435 U.S. 790-791 (1978); *Citizens Against Rent Control v. City of Berkeley*, 454 U.S. 295 (1981); *Meyer v. Grant*, 486 U.S. 426 note 7 (1988).

To better understand the question at hand one has to discern the actual content of the concepts of both corruption and inequality in the SCOTUS's jurisprudence. In this context, corruption and inequality have a very complex relationship and their meanings to a certain degree overlap, since corruption - and even more the appearance of corruption - as far as campaign finance is concerned, is not so much about bribery as it is about the risks interest group politics pose - hence inequality.[118] While campaign contributions are often perceived by the public as being as corrupting as outright bribery, such an equation is simply not true. A campaign contribution, even when given on a *quid pro quo* basis, is not like a bribe in the sense that it does not go into a candidate's pocket. The only way to spend it is on a candidate's campaign, at least under normal circumstances.[119] In essence, that money is used to gather - directly or indirectly - votes. That is true even more in the case of independent campaign expenditures (expenditures made without a candidate's approval). A campaign contribution lacks the element of unjust enrichment, which is what makes bribery universally and unconditionally unacceptable.[120]

There is of course the counterargument that, by spending the funds of campaign contributions, candidates may well be substituting it for funds out of their own resources. Certainly, such a possibility cannot be ruled out, but at the U.S. federal level personal resources usually amount to a tiny fraction of the expenditures involved in an election campaign.

Bearing in mind this difference between outright bribery and campaign contributions and, assuming there is a relationship between the money candidates spend on their campaigns and the votes they receive, one could reasonably argue that campaign contributions are not that much different from votes.[121] If a contribution could represent a fraction (or even a multiple, depending on its size) of a vote, and one is free to pledge one's vote to a candidate, what is wrong with pledging a campaign contribution and how can this justify the restriction of a constitutional right by legislation aimed at regulating campaign finance?

Of course, a vote is not exactly the same thing as a campaign contribution or expenditure,[122] but the similarities between voting and contributing have already been established in the previous paragraph; however, their different treatment is not only known, but also widely accepted. Contributing has the same objective as voting, namely

118 Stephen E. Gottlieb, 'The Dilemma of Election Campaign Finance Reform' (1989) 18 Hofstra L. Rev. 213, 239-240.

119 An example of abnormal circumstances would be the arrangement under which members of the U.S. House of Representatives retiring by 1992 got to keep any unused campaign contributions for their personal use, Frank J. Sorauf, *Inside Campaign Finance: Myths and Realities* (Yale University Press 1992) 235 n 2.

120 David A. Strauss, 'What is the Goal of Campaign Finance Reform' (2011) 1995 Univ. Chic. Leg. Forum 141, 148.

121 David Strauss, 'Corruption, Equality and Campaign Finance Reform' (1994) 94 Colum. L.Rev. 1369, 1372-1373.

122 Ibid. 1383.

influencing the outcome of an election. Furthermore, contributing has an expressive value, even if one accepts the distinction established in the *Buckley v. Valeo* decision between contributions and independent expenditures and discussed previously,[123] whereby the First Amendment value in the first case is inferior, as it stems from the volitional value of the contributor and is exhausted when the funds are transferred to the candidate,[124] while in the latter case it is retained as long as it conforms to the expressive purpose of the spender. So, even in the case of contributions – as opposed to independent expenditures – spenders give money because they share political, social and economic beliefs with the recipients and want to attempt to have these beliefs affect the policies of the government.

When the SCOTUS accepts that corruption is a legitimate concern of the government that can excuse its interference with the free expression of its citizens in principle, it must have a compelling reason to disregard the similarities between voting and contributing noted above. What the SCOTUS refers to as corruption, the implicit or explicit exchange of a campaign contribution for official action, is only a derivative problem,[125] or – to use a medical analogy – a symptom, but not the disease. The underlying 'disease' is inequality, or the very thing the SCOTUS has accepted as not being a compelling and legitimate government concern to restrict the free speech right of the First Amendment.[126] A crucial difference between casting a vote and making a campaign contribution or an independent expenditure in favor of a candidate is the way the means to take each action have been distributed amongst the electorate. In the first case, the electorate is empowered to vote according to the principle of equality or 'one person, one vote'.[127] The principle of 'one person, one vote' is both amazing and spectacular in its simplicity. It establishes a very simple and relatively easy to implement system (the main difficulty being in apportioning seats in the legislative bodies to voting districts so as the voters of various districts have all the same voting power as much as possible) to distribute rights for political participation and expression. In the latter case, making a contribution, prospective contributors are able to express themselves politically according to their wealth and affluence, and wealth is most certainly not equally distributed. More importantly, it seems that there is no conception of the principle of equality in the field of campaign finance that would seem even remotely plausible and easy to administer the way the concept of 'one person, one

123 Supra n 36.

124 In the words of SCOTUS' Justice J. Thomas in a concurring but partly dissenting opinion, where he is critical of the distinction established the *Buckley v. Valeo* decision 'contributions have less First Amendment value than expenditures because they do not involve speech by the donor, *Colorado Republican Federal Campaign Committee v. FEC*, 518 U.S. 638 (1978).

125 Strauss 1994 (n 121) 1370.

126 Gottlieb (n 118) 229.

127 And one could argue that 'one person, one vote' is a good counterexample of how restricting the speech of some elements of society in order to enhance the relative voice of others is not such a foreign to the First Amendment concept, at least as the SCOTUS would let us think, Strauss 1994 (n 121) 1383.

vote' is applied in voting. This results in a tension between the inalienable equality of citizens and the enormous inequality of wealth, inherent in any democratic society with a market economy.[128]

There is another fundamental difference between the right to vote and the right to contribute, and that is their respective subjects. While the right to vote belongs only to natural persons, the same does not apply to the right to free speech which is protected by the First Amendment of the U.S. Constitution, an expression of which is contributing directly or indirectly to a candidate. The U.S. legal system and the jurisprudence of the SCOTUS have long recognized extensive rights to collective entities, especially corporations. Starting with a 19th century decision, *Santa Clara County v. Southern Pacific R. Co.*,[129] which has been taken to affirm that a company was entitled to protection under the Fourteenth Amendment to the U.S. Constitution,[130] thus establishing the doctrine of corporate personhood, the SCOTUS has progressively recognized extensive constitutional rights and prerogatives to corporations. Of course, constitutional rights enjoyed by corporations are not as many as those enjoyed by natural persons, but they include the rights to equal protection under the law, to free speech, to privacy and – quite recently – the right to religious liberty.[131] On the other hand, the right against self-incrimination for example is not recognized to corporations, since this right, protected under the Fifth Amendment to the U.S. Constitution,[132] can be exercised only on an individual basis and is not available to persons acting as a group.[133] The right against self-incrimination is a good example of a constitutional right not recognized to corporations because, just like it, the right to vote is a right which can be exercised only on an individual basis. There lies the great difference between the right to vote and the right to contribute, which sometimes seems to be ignored by those using analogies between those two.[134]

3.3 The U.S. Federal Campaign Finance System: Current Legislation and Typology

In the U.S. the legal text which mainly regulates campaign finance remains the Federal Election Campaigns Act (FECA). Public campaign finance is rather limited and remains

128 Gottlieb (n 118) 232.

129 *Santa Clara County v. Southern Pacific R. Co.*, 118 U.S. 394 (1886).

130 See supra n 90 for the text of the relevant section of the Fourteenth Amendment to the U.S. Constitution.

131 *Burwell v. Hobby Lobby Stores, Inc.*, 573 U.S. ___ (2014), docket no 13-354.

132 See supra n 89 for the text of the Fifth Amendment to the U.S. Constitution.

133 *U.S.A. v. S. Steve Sourapas and Crest Beverage Company*, 515 F.2d 295 (9th Cir. 1975).

134 For example, Strauss 1994 (n 121) 1373; Strauss 2011 (n 120) 148. To be fair, one has to acknowledge that such views were expressed before the SCOTUS delivered its decision in *Citizens United v. FEC*, 558 U.S. 310 (2010).

optional. The regulation is centered on private campaign financing because it is private money of which the funds flowing in politics mainly consist.

3.3.1 *Public Campaign Finance*

At federal level direct public funding is granted only in connection to presidential elections to party nominating conventions, general election candidates and primary election candidates, in that order of priority.[135] A Presidential Election Campaign Fund is established[136] through voluntary contributions of individual tax payers.[137] The per candidate (or per party, in the first case) limits for the three aforementioned categories are $4,000,000, $20,000,000 and $10,000,000 times an inflation (or 'living' as it is called) adjustment respectively.[138] The candidates for the Presidential Elections which represent the major parties receive equal payments from this fund,[139] while financial support for candidates from minor and new parties is provided as well.[140] Candidates are ranked based on the electoral success of the previous candidates of their respective parties. Therefore, a candidate is considered to belong to a major party when his predecessor achieved in the previous elections at least 25% of the total number of votes,[141] while candidates from minor parties are those whose predecessors were ranked from 5% to less than 25%.[142] The eligibility for payments from the Presidential Election Campaign Fund is conditioned upon certain limitations including most importantly an overall spending limit, but also abiding by spending limits in each state, keeping financial records and permitting an extensive campaign audit.[143]

What should be underlined is that the acceptance of this contribution is optional, and candidates can opt out if they wish to use in a more unrestricted way and quantity, funds raised by private parties for their campaigns, as they have to certify that they will not incur campaign expenses in excess of the payments they are entitled to, nor accept any private contributions (except in the case of insufficient amounts in the fund, and that only to the extent necessary to cover the deficiency);[144] they must also conform to a $50,000 personal spending limit. Furthermore, with regard to presidential primary

135 GRECO Eval III, U.S.A. Evaluation Report Theme II (2011) 8 §33.
136 26 USC Section 9006 (a).
137 Ibid. Section 6096.
138 Taking into account this adjustment, the actual amounts during the 2008 presidential election were $16,820,000, $84,100,000 and $42,050,000 respectively, GRECO Eval III, U.S.A. Evaluation Report Theme II (2011) 8-9 §35.
139 26 USC Section 9004 (a)(1).
140 Ibid. Section 9004 (a)(2) & (3).
141 Ibid. Section 9002 (6).
142 Ibid. Section 9002 (7).
143 Ibid. Section 9003 (a).
144 Ibid. Section 9003 (b) for major parties and (c) for new and minor ones.

candidates, a Presidential Primary Matching Payment Account is established,[145] from where candidates seeking nomination by a political party for election to the office of President can receive direct public funding to match contributions from individual donors, up to $250 per individual.[146] In the case of primary election candidates, the maximum amount to be granted equals half the spending limit amount, depending also on the number of individual contributions the candidate has attracted, as it is based on a contribution matching system, while in the case of nominating conventions and the general election candidates of the major parties the amount equals that of the spending limits. The Internal Revenue Code includes strict reporting obligations by the candidates to the FEC for both types of funding.

The strings attached seem to have been deemed as excessive by the Democratic Party's candidate in 2008 (and future president) Barak Obama, who chose to decline public funding not only for the primary, but also for the general election, even though previously he had stated that he would accept public funds.[147] Instead of the approximately $126 million of public funding, to which he was entitled for both the primary and general election, he managed to raise about $754 million, or about six times more.[148] In 2012 both major party presidential candidates opted out of the public finance program entirely,[149] and the reversal of this trend in the future seems highly unlikely. Public funding was even more enfeebled after the adoption of Gabriella Miller Kids First Research Act, which amended the Internal Revenue Code by terminating public financing of nominating conventions and transferring the funds to a 10-Year Pediatric Research Initiative Fund.[150]

3.3.2 Private Campaign Finance

Political parties and candidates opting to use private funds for their campaigns are not themselves directly involved in political financing activities, but such activities are carried out through political committees which are in charge of raising campaign funds,

145 Ibid. Section 9037.

146 Ibid. Section 9034 (a).

147 Mutch 2014 (n 10) 168; Charles Funderbunk, 'Political Corruption: Causes and Consequences' in Charles Funderbunk (ed.), *Political Corruption in Comparative Perspective: Sources, Status and Prospects* (Ashgate 2012) 33.

148 GRECO Eval III, U.S.A. Evaluation Report Theme II (2011) 10 §40.

149 Mutch 2014 (n 10) 168.

150 26 USC Section 9008.

receiving campaign contributions, making campaign expenditures and filing financial reports[151]

The jurisprudence of the SCOTUS has provided significant guidance about how the legislative framework on contribution limits should be framed. It has consistently ruled that contribution limits are allowed to be imposed 'as long as the government demonstrates that they are 'closely drawn' to match a 'sufficiently important interest'.[152] The FECA regulates in a detailed manner contribution limits and prohibitions on private funding. Table 1 of the Appendix illustrates what limitations are applicable for every type of donation to different recipients.[153] Donors can be individuals, candidate committees, Political Action Committees (PACs)[154] multicandidate and non-multicandidate, as well as state, national, district and local party committees.[155] The latter, according to table 1, are not limited on their contributions to state, national, district and local committees. However, the following persons are prohibited either to contribute or to incur any expenditure for the support of political parties: corporations,[156] national banks,[157] labor organizations,[158] other federally chartered corporations,[159] federal government contractors[160] and foreign nationals.[161] Apart from the aforementioned donors, FECA also prohibits contributions that are made in the name of another person[162] as well as contributions in cash which exceed $100.[163]

With regard to limitations on expenditure, the SCOTUS has introduced an even stricter standard in assessing the constitutionality of those restraints. According to its consistent case law, the relevant restrictions should be 'narrowly tailored' so as to support a 'compelling interest'.[164] Limitations on campaign spending have been

151 FECA: Federal Elections Campaign Laws, Section 30101, subsection 4. According to it, a political committee may be: a) a committee, club, association, or other group of persons if it receives more than $1,000 in contributions or makes aggregate expenditures of more than $1,000 during a calendar year, b) a segregated fund or, c) a local committee of a political party receiving contributions of more than $5,000 or making payments not qualifying as contributions or expenditures above $5,000 or makes contributions or expenditures of more than $1,000 per calendar year.

152 *Randall v. Sorrell*, 548 U.S. 247 (2006).

153 See Table 1 in FECA's Appendix.

154 PACs are private organizations that raise money pooling political contributions, which then use to make political campaign contributions or expenditures; they are subject to the provisions of Title 527 of the Internal Revenue Code (formally, the Internal Revenue Code of 1986), 26 USC 527, about political organizations.

155 FECA: Federal Elections Campaign Laws, Section 30116.

156 Ibid. Section 30118 (a).

157 Ibid.

158 Ibid.

159 Ibid.

160 Ibid. Section 30119 (a).

161 Ibid. Section 30121 (a).

162 Ibid. Section 30122.

163 Ibid. Section 30123.

164 *FEC v. Wisconsin Right to Life, Inc.*, 551 U.S. 464 (2007).

abolished after the ruling of Buckley v. Valeo because those restrictions would constrain the right to free speech as enshrined in the First Amendment to the Constitution.[165] Therefore, although the 1974 Amendment to the FECA originally restricted not only contributions, but also expenditures, since *Buckley* there are no limits on campaign expenditures in the U.S. campaign finance regulatory framework.

There are however coordinated party expenditure limits applicable to national, state and local party committees. In this regard, the law provides that the national committee of a political party may not make any expenditure in connection with the general election campaign of any candidate for the office of the President of the United States who is affiliated with such party, that exceeds an amount equal to 2 cents multiplied by the voting age population of the United States plus a cost of living adjustment.[166] In the case of a candidate for election to the office of Senator, or in that of Representative from a State which is entitled to only one Representative, the limit for the national committee of a political party or a State committee of a political party shall be equal to 2 cents multiplied by the voting age population of the State or $20,000 plus a cost of living adjustment, whichever is greater.[167] In any other State, the coordinated party expenditure limit for candidates to the House of Representatives shall be $10,000.[168] However, apart from the expenditure limits mentioned above, party committees can make unlimited independent expenditures to advocate in favor or against any candidate. Only presidential candidates who accept public funding for general elections are subject to a spending limit. This limit was originally established as $20 million plus a cost of living adjustment,[169] the actual amount allowed for the 2016 presidential election having risen to $48,070,000.

Finally, the U.S. campaign finance system regulates closely the activity of political committees.[170] All political committees have to file reports of receipts and disbursements which should contain the name and the address of the person who contributes or incurs an expense, mentioning also the date and the exact amount of the contribution or expenditure.[171] Reports can be distinguished between those submitted on a monthly and those submitted on a quarterly basis. On a monthly basis reports are submitted to the FEC by national party committees (during and outside the campaign periods),[172] by State, district and local party committees which have at least $5,000 of aggregate receipts and disbursements for Federal election activity in a calendar year,[173]

165 *Buckley v. Valeo*, 424 U.S. 39-51 (1976).
166 FECA: Federal Elections Campaign Laws, Section 30116 (d)(2).
167 Ibid. Section 30116 (d)(3)(A).
168 Ibid. Section 30116 (d)(3)(B).
169 Ibid. Section 30116 (b)(1)(B).
170 Ibid. Section 30104 (a)(4)(B) (reporting obligations of political committees) and Section 30104(e)(1) (specific reporting rules for national and congressional party committees).
171 Ibid. Section 30104 (a) & (b).
172 11 CFR, §104.5 (c)(4).
173 Ibid. §300.36 (b)(2), (c).

and by the principal campaign committee of a presidential candidate if on 1 January of an election year, it received contributions or made expenditures aggregating $100,000.[174] The latter, if their contributions or expenditures are lower than $100,000, are required to submit only quarterly reports. Beyond the temporal limits of the electoral campaign period (the year in which there is a regularly scheduled election for which the candidate associated with a committee is running for or seeking nomination) it is upon the discretion of the principal campaign committee of a presidential candidate to submit the reports either on a monthly or on a quarterly basis, after submitting a written notification to the FEC.[175] In the same vein, principal campaign committees of a House of Representatives or Senate candidate have to submit quarterly reports both during and outside the electoral period, as well as, in years of elections, pre-election and post-election reports (being complete as of 20 days before and after the election respectively).[176]

3.3.3 *Assessment*

In accordance with the typology adopted about campaign finance systems in relation to the source of the funding and bearing in mind (i) the limited and optional character of public campaign finance in the U.S. and (ii) the reality of the U.S. political system basing its financing largely on private contributions, this system may be characterized as a private campaign finance system with certain public campaign finance elements.

3.4 Supervision and Enforcement: The Federal Election Commission

In the U.S., an independent agency responsible to supervise and apply the Federal Election Campaigns Act (FECA) called the Federal Election Commission (FEC) was already established in 1974,[177] and the institutional supervision and regulation of campaign finance is a long-established tradition, at least compared to the rather nascent systems in Greece and the U.K. In line with the pattern adopted above, the present section aims to present this body from a structural and organizational and examine certain of its strengths and inefficiencies.

174 FECA: Federal Elections Campaign Laws, Section 30104 (a)(3)(A).
175 Ibid. Section 30104 (a)(3)(A).
176 Ibid. Section 30104 (a)(2).
177 By Federal Election Campaign Act Amendments of 1974, and already discussed in 3.1.2.

3.4.1 Structure

The FEC is composed of six members, appointed by the President of the United States upon the advice and consent of the United States Senate.[178] Previously, before the United States Court of Appeals for the District of Columbia Circuit issued its decision in the *FEC v. NRA Political Victory Fund* case[179] in 1993, the Secretary of the Senate and the Clerk of the House of Representatives also participated in the FEC as *ex officio* non-voting members, but their participation was found unconstitutional as violating the principle of separation of powers.

The Members of the Commission are chosen based on their experience, integrity, impartiality and good judgment. Apart from this general requirement, the FECA provides that, at the time of the appointment, FEC's Members should not hold office in the executive, legislative, or judicial branch or be engaged with business, vocation or employment in those branches. In the case of employment, the relevant Member should cease the prohibited activity at least 90 days before their appointment.[180]

The six members of the Commission are appointed for six years[181] and no more than three members should be affiliated with the same political party.[182] Members may continue with their duties, after the expiration of their term, until the moment of the appointment of their successor.[183] In case a vacancy occurs before the expiration of the incumbency period, the position is filled until the expiration date of the position at hand.[184] The procedure of appointment is applicable *mutatis mutandis* with regard to the fulfillment of a vacancy.[185] Two members of the Commission are elected by the Commission annually as Chairman and Vice Chairman respectively, with the sole restriction that they should not belong to the same political party. However, all the Members of the Commission shall rotate in the role of Chairman, and will all serve in that role once during their term. The Vice Chairman assumes the role of the Chairman in case of absence or disability of the Chairman, or when this position remains vacant for any reason.[186]

---

178 Federal Election Campaign Laws, Section 30106, Federal Election Commission, (a) (1).

179 *FEC v. NRA Political Victory Fund*, 6 F.3d 821 (D.C. Cir. 1993). It should be noted that the case reached the SCOTUS, but the Supreme Court did not enter into the merits of the case and dismissed it, finding that the FEC had failed to obtain the Solicitor General's authorization to file its petition before the Court and lacked the capacity to do so on its own, *FEC v. NRA Political Victory Fund*, 513 U.S. 88 (1994); thus the decision of the U.S. Court of Appeals for the District of Columbia that had found unconstitutional the participation of the Secretary of the Senate and the Clerk of the House of Representatives was affirmed.

180 Federal Election Campaign Laws, Section 30106, Federal Election Commission, (a) (3).

181 Ibid. Section 30106, Federal Election Commission, (a) (2) (A).

182 Ibid. Section 30106, Federal Election Commission, (a) (1).

183 Ibid. Section 30106, Federal Election Commission, (a) (2) (B).

184 Ibid. Section 30106, Federal Election Commission, (a) (2) (C).

185 Ibid. Section 30106, Federal Election Commission, (a) (2) (D).

186 Ibid. Section 30106, Federal Election Commission, (a) (5).

The Commission meetings are taking place once a month, with the possibility of further meetings upon the request of any Member.[187] The Commission is obliged to prescribe in writing the rules of its conduct, to maintain an official seal and to have its principal office in proximity to the District of Columbia. However, the powers of the Commission are not territorially limited and it can exercise them anywhere in the United States.[188]

With regard to the decision-making process of the Commission, the FECA provides that any decision of the Commission should be taken with majority voting. The Members are prohibited from delegating their decision-making powers.[189] Finally, the Commission is assisted a staff Director and a General Counsel;[190] upon request, the Commission may be assisted by personnel of other agencies and departments.[191]

3.4.2 Powers

The Commission is assigned to audit all financial data, investigate and, in case of violations of law, impose fines or report such violations to the relevant authorities. Its mandate consists of (i) enforcing FECA's limitations and prohibitions; and (ii) administering the Presidential Campaign Fund.[192] It may also render advisory opinions and submit legislative recommendations.

The FEC may commence the investigation procedure on its own initiative; more often, though, the enforcement starts after the filing of a complaint[193] by persons alleging a violation of the law.[194] The Commission may not conduct any investigations or take any other actions solely on the basis of an anonymous complaint.[195] Upon receiving the complaint, the Commission notifies the alleged infringer in order for that individual or party to respond to the alleged violation. If the Commission suspects that the alleged infringer has committed or may commit a violation, it launches an investigation[196] and collects information by asking for reports, witness statements[197] and disclosure of information, if necessary.[198] In case a breach of law is confirmed, the Commission may seek for conciliation and impose fines[199] or report the infringement to

187 Ibid. Section 30106, Federal Election Commission, (d).
188 Ibid. Section 30106, Federal Election Commission, (e).
189 Ibid. Section 30106, Federal Election Commission, (c).
190 Ibid. Section 30106, Federal Election Commission, (f) (1).
191 Ibid. Section 30106, Federal Election Commission, (f) (3).
192 26 USC Chapter 95.
193 GRECO Eval III, U.S.A. Evaluation Report Theme II (2011) 23 §108.
194 Federal Election Campaign Laws, Sections 30115-30126.
195 Ibid. Section 30109: Enforcement, (a) (1).
196 Ibid. Section 30107: Powers of the Commission, (a) (9).
197 Ibid. Section 30107: Powers of the Commission, (a) (1-3).
198 Ibid. Section 30107: Powers of the Commission, (c).
199 Ibid. Section 30109: Enforcement, (a).

the appropriate law enforcement authorities.[200] In the Commission's discretion, an apparent knowing and wilful violation of the FECA or the provisions about the Presidential Campaign Fund or the Presidential Primary Matching Account may be referred to the Attorney General of the U.S.; in such a case the latter shall report the relevant actions to the perpetrator and investigate the claim.[201] The Commission may also initiate civil actions for the enforcement of campaign finance law,[202] while the criminal aspect of the infringement falls under the exclusive competence of the Department of Justice.[203]

Furthermore, the Commission possesses significant advisory powers, as it may issue guidance addressed to political parties and candidates, as well as to the legislature. One FEC power is to render advisory opinions,[204] when a person, a candidate or an authorized committee asks for one. The Commission issues the opinion in written form and provides insights into the transactions or the activities concerned that form the base of the question asked.[205] Before issuing its opinion, however, the FEC should first make public the request for an advisory opinion and accept feedback in the form of written comments by any interested party.[206]

Another important function of the FEC concerns the submission of legislative recommendations or comments on legislation, when requested by the Congress *in toto* or by individual Members of it.[207] Furthermore, the Commission, in common with the national committee of any political party or any individual eligible to vote in any election for the office of President, may institute proceedings before the competent courts for a judgment (including a declaratory judgment) in the appropriate district court of the U.S. in order to construe the constitutionality of any provision of the FECA.[208] It also has the duty of providing guidance to all regulated parties by prescribing forms for the implementation of the FECA and by publishing a manual proposing methods of bookkeeping and reporting. The FEC shall also maintain an index of designations, reports and statements,[209] and ensure the widest publicity of those details, through reports and other information posted on its own website.[210]

---

200 Ibid. Section 30107: Powers of the Commission, (a).
201 Ibid. Section 30109: Enforcement, (a)(5), (c).
202 Ibid. Section 30107: Powers of the Commission, (e).
203 GRECO Eval III, U.S.A. Evaluation Report Theme II (2011) 22 §101.
204 Federal Election Campaign Laws, Section 30107: Powers of the Commission, (a) (7).
205 Ibid. Section 30108: Advisory opinions, (a).
206 Ibid. Section 30108: Advisory opinions, (d).
207 Ibid. Section 30107: Powers of the Commission, (d) (2).
208 Ibid. Section 30110: Judicial Review.
209 Ibid. Section 30111: Administrative provisions, (a).
210 Ibid. Section 30112: Maintenance of website of election reports, (a).

3.4.3 *Assessment*

3.4.3.1 Strengths

In the pre-Watergate period it had been argued that the initial failure to reinforce the framework of campaign finance in the U.S. can be seen in the lack of an effective institutional mechanism to monitor the application of the electoral law.[211] Therefore, FEC's role as a monitoring mechanism was perceived as an evolution aiming at enhancing public trust and certainty on proper law enforcement. Interestingly, while the majority of scholarship is devoted to addressing FEC's inefficiencies, certain positive features can be distinguished.

Already at a preliminary note, FEC's track record in enforcing campaign finance laws cannot be doubted despite any inefficiency that may be noticed.[212] In monitoring the public finance provisions, the Commission's work may be highly endorsed, especially during presidential elections, when the FEC has access to the largest proportion of its available resources. In the performance of one of FEC's fundamental powers, namely reporting on and disclosure of campaign funding, the Commission's strong and consistent operation can be positively perceived as a move towards establishing more transparency, thus safeguarding the application of the electoral law.[213] Another positive feature of the Commission can be seen in the provision of advisory opinions, which create precedent for similar questions of law and ensure its consistent application.[214] Outside of the judicial system, the interpretation of the law is strictly tied to the Commission, marginalizing the role of the Congress on how the existing law should apply. The sole way to question the Commission's interpretation is either through the judicial route or through a legislative amendment.[215]

3.4.3.2 Inefficiencies

Despite the aforementioned positive insights, it has been fiercely noticed that the Commission 'has never been the independent and effective arbiter that advocates of reform were promised in the wake of Watergate'.[216] Notwithstanding the role of the

211 William C. Oldaker, 'Of Philosophers, Foxes, and Finances: Can the Federal Election Commission Ever Do an Adequate Job?' (1986) 486 Ann. Am. Acad. Political Soc. Sci. 133-134.

212 Michael M. Franz, 'The Devil We Know? Evaluating the Federal Election Commission as Enforcer' (2009) 8 Election Law J. 167, 186.

213 Oldaker (n 211) 145.

214 FEC's advisory opinions help to promote certainty about the law, since they clarify the way the Commission interprets it. For example, in 1979 an advisory opinion sought by the Democratic Party of Virginia about the ability of its various committees (not all of them registered with the FEC) to transfer funds amongst themselves, in order to balance the finances of those of the committees that ended up with deficits in their budgets, has provided the relevant framework applicable ever since, see Federal Election Commission, Advisory Opinion 1979-30.

215 Franz (n 212) 169.

216 Harvard Law Review, 'Eliminating the FEC: The Best Hope for Campaign Finance Regulation?' (2018) 131 Harv. Law Rev. 1421, 1442.

SCOTUS in shaping campaign finance legislation by introducing the one or the other constitutional interpretation on campaign finance, the goal to introduce an institutional mechanism capable to 'remove whatever influence big money and special interests may have on [the] Federal electoral process'[217] can be considered not only overambitious, but to a significant extent unrealized – so far.

The first and crucial challenge to the FEC's effectiveness lies in the highly paradoxical relationship between the Commission and the Congress. On the one hand, the Commission, as a regulator, addresses its actions against the members of the Congress, while on the other hand, the Congress keeps a tight rein on the Commission by restricting its functional independence.[218] FEC's role in monitoring one of the most sensitive congressional activities, the re-election effort, is constrained through the influential position of the Congress. A historical recourse from the early years of the Commission's works may well illustrate the interventionist attitude of the Congress through the exercise of veto rights on FEC's proposed regulations, legislative initiatives to eliminate the Commission's role, and its power to impose budgetary restrictions on the Commission.[219] As a result, the Commission's actions against the Congress may eventually be regarded as actions against its own boss. While these facts may *prima facie* seem to be external to the institutional design of the Commission, it has been observed that this pressure has been internalized, leading the Commission to adopt a more conciliatory attitude with regard to the legislature, resulting in a *sui generis* self-restriction.[220]

Another source of criticism focuses on the Commission's several structural inefficiencies, namely the failure of the interest representation model as the FEC's foundation, the 'deadlock' votes in the decision-making process and the lack of strict requirements to impede illegitimate connections between FEC members and politics.

In fact, the Commission's structural design as introduced by the law[221] has been premised on the interest representation model; this was an effort for such structure to reflect the widest range of interests possible, thus restricting the exercise of administrative discretion.[222] Despite the popularity of this system in the 1960s and 1970s, when diminished faith in the objectivity of professional administrators led to an attempt to achieve the rather impractical ideal of the full and fair participation of interest groups in agency processes,[223] its inefficiency when used in relation to campaign finance is quite

217 Gerald Ford, *Statement on the Federal Campaign Act Amendments of 1974*, 15 October 1974, www.presidency.ucsb.edu/documents/statement-the-federal-campaign-act-amendments-1974 last accessed 6 November 2019.

218 Oldaker (n 211) 136.

219 Ibid.; also Robert E. Mutch, *Campaigns, Congress and Courts* (Praeger, 1988) 88-92.

220 Eliminating the FEC (n 202) 1431.

221 Including the two non-voting members.

222 Elena Kagan, 'Presidential Administration' (2001) 114 Harv. Law Rev. 2245, 2253.

223 Ibid. 2253-2254.

flagrant. This happens due to the fact that interest representation works best when opposing interest groups are engaged in the output of agency decision-making being as favorable as possible to their own interests, while FEC's inaction – rather than action – is better serving the interests of all groups concerned, i.e. the inaction of the Commission gives a wider leeway for deviations to political parties.[224]

Another disadvantage may be found in the even number of its members, leading to 3-3 deadlocks and strengthening institutional bias through inaction.[225] 'Deadlocked' votes show the main point of policy divergence within the Commission. The high threshold of four votes in favor or against an issue results in leaving questions of law, regulation, or enforcement, unresolved. It is remarkable that, despite the high potential for policy disagreements in an enhanced complexity sector like campaign finance, the Commission's inaction is not derivative of such complexity, but rooted in the ill-formed Commission's structure.

On the one hand, it has been argued that the maintenance of this decision-making model might have been expected or even intended by Congress that was aiming at impeding the Commission's consensus and restricting its regulatory reach. On the other hand, there are voices echoing that such a model has been placed to ensure that the Commission will proceed solely through a wider consensus of mixed, bipartisan majorities.[226] Promoting bipartisan consensus on how campaign finance is regulated should be considered beneficial to democracy. However, the latter view may be criticized as both unconvincing and pre-textual because, as bitter experience of FEC's inaction has demonstrated. Several examples of deadlocks can be mentioned, such the one of the complaint that a company during the 2012 presidential election obliged its employees to actively contribute on political rallies and campaigns,[227] or another in the early 2015 on a dispute concerning simple donation disclosure and illegal coordination between candidates and affiliated super PACs,[228] which can only confirm that, no matter what the intentions of the legislature were when designing FEC's structure, such structure eventually creates impediments to efficient regulatory enforcement.

In addition, the rather vague requirements for the selection of the members of the Commission in combination with the interest representation model structure not only fail to isolate the Commission from political influence, but actually encourage strong

---

224 Eliminating the FEC (n 216) 1428.

225 Ibid. 1431.

226 R. Sam Garrett, 'The Federal Election Commission: Overview and Selected Issues for Congress' (Congressional Research Service 2015) 11-14 https://digital.library.unt.edu/ark:/67531/metadc795891/m1/1/high_res_d/R44318_2015Dec22.pdf last accessed 6 November 2019.

227 Melissa Yeager, 'Deadlock over political coercion at work causes 3 FEC commissioners to issue scathing statement' (Sunlight Foundation, 24 May 2016) https://sunlightfoundation.com/2016/05/24/deadlock-over-political-coercion-at-work-causes-three-fec-commissioners-to-issue-scathing-statement/ last accessed 6 November 2019.

228 Megan R. Wilson, 'FEC deadlocked on 'dark money'' (The Hill, 2th of November 2015) https://thehill.com/homenews/campaign/232582-fec-deadlocked-on-dark-money last accessed 6 November 2016.

partisanship between its members. These broadly defined requirements do not provide for a solid standard to block the appointment of Commissioners who maintain strong links with the leaders of the parties represented in the Congress.[229] Consequently, the facilitation of inaction through the introduction of the four-vote majority rule in a six-member body, entangled with the provision that three members of the same party can be represented at the Commission, collectively amount to institutional bias and substantially restrict FEC's regulatory capabilities.

Apart from structural disadvantages, FEC's ineffectiveness can also be witnessed at the enforcement level, especially in relation to issues arising out the structural inefficiency. For instance, one of the core functions of the Commission is to audit the various campaign expenditures. However, a series of administrative and functional restraints impede the successful carrying out of this function. First, the Commission often fails to initiate an *ex officio* investigation, being often internally constrained in pursuing enforcement actions upon the receipt of a complaint because of the requirement of four positive votes for the initiation of the enforcement process in the context of the high degree of Commission's politicization further impedes its actions. Furthermore, and closely related to the ease with which a deadlock may arise, the exercise of its discretionary power on whether to act or not, has received further criticism because of the Commission's focus on 'petty infractions' rather than on important issues of campaign financing. Finally, the enforcement procedure is further restricted for financial reasons as the percentage of the available budget for those actions fluctuates between 10-20% of the FEC's total budget.[230]

Issues such as the even number of the Commissioners undoubtedly impact on the mechanism's function but have been highly neglected from legislative debates and amendments, so far.[231] These inefficiencies have incited scholars and other stakeholders to suggest a radical reform of the existing Commission by proposing structural and functional amendments to be adopted.[232] A great part of those proposals is mirrored in the recently proposed amendments to the FECA, namely the Restoring Integrity to America's Elections Act Bill,[233] introduced on 6 April 2017. It proposed the reduction of FEC's members from eight to five and the elimination of the Commissioners belonging to the same party from three to two; Furthermore, the proposal aimed to strengthen the institution's independence and effectiveness through the recommendation of the candidate members by a Blue Ribbon Advisory Panel,[234] the revision of the

229 Mutch 1988 (n 219) 104-106.
230 Oldaker (n 211) 141-142.
231 Eliminating the FEC (n 216) 1432-1433.
232 Franz (n 215) 185; Garrett (n 226) 17.
233 H.R. 2034 – 115th Congress (2017-2018).
234 In the U.S. a Blue Ribbon Committee or Panel is a group of exceptional individuals appointed to investigate, study or analyze a particular question, usually enjoying a high degree of independence from political or other influence.

Commission's powers and the allocation of those powers among the members and the Chairman.[235]

3.5 Corruption Issues and GRECO's Evaluation

3.5.1 Campaign Contributions and Influence

There is more than one bone of contention regarding the role of money in U.S. politics. Besides the perceived need of ever increasing amounts of money to be spent for electoral campaigning, there is also disagreement about the kind of influence these amounts secure for the donors behind them. It should be noted, however, at least as far as for the ever increasing amounts of money necessary for election are concerned, the increase is not as dramatic as they would seem, especially if inflation is taken into account;[236] nor should it be inferred from these concerns that a return to a less corrupted from money past is envisioned, especially since, as Judge Richard Posner has once remarked, 'the clock cannot be turned back, especially to a time that never existed'.[237] As for influence, it is very difficult to ascertain the exact effect of donations, since are they hardly ever accompanied with *quid pro quo* offers, seasoned lobbyists and contributors not only avoiding making such offers, but also scorning anyone that would.[238] Officially, donating for a politician's election is aimed at strengthening the political views that said politician needs to advocate for and legislate if elected; as vividly put by former (1978-1989) Democratic Congressman from California Tony Coelho, what is sold is not legislation, only the right to be heard;[239] of course, this begs the question, why should citizens need to pay to be heard by their elected representatives. Anyway, whether the amounts of political money involved are indeed excessive or not, or whether they constitute bribes or not, may well be beyond the point. The effects of perceived corruption on the political institutions can be very real, even when one could argue that the corruption is fictitious. To quote the old proverb, Caesar's wife must be above

235 The Bill was referred to the House Committee on House Administration and appeared to have been quietly forgotten. On 14 February 2019 it was reintroduced under the same name as H.R. 1272 - 116th Congress (2019-2020) and referred once more to the House Committee on House Administration.

236 Michael Johnston, *Syndromes of Corruption: Wealth, Power, and Democracy* (CUP 2005) 66.

237 The remark was made in a review of a book by Mary Ann Glendon with the rather provocative title 'A Nation under Lawyers: How the Crisis of the Legal Profession is Transforming American Society', Richard Posner, *New Republic* (New York, 31 Oct 1994) 40. See also Collins and Skover (n 22) 14-15 about how even Abraham Lincoln ('Honest Abe') manipulated campaign finance by buying a German-language newspaper, the Illinois Staats Anzeiger, then leased it back to its previous management, so as to maintain the fiction of independence, on the condition to endorse Lincoln's Party; the German vote helped Lincoln secure victory in seven key northwestern states in the next election.

238 Ibid. 70.

239 Jay Hedlund, 'Lobbying and Legislative Ethics' in Anne Marie Donahue (ed), *Ethics in Politics and Government* (Hw Wilson Co 1989) 126, quoted in Funderbunk (n 147) 33-34.

suspicion. Although perceived corruption does not conform to the definition given in Chapter 2, and so would be beyond the scope of this study, it merits some discussion, as at least some of its effects on the political system are not only real, but also very similar the first to suffer from it is the system's credibility.

To the extent the U.S. public becomes convinced of certain negative aspects of the political system and their connection with money politics, the veracity of such connections becomes superfluous. Beliefs, such as that the legislature acts in accordance with the interests of contributors rather than the country, that the political system is so extensively controlled by special interests that it is unable to respond to the country's needs, or that corporations have too much power and influence on government policy in comparison to public opinion, are widely accepted, according to numerous surveys.[240] Furthermore, such beliefs are also accompanied by the disrepute attached to the candidates managing to get elected, as it is widely held amongst the public that elections are for sale to the candidates that can raise the most money rather to the best candidates for the job, and that good people are discouraged by the system from running for office due to the high costs of campaigning.[241] These widespread beliefs of the public damage the vitality and credibility of electoral politics, subverting the entire political system. Of course, as buying influence is an expensive game, it is no wonder why the majority of voters, who cannot afford it, are so suspicious of the political system.

3.5.2 *Incumbents and Challengers*

The credibility of the electoral process is further undermined by the great advantages enjoyed by incumbents campaigning for re-election in comparison to challengers running against them. In the U.S. the amounts of money funneled into electoral campaigning is usually determined by how much challengers are able to raise, that amount usually being then easily exceeded by incumbents.[242] Contributors, being aware of how unlikely it is for challengers to be elected, offer them very little 'hard money',[243] thus creating a self-fulfilling prophesy in this respect.[244] Since the introduction of the BCRA, which sought amongst others to ban 'soft money', the ability of the parties' leaders to help challengers via party advertising and activities was further diminished. Incumbents' security is so extensive, that contributions to them may more closely resemble protection money.[245]

240 Johnston (n 236) 66.
241 Ibid.
242 Ibid. 69.
243 See supra n 43 about the distinction between 'hard money' and 'soft money'.
244 Johnston (n 236) 69.
245 Ibid. 70.

In fact, the percentages of incumbents seeking re-election are notably high in the case of U.S. representatives or U.S. senators,[246] while at the same time in presidential races since 1951, when the Twenty-second Amendment to the U.S. Constitution[247] barring candidates from running for a third term as presidents came into effect, only three incumbent presidents failed to be re-elected for a second term (Gerald Ford in 1976, Jimmy Carter in 1980 and George H. W. Bush in 1992).[248] In the case of presidential elections, incumbent advantage is further enhanced by the provisions of the FECA regarding public funding, which benefit the two established parties that have been taking turns in the White House from the md 19th century. This is because all new parties and independent candidates have to exceed the relatively high threshold of 5% of the popular vote in order to be entitled to a fraction only of the public funding provided to the candidates of the two major parties, and that only after the election.

3.5.3 *Legitimacy of the Political System*

The undermining of the political system's credibility by its corrupt practices, as these are perceived by much of the public, outline a systemic corruption problem in the U.S. according to the authors of the GRECO report. As long as the public opinion thinks that the whole campaign finance regime is corrupting, the institutions regulating the connections between wealth and power in the electoral process (most notably the FEC) face serious credibility issues.[249] Furthermore, the advantages enjoyed by incumbents in comparison to challengers reduce political competition and the value of voting as a means of accountability, with voter participation taking place in a setting of little real competition for many offices.[250] The U.S. is a country of great capital aggregation, and wealth interests have traditionally been very powerful. Contributions by such interests are made with expectations of the donors well beyond the means and, sometimes, even the imagination of the average citizen. It is hard to regulate the flow of money from such

246 Ibid.

247 The text of the relevant section of the Twenty-Second Amendment to the U.S. Constitution has as follows: 'Section 1. No person shall be elected to the office of the President more than twice, and no person who has held the office of President, or acted as President, for more than two years of a term to which some other person was elected President shall be elected to the office of the President more than once. But this Article shall not apply to any person holding the office of President when this Article was proposed by the Congress, and shall not prevent any person who may be holding the office of President, or acting as President, during the term within which this article becomes operative from holding the office of President or acting as President during the remainder of such term.'

248 And Gerald Ford was a special case anyway: He replaced President Richard Nixon after the latter resigned in 1974 during his second term, having already replaced Spiro Agnew in the office of Vice-President when he resigned in 1973, thus serving as Vice-President and subsequently President of the U.S. without having been elected to either of these offices.

249 Johnston (n 236) 72.

250 Ibid.

interests to the political arena, as the more complex a law is, the more ingenious become the methods of circumventing it,[251] and the Supreme Court, although very active in reviewing relevant legislation, often cannot reach the practices circumventing it. The ability of such interests to contribute large amounts of money is the result of their power at least as much as the cause of it.[252]

When the majority of the citizens become suspicious of a state's political system, that state's capacity to elicit the loyalty of them is degraded; if politics becomes – or is perceived to have become – an extension of the markets, the system risks losing the trust of the citizens.[253] This systemic corruption problem serves also as a reminder of why using mainly GDP and other related economic indices to evaluate corruption on a global scale is not a reliable method.[254] Realizing that the U.S., the strongest economic power in the world, suffers from such systemic corruption issues just by its public opinion's perception of its political financing processes helps expand one's perspective of corruption all over the globe.

3.5.4 GRECO's evaluation on Party Funding Transparency

Since the election system in the U.S. has a few very particular characteristics, which do not correspond to what applies in the other two countries under examination (the U.K. and Greece), it is interesting to examine how these were perceived and commented on in the GRECO Evaluation Reports. One of those characteristics that GRECO focused on is that it is extremely candidate-centered, with the candidates, despite belonging to or being affiliated with a particular political party, enjoying wide autonomy, running their campaigns as separate entities from that party.[255] The political parties themselves are broad structures rather loosely organized, quite contrary to what applies in the U.K. and in Greece (and in most European countries); it is interesting to note that the two major parties in the U.S. (the Democratic and the Republican ones) have no legal personality at all.[256] As such, the parties are not directly involved in the flow of political money. Instead, financing is handled by political committees, which are the formal organizations that political parties and candidates are required to have in order to deal with the financial issues of their campaigns.[257]

251 Mutch 2014 (n 10) 170.
252 Johnston (n 236). 71.
253 Ibid. 70.
254 See Chapter 2 n 13-15.
255 GRECO Eval III, U.S.A. Evaluation Report Theme II (2011) 6 §23; also, Johnston (n 236) 69.
256 GRECO Eval III, U.S.A. Evaluation Report Theme II (2011) 5 §21.
257 See supra n 154.

There is a wide variety of political committees engaged with political campaign financing in the U.S.: besides the political party committees[258] at the federal, state or local level, and the authorized committees provided for by the FECA,[259] there are the PACs (political action committees), already mentioned above, which are broken down into two groups, the non-connected committees, which are political committees not affiliated with a party or a candidate, and the separate segregated funds, which are political committees established and administered by a corporation, labor union, membership organization or trade association;[260] their number has increased significantly since the introduction of the FECA, and in 2011 there were approximately 11,000 political committees, while the political party committees numbered about 400.[261]

An issue of concern for campaign finance reformers all over the world is that of anonymous donations and GRECO Evaluation Reports always attempt to establish the limits placed on them. In the U.S., the provisions of the FECA imply a cap of $50 on anonymous donations to candidates or political committees, since they require that the accounts of such recipients must contain the name and address of any person making a contribution in excess of that amount, along with the date and the amount itself, while for amounts above $200 the identity of the contributor, including address, occupation and employer, must be recorded.[262] No contributions over $100 in cash are allowed.[263] The same restrictions applying to anonymous donations above $50 – recording of name and address – apply to the disbursement of any amount above $50 as far as the identity of the recipient is concerned. As for loans, the FECA considers that in order for a loan or line of credit not to be considered a contribution, it must be made on a basis that insures repayment, evidenced by a written instrument, and subject to a due date or amortization schedule, while it bears the lending institution's usual and customary rate for that category of loan.[264] There are also other provisions about loans, how these may be considered as contributions and how their repayment can or (in the case of unlawful loans) cannot reduce the amount of such contributions, as well as about the possible endorsement or guarantee of the outstanding balance of loans.[265]

258 A political party committee is a political committee that represents a political party and is part of the party's official structure at the federal, state or local level, 11 CFR 100.5 (e) (4).

259 According to the FECA, 2 U.S.C. 431(6), an authorized committee is a committee designated (or not disavowed) by a candidate to receive contributions or to make expenditures on the candidate's behalf.

260 Separate segregated funds may have their administration and solicitation expenses covered by their sponsoring organization, however they may not solicit contributions from the general public, Trevor Potter, 'The Current State of Campaign Finance Law' in Anthony Corrado, Thomas E. Mann, Daniel R. Ortiz, Trevor Potter, *The New Campaign Finance Sourcebook* (Brookings Institution Press 2005) 51.

261 GRECO Eval III, U.S.A. Evaluation Report Theme II (2011) 7 §26.

262 GRECO Eval III, U.S.A. Evaluation Report Theme II (2011) 31 §138.

263 Ibid. See also supra n 163.

264 GRECO Eval III, U.S.A. Evaluation Report Theme II (2011) 12 §53.

265 Ibid. §§54-57.

The main means of campaign finance regulation in the U.S. is in the form of contribution limits in tandem with disclosure requirements for – limitless – independent spending. Of course, the data concerning aggregate limits on contributions quoted in the relevant Evaluation Report of GRECO[266] have become largely irrelevant in the aftermath of the *McCutcheon v. FEC* decision, which struck them as unconstitutional.[267] As far as transparency goes, however, the Evaluation Report of GRECO was concerned about the participation in political financing of certain tax-exempt groups,[268] to which some important disclosure requirements do not apply. These are the groups organized under section 501(c) of the Internal Revenue Code and, mainly, social welfare organizations such as environmental protection or civil rights groups organized under 501(c)(4), labor unions under 501(c)(5) and business associations under 501(c)(6).[269] These tax-exempt organizations, to the extent that they are primarily engaged in activities that further their aforementioned exempt purposes, can also make issue-advocacy expenditures, without having to reveal their donors if their contributions were less than $5,000, but even above that threshold, the relevant information of the donor's identity submitted to the Internal Revenue Service is considered tax information and thus pursuant to section 6103 of the Internal Revenue Code cannot be made public.[270] Moreover, as noted in the GRECO Evaluation Report, there is no specific rule for accessing what constitutes the primary activity of tax-exempt organizations.[271]

Due to the issues above, but also admitting that nothing more than a possible indirect link can be found between some tax-exempt organizations and specific candidates or parties, GRECO in its Evaluation Report suggested that the U.S. should 'seek ways to increase the transparency of funding provided to organizations such as those defined in section 501(c) of the Internal Revenue Code when the purpose of the donation/funding is intended to independently affect the election of a particular candidate or candidates',[272] one of its three recommendations in respect of transparency of party funding.[273]

In response to what – even before the GRECO Evaluation Report – has been perceived as a weak link of the campaign finance regulation regime, that is the lack of transparency

---

266 Ibid. §69.

267 Supra n 108.

268 According to section 501(c)(3) of the Internal Revenue Code, political intervention is the participation in, or intervention in (including the publishing or distributing of statements) any political campaign on behalf of or in opposition to any candidate for public office.

269 Mutch 2014 (n 10) 174. It should be noted that the appellant in *Citizens United v. FEC* was such a group; specifically, it was organized under section 501(c)(4).

270 Ibid.; GRECO Eval III, U.S.A. Evaluation Report Theme II (2011) 20 §93.

271 Ibid. 33-34 §144.

272 Ibid. 34-35 §146 and 38-39 §162.

273 The other two recommendations being of a rather technical nature, namely the electronic filing and thus the speedier processing of public disclosure of financial reports concerning Senate elections, as well as measures to prevent deadlocks arising in the decision-making process of the FEC, ibid. 32-33 §141 and 36 §151 respectively.

where contributions by section 501 (c) organizations are involved, six different legislative initiatives have taken place during the years 2012 and 2013 addressing the issue about which GRECO has raised its concerns; however, not a single one was successful.[274] Despite that, GRECO concluded that its recommendation was dealt with in a satisfactory manner[275] and has stood by that conclusion[276] even though that after more than five years since its original Evaluation Report nothing tangible has come out of the said recommendation, noting how the (failed) legislative attempts reflected the interest shown by the U.S.

At the outset, it seems that GRECO focuses on the rather rigid campaign finance structure of the U.S. – on both legislative and jurisprudence grounds – acknowledging broadly its ability to tackle political corruption, the abuse of public office for private gain; it does, however, focus on the transparency concerns that certain tax-exempt organizations pose for the whole system. As we will be able to realize in the relevant sections of Chapters 4 and 5, such concerns are limited in comparison to the critique the U.K. and especially the Greek campaign finance systems received by GRECO; this is probably an indication of a *sui generis* trust the U.S. system creates to third party reviewers, despite the rather limited public endorsement the very same system has in the U.S., and the failure of its political personnel and judiciary to tackle vital anomalies recognized within the system.

274 GRECO Eval III, U.S.A. Compliance Report (2014) 15 §53.

275 Ibid. 15§55.

276 GRECO Eval III, U.S.A. Addendum to the Second Compliance Report (2014), p. 7 §33.

Chapter 4 Campaign Finance Regulation in the U.K.

4.1 Historical Background, Main Characteristics and Constitutional Aspects

The U.K. campaign finance regime prior to the enactment of the Political Parties, Elections and Referendums Act 2000 (PPERA) was based on a 19th century Act, the Corrupt and Illegal Practices Prevention Act 1883.[1] Besides being partial and fragmented[2] (not unlike the U.S. legal framework prior to the 1974 Amendment to the FECA), it was also rather ineffective, as it was limited to regulation at the constituency level and failed to regulate campaign expenditure at the national level (as originally demonstrated since 1952 already in the *R v. Tronoh Mines Ltd* case),[3] even though it provided for very strict expenditure limits, namely for limits to what each party and candidate can spend when campaigning for office.

Although the original Act of 1883 did not regulate expenditures incurred by third parties, after the Representation of the People Act 1918, the limits placed on independent expenses, namely to out of own pocket expenses incurred by parties and candidates incurred were so low, as to render them meaningless. This was the reason the U.K. lost in the *Bowman v. United Kingdom* case before the European Court of Human Rights in 1998,[4] which found that the legislation in force violated Article 10 of

1 Navraj Singh Ghaleigh, 'Expenditure, Donations and Public Funding under the United Kingdom's Political Parties, Elections and Referendums Act 2000 - And Beyond?', in KD Ewing and Samuel Issacharoff (eds), *Party Funding and Campaign Financing in International Perspective* (Hart Publishing 2006) 35.

2 Ibid. 36.

3 Ibid. 37. In this particular case the Central Criminal Court of England and Wales held that the Representation of the People Act 1918 did not cover expenditures on nation-wide propaganda '... even though the general political propaganda does incidentally assist a particular candidate', *R v. Tronoh Mines Ltd* [1951] 1 All ER 697, 700.

4 *Bowman v. the United Kingdom* ECHR 1998-I 175. At the time, the limit was set by s 75 of the Representation of the People Act 1983 at £5.

the European Convention of Human Rights[5] on the freedom of expression in conjunction with Article 3 of Protocol 1 to the Convention[6] on the right to free elections. The case shall be further analyzed later in the present Chapter.

4.2 The Transformation of the U.K. Campaign Finance Regulation Regime

4.2.1 *The PPERA*

The decision in *Bowman v. United Kingdom* came at about the same time as a number of national constitutional innovations, such as the Scottish and Welsh devolutions, which changed the landscape of elections in the U.K., as well as on top of revelations about potential *quid pro quo* campaign donations.[7] These led to increasing demands for an effective campaign finance regulatory system. The outcome was the Political Parties, Elections and Referendums Act (PPERA), which radically transformed the regulatory framework for electoral parties in the U.K., affecting almost every aspect of donating to, spending by and accounting for of political actors, at both the constituency and the national level.[8]

Examining the PPERA, one must start from the keystone of its architecture, which is the Electoral Commission.[9] The Electoral Commission will be further elaborated on towards the end of the present Chapter, but a broad outline is in order here. The PPERA confers on the Commission a wide range of responsibilities and supervisory powers and even some limited legislative powers.[10] The Commission's main task,

5 The text of Article 10 of the European Convention of Human Rights has as follows: '1. Everyone has the right to freedom of expression. This right shall include freedom to hold opinions and to receive and impart information and ideas without interference by public authority and regardless of frontiers. This article shall not prevent States from requiring the licensing of broadcasting, television or cinema enterprises. 2. The exercise of these freedoms, since it carries with it duties and responsibilities, may be subject to such formalities, conditions, restrictions or penalties as are prescribed by law and are necessary in a democratic society, in the interests of national security, territorial integrity or public safety, for the prevention of disorder or crime, for the protection of health or morals, for the protection of the reputation or rights of others, for preventing the disclosure of information received in confidence, or for maintaining the authority and impartiality of the judiciary.'

6 The text of Article 3 of Protocol 1 to the European Convention of Human Rights has as follows: 'The High Contracting Parties undertake to hold free elections at reasonable intervals by secret ballot, under conditions which will ensure the free expression of the opinion of the people in the choice of the legislature.'

7 See Chapter 1, note 39. In the wake of the Formula 1 scandal a new word entered the vernacular in the U.K., with a million pounds being referred to in less reverential circles as a 'Bernie', after Bernie Ecclestone, who was the donor involved in the scandal, KD Ewing, 'The Disclosure of Political Donations in Britain' in KD Ewing and Samuel Issacharoff (eds), *Party Funding and Campaign Financing in International Perspective* (Hart Publishing 2006) 59.

8 Ghaleigh (n 1) 35.

9 Ibid. 42.

10 PPERA sch 8 (3).

though, is enforcement. One of the reasons of the perceived ineffectiveness of the pre-PPERA framework was that its enforcement was not the responsibility of a single, dedicated body.[11] In respect of its role as the state organ responsible for monitoring and enforcing conformity with the PPERA's provisions, the Electoral Commission bears a strong resemblance to the FEC in the U.S. and is a huge improvement over the pre-PPERA regime. Unlike the FEC, however, the members of the Commission are selected and appointed on the basis of near total absence of political experience, given that not only is party affiliation or previous service in office not required for the appointment, but it was actually the main reason of ineligibility,[12] at least until the introduction of nominated Commissioners in 2009, a novelty analyzed later in this Chapter in 4.4.1.

As far as expenditure limits are concerned, the PPERA addressed the main problem of the previous regime, namely the limits of only at the constituency level regulation. The need for national expenditure limits and the lack of an adequate nationally applicable regulatory framework were perhaps the most important aspect of the faults of the pre-PPERA regime identified by the Neill Committee.[13] The PPERA establishes a national limit on expenditures by political parties of £30,000 per seat contested in a general election,[14] which in theory can mean a total sum of up to £19,500,000 for the 650 seats of the House of Commons.[15] Furthermore, the PPERA introduces limits on expenditures by third parties at the national level along with the notion of 'recognized third parties',[16] which are obliged to notify the Electoral Commission of their intention to spend £10,000 or more at a general election in England or £5,000 or more each for Scotland, Wales or Northern Ireland.[17] The maximum aggregate limits are different for each constituent part of the U.K., ranging from £810,000 for England to £27,000 for Northern Ireland.[18] There are also different limits on expenditures by parties and 'recognized third parties' for the elections to the European Parliament.[19] The restrictions at the national level function in conjunction with those already in place at the local/constituency level. Of course, the limit on individual expenditures has increased[20] to satisfy the strictures of the *Bowman v. United Kingdom* decision, which will be analysed in detail below. The PPERA also contains provisions to avert possible ways of bypassing the restrictions imposed by it,

11 Ghaleigh (n 1) 43.
12 Ibid. The ineligibilities are listed in s 3 (4) of the PPERA.
13 Committee on Standards in Public Life, 'The Funding of Political Parties in the United Kingdom' (Cm 4057-I, 1998) ch 10. Lord Neill succeeded Lord Nolan as chairman of the Committee in 1997.
14 PPERA, sch 9 (3).
15 Only in theory, as British parties do not contest the Northern Irish seats.
16 PPERA, s 88.
17 Ibid. s 94 (4) and (5).
18 Ibid. sch 10 (3).
19 Ibid. sch 9 (4) and sch 10 (4) respectively.
20 From £5 to £500, ibid. s 131, which amended s 75 of the Representation of the People Act 1983.

so for example the free or discounted use (by more than 10%) of property, facilities or services is to count as an expenditure at the market and not the given rate.[21]

One of the main issues of the PPERA is that it introduces the notion of a regulated period in regard of expenditures which amounts to 365 days, the 365 days ending with the date of the poll of the election.[22] At the time of the enactment of the PPERA, the Parliament was customarily dissolved by royal proclamation by virtue of the Royal Prerogative (in practice on advice of the Prime Minister), only the maximum duration of the parliament (the period beginning with the first meeting of the new parliament) being set at five years under the Parliament Act 1911.[23] As there were no fixed dates for elections, but these were rather announced four to six weeks prior to the polling day, the provision of a regulated period of 365 days made it practically impossible for those intending to incur expenditures regulated by the PPERA to accurately time these expenditures.[24]

Even worse, as far as equality before the law goes, such a provision left open the possibility of abuse by the party in power. As it could effectively determine the polling date by the Prime Minister advising the monarch to dissolve the parliament, it could possibly manage its electoral campaign and its expenditures in full knowledge of the quantitative and temporal constraints imposed by the PPERA,[25] while the other parties could theoretically remain completely ignorant of the time of the impending election.

This particular problem seems to have been eased with the enactment of the Fixed-Term Parliaments Act 2011, which repealed the Septennial Act 1716 and which provides for elections taking place on fixed dates (in principle, the first Thursday in May in the fifth calendar year following that in which the polling day for the previous parliamentary general election was held)[26] and thus has made timing more predictable. It did not solve the problem, however, as recent experience has shown: the last U.K. general election took place on June 8 2017, only two years and a month after the previous one, which had taken place on May 7 2015, after being called by the Prime Minister according to section 2 of the Fixed-Term Parliaments Act, which provides for an early dissolution of Parliament by means of a House of Commons vote by a supermajority of two thirds of the entire membership of the House. Such a vote took place on April 19 2017, one day after the Prime Minister announced her intention to seek election on June 8, and the motion for an early general election passed with a majority meeting the requirements of the Act. Even though no significant data relating to how such an early election affected the campaign expenditures of the parties have been published, it is evident that no kind of

21 Ibid. s 73.
22 Ibid. sch 9 (7).
23 Parliament Act 1911 s 7. It amended the Septennial Act 1716 which provided for a maximum duration of parliament of 7 years.
24 Ghaleigh (n 1) 47.
25 Ibid.
26 Fixed-Term Parliaments Act 2011 s 1.

timing or scheduling to meet the requirements of the PPERA could have survived the derailment caused by this snap election. And just to demonstrate the innate limits of the Fixed-Term Parliaments Act 2011, on 31 October 2019, two days after the introduction of the relevant bill, the Early Parliamentary General Election Act 2019 came into effect, providing for an early parliamentary general election to take place on 12 December 2012, the Act becoming automatically spent on the conclusion of the election; the criticism regarding the advantages offered by unscheduled elections to the political party in power is even more applicable in this case, as not even the aforementioned supermajority, and thus the consent of a – a part at least – of the opposition, was required.

Besides reforming the regulatory regime of election expenditures, the PPERA did the same on contributions to political parties and candidates. As is also the case with the relevant legal framework in the U.S. and in Greece, the PPERA places restrictions on the persons of the donors based on their electoral connection to the U.K. by introducing the notion of 'permissible donor' in order for a person to be allowed to contribute.[27] Unlike U.S. and Greek legislation however, which use nationality as its sole criterion for natural persons in this respect, according to the provisions of the PPERA 'permissible donor' for natural persons means all individuals who are on the electoral rolls (not simply all nationals), while for legal persons the main criterion is the place of registration.[28] However, the PPERA does not restrict in any way the amount of contributions: there is no maximum limit, except that all donations over £7,500 at the national level and £1,000 at the local level have to be reported.[29] There are many safeguards in PPERA's relevant provisions to ensure that parties will not be able to evade the disclosure rules by breaking down the donations given to them into smaller amounts or accepting them over longer periods of time.[30]

A final important aspect of the PPERA regarding donors' permissibility that should be noted concerns the introduction of shareholder consent for corporate contributions. Prior to the PPERA's enactment, there were restrictions on trade unions donations, which had to have passed a resolution approved by the majority of their members voting in order to seek the furtherance of political objects [*sic*] and be able to donate to this purpose;[31] any contributions would only come from a separate fund; members of the unions could be exempted from contributing to these political funds without any disadvantage to their rights.[32] The Trade Union Act 1984, furthermore, required the

27 PPERA, s. 54 (1).

28 Ibid. s 54 (2). As far as natural persons are concerned, see also s 141, amending the Representation of the People Act 1985 as amended by the Representation of the People Act 2000, and shortening the period a non-resident retains the right to vote from 20 to 15 years.

29 Ibid. s 62. Subsection 11 refers to local units of party organization as 'accounting units'.

30 See KD Ewing (n 7) as to how PPERA's provisions attempt to achieve this.

31 Trade Union Act 1913, s 3 (1).

32 Ibid.

repetition of ballots every ten years for the continuance of the political funds.[33] There were no similar restrictions placed on corporations and their contributions, even though there were valid concerns about the risk of conflicts of interest on the part of the directors, as well as about the possibility of shareholder opposition.[34] Of course, due to its affiliation with the trade unions, the Labour Party was greatly disadvantaged by this regime, while the Conservative party, which was supported mainly by corporate donations, faced no similar burdens.[35] The inconsistency between trade union and corporate contributions was addressed by the PPERA, which amends company law (specifically, the Companies Act 1985) to include the principle of shareholder consent in the form of the requirement of an approval resolution to allow corporate donations or expenditures.[36]

4.2.2 Free Airtime and Other Means of Public Financing to the Political Parties

The PPERA regime did not alter the pre-existing ban on political advertising in broadcast media. Such a ban has been in existence even before the launch of commercial television, although the first time a distinction was drawn between commercial and political advertisements was with the Television Act 1954.[37] The ban has been offset by party political and election broadcasts, which are provided for free by the BBC (by convention) and certain independent broadcasters (by law),[38] and offer political parties direct access to the broadcast media. This free airtime during the election period and at certain other dates of the political calendar[39] is not dissimilar to that offered to political parties in Greece by the relevant provisions of its legislation during the election period and is, perhaps, the inspiration for it, as we will analyse further in Chapter 5; note, however, that in the election regulation framework in Greece, there is no prohibition of paid political advertising in the broadcast media.

Free airtime is one of the means used in the U.K. political regulatory regime to subsidize the political parties, without actually providing them with funds. Other similar means include free access to public buildings for holding meetings during campaigning periods and free – but limited use – of the postal system.[40] Grants of state

33 Trade Union Act 1984, s 12.
34 Ghaleigh (n 1) 39.
35 Ibid. 38. For some hard data about the dependence of the Labor Party on trade unions' contributions see KD Ewing (n 7) 69-70.
36 PPERA, s 139 and sch 19.
37 Jacob Rowbottom, 'Access to the Airwaves and Equality: The Case against Political Advertising on the Broadcast Media' in KD Ewing and Samuel Issacharoff (eds), *Party Funding and Campaign Financing in International Perspective* (Hart Publishing 2006) 77-78.
38 Alan Grant, 'Party and Election Finance in Britain and America: A Comparative Analysis' (2005) 58 Parliam. Aff. 71, 74.
39 Ibid.
40 Ghaleigh (n 1) 53.

aid directly to political parties (as in many European countries, including Greece) or providing tax incentives to potential donors (as in the U.S., both at the state and the federal level) have never garnered much support in the U.K.[41] There were, however, some other, more indirect, ways of providing at least a limited amount of funds to political parties, even before the enactment of the PPERA. Such are the Short/ Cranborne schemes which fund opposition parties to fulfil more effectively their parliamentarian function, and which will be analysed further in the present Chapter in 4.3.1.

A further source of state funding is the Policy Development Grant, a global annual fund of £2,000,000 to be distributed by the Electoral Commission to political parties for the purpose of developing policies to be included in any manifesto; this Grant was introduced by the PPERA.[42] Even though the amount is rather modest, it greatly enhances the ability of parties to engage in long term research without the fear of spreading their scarce resources too thin.[43] Its purpose is similar to that of one of the three different forms of state subsidies to political parties in Greece, namely the research and educational subsidies, as it will be further elaborated upon in the next Chapter.

Although direct state aid has not been very popular in the U.K., its importance is increasing, as well as the reliance of the parties on it: over the period 2001-2004, for example, public funds amounted to some £11.9 million out of the approximately £36 million in donations reported by the Conservative Party.[44]

4.2.3 *Freedom of Expression and the PPERA:* Bowman v. The United Kingdom

4.2.3.1 The Background

The issue of freedom of expression in relation to campaign finance regulation has been shaped in the U.K. mainly by the *Bowman* case in the proceedings before the European Court of Human Rights.[45] In this respect, it is worth to delve deeper into the case, especially as it highlights another interesting aspect of any constitutional issues that may arise with campaign finance regulation in the U.K., which applies also for Greece (but not for the U.S.): the subjection of any relevant legislation not only to constitutional restrictions imposed by the domestic legal system, but to international law as well, namely the European Convention of Human Rights (ECHR).

It should perhaps be recalled at this point that, at the time the *Bowman* first arose (1992), the ECHR had not yet become part of U.K. law, since the Human Rights Act 1998, which transposed the Convention into U.K. law, had not yet come into force (it

41 Ibid. 39-40.
42 PPERA, s 12.
43 Ghaleigh (n 1) 53-54.
44 KD Ewing (n 7) 71-72.
45 *Bowman v. the United Kingdom* ECHR 1998-I 175.

came into force on October 2, 2000). The U.K. legal system being dualistic, this meant that the Convention could not be invoked before the domestic courts of law and its provisions did not bind them. Even if this *lacuna* could usually be overcome by the interpretation of rules of domestic law in such a way, as not to bring them into conflict with the Convention,[46] that was simply not possible in this case, as there was no room for such an interpretation.

Ms. Phyllis Bowman, the applicant before the European Court of Human Rights, was the executive director of an anti-abortion society numbering approximately 50,000 members. The society was seeking changes to U.K. legislation on abortion and embryo experimentation. As these issues are considered by the two major political parties to be of moral nature and their members of Parliament are allowed to vote according to their conscience, the applicant and her society believed that it was important to inform voters on the opinions of the candidates standing for the parliamentary elections of April 1992 on the matter.[47] In this respect, they arranged for the distribution of one and a half million leaflets throughout the country, including 25,000 in the constituency of Halifax; the leaflets started with a disclaimer of sorts reading: 'We are not telling you how to vote, but it is essential for you to check on Candidates' voting intentions on abortion and on the use of the human embryo as a guinea-pig.'[48] They went on to describe the opinions of candidates as perceived by the society; in the constituency of Halifax, the leaflets described in positive terms the positions of the Conservative and the Liberal Democrat candidates, while the opposite happened to the positions of the Labour party candidate, who was characterized as 'a leading pro-abortionist'.[49]

Subsequently, Ms. Bowman was charged with an offence under the Representation of the People Act 1983, which according to subsection 75 (1), as it stood at the time, prohibited expenditure of more than £5 by an unauthorized person during the period before an election with a view to promoting or procuring the election of a candidate.[50] Although the text of the leaflets was not promoting the election of a particular candidate, but rather the exact opposite, the House of Lords had in its case law interpreted this to include the intention to prevent the election of a particular candidate or candidates.[51] If found guilty of what subsection 75 (5) described as a 'corrupt practice', she was liable to imprisonment of up to one year or a fine.[52] At her trial, Ms. Bowman was acquitted by the jury at the direction of the judge for a procedural reason, as the summons charging

---

46 W.M.E Thomassen, 'The European Convention of Human Rights (ECHR) and the Position of the National Judge' in A.S. Muller and M.A. Loth (eds.), *Highest Courts and the Internationalisation of Law: Challenges and Changes* (Hague Academic Press 2009) 115.

47 *Bowman v. the United Kingdom* ECHR 1998-I 175, 179.

48 Ibid. 180-181.

49 Ibid. 181.

50 Representation of the People Act 1983 as amended by the Representation of the People Act 1985, subsection 75 (1). The original amount in the Representation of the People Act 1983 was 50p.

51 *Bowman v. the United Kingdom* ECHR 1998-I 175, 183.

52 Representation of the People Act 1983 as amended by the Representation of the People Act 1985 s 168 (1).

her with the offence had not been issued within the proscribed time-limit of one year since the alleged corrupt practice took place,[53] so the issue of freedom of expression in this case was never actually examined by a U.K. court of law.

4.2.3.2 The Proceedings before the European Court of Human Rights

The initial application to the European Commission of Human Rights was brought jointly by Ms. Bowman and the society of which she was the executive director; however, it was declared inadmissible in regard of the latter, because it was found that the society could not claim to be itself a victim by virtue of Ms. Bowman's prosecution.[54] The U.K. government had also submitted a preliminary objection that Ms. Bowman could not properly be considered a victim according to Article 25 of the European Convention of Human Rights,[55] as the trial judge had directed the jury to acquit her, and thus the case was *in toto* inadmissible; nevertheless, both the Commission and the Court dismissed the U.K.'s allegation, on the grounds that the prosecution of Ms. Bowman constituted itself a measure of implementation taken against her. Moreover, the Court considered that the acquittal was based on a procedural reason, and that the strong indication given to her that, unless she modified her behavior during future elections she ran the risk of being prosecuted and possibly convicted and punished, had to be judicially reviewed.[56]

The applicant submitted that there had been a violation of her right to freedom of expression protected under Article 10 of the ECHR.[57] Although the U.K. government contented that the relevant provisions of the Representation of the People Act 1983 restricted only the freedom of unauthorized persons to incur expenses in a parliamentary election and not their freedom of expression, the Court rejected the argument, and examined whether the restriction could be regarded as falling within the exception established in paragraph 2 of Article 10 as being prescribed by law, pursuing a legitimate aim and being necessary in a democratic society. Answering in the affirmative the first question, it moved to examine the other two. It concluded that section 75 of the Representation of the People Act 1983 sought to secure equality between candidates in an election and thus recognized equality within the context of campaign finance regulation

53 Ibid. s 176 (1).

54 *Bowman v. the United Kingdom* ECHR 1998-I 175, 184.

55 The text of the relevant section of Article 25 of the ECHR, as it stood at the time, has as follows: '1. The Commission may receive petitions addressed to the Secretary-General of the Council of Europe from any person, non-governmental organisation or group of individuals claiming to be the victim of a violation by one of the High Contracting Parties of the rights set forth in this Convention, provided that the High Contracting Party against which the complaint has been lodged has declared that it recognises the competence of the Commission to receive such petitions. Those of the High Contracting Parties who have made such a declaration undertake not to hinder in any way the effective exercise of this right.'

56 *Bowman v. the United Kingdom* ECHR 1998-I 175, 185.

57 See supra n 5 for the text of Article 10 of the ECHR.

as a legitimate government aim.[58] Then, it focused its examination on the necessity of such a restriction in a democratic society and the proportionality of the measure to the stated aim.

The U.K. government maintained that the restriction was no more expansive than necessary and listed other means that Ms. Bowman could have used to communicate her message, such as starting her own newspaper, having letters or articles published in the press, giving interviews on radio or television, standing for election herself, or publishing leaflets with the purpose of informing the electorate without promoting or opposing any particular candidate.[59] The Court considered the possible violation of Article 10 under the prism of Article 3 of Additional Protocol No. 1 to the European Convention of Human Rights establishing the right to free elections, noting that, although freedom of expression is a precondition for free elections, at times the two rights may come into conflict.[60]

The member states to the ECHR enjoy a margin of appreciation, which the Court has incessantly emphasized,[61] in striking a balance between those rights when they come into conflict. The Court found that the measure adopted by the U.K. was disproportionate to its aim, remarking that the other means of disseminating information proposed by the U.K. government in its submission were of markedly reduced effectiveness or increased cost, and thus found the respondent state in violation of Article 10.[62] It should be noted that it was not the concept of a limit on third parties' expenses that was found to violate the right to freedom of expression, but the very exceptionally low limit of £5 that was found disproportionate. Being an international tribunal, the European Court of Human Rights determined that its finding of a violation was sufficient just satisfaction for any non-pecuniary damage suffered by the applicant.[63]

The Court's decision of a violation of Article 10 was reached by a 14 to 6 majority of its members. There were three partly dissenting opinions: one by Judge Valticos (Greece), one joint one of Judges Loizou (Cyprus), Baka (Hungary) and Jambrek (Slovenia) and one by Judge Freeland (U.K.) joined by Judge Levits (Latvia). There are interesting points in all three, but of particular interest is a point made in the last two, concerning the relationship of section 75 to section 76 of the Representation of the People Act 1983. These two partly dissenting opinions touch upon the interdependence of the two sections: as section 76 seeks to restrict the expenses of the candidates themselves,

---

58 *Bowman v. the United Kingdom* ECHR 1998-I 175, 187.

59 Ibid. 187-188.

60 Ibid. 188-189.

61 D. Grimm, *Domestic Courts and International Courts*, in A.S. Muller and M.A. Loth (eds.), *Highest Courts and the Internationalisation of Law: Challenges and Changes* (Hague Academic Press 2009) 125.

62 *Bowman v. the United Kingdom* ECHR 1998-I 175, 189-190.

63 Ibid. 190.

section 75 is necessary to prevent the circumvention of these restrictions by third persons.[64] In their joint opinion, Judges Loizou, Baka and Jambrek elaborated on how the restrictions of the Representation of the People Act 1983 seek to prevent the manipulation of candidate by pressure groups, while Judge Freeland focused on (i) how, despite section 75, Ms. Bowman and her society managed to circulate one and a half million leaflets without any hindrance and (ii) on the actual possibility of her being acquitted based on substantive grounds had she not been acquitted on procedural grounds. All three decisions stress the importance of equality and fairness in the elections as a legitimate government concern.

4.2.3.3 The Assessment by the Committee on Standards in Public Life

The *Bowman v. United Kingdom* judgment received particular attention in the Fifth Report of the Committee on Standards in Public Life.[65] The Committee approached the issue from two viewpoints: (i) the maximum amount of independent expenses *in concreto*; and (ii) the legality of restrictions on independent expenses *in abstracto*. On the first issue, after a brief discussion of the relevant parameters to be taken into account, it reached the conclusion to propose a maximum amount in the order of £500.[66] On the second issue, its reasoning focused on the compatibility of restrictions on independent expenses with Article 10 of the ECHR. While remarking on the differences of the said Article with the free speech right as laid down in the First Amendment of the U.S. Constitution, which according to the Committee is given a much more absolutist interpretation,[67] it relied on the more flexible standards of paragraph 2 of Article 10 in conjunction with the right to free elections protected by Article 3 of Additional Protocol No. 1 to the ECHR, and concluded that, by utilizing its margin of appreciation, a state party to the Convention may impose reasonable limits on the right to freedom of expression for a strictly defined period before or during an election.[68] In reaching this conclusion, the Committee made special reference to the joint partly dissenting opinion of Judges Loizou, Baka and Jambrek, as well as to 'clear indications' (as perceived by the Committee) that the European Court of Human Rights would be sympathetic to a 'level playing field' argument.[69] What the Court objected to, according to the Committee's assessment of the *Bowman* decision, was not the imposition of a limit in general to independent expenses, but rather the derisory limit

64 Ibid. 195-196 (para 5 of joint partly dissenting opinion of Mr. Loizou, Mr. Baka and Mr. Jambrek); ibid. 198-199 (para 5 of partly dissenting opinion of Sir John Freeland, joined by Mr. Levits).

65 Committee on Standards in Public Life, 'The Funding of Political Parties in the United Kingdom' (Cm 4057-I, 1998) 126-131.

66 Ibid. 129.

67 Ibid. 130 and in Appendix II of the Report at 211-212.

68 Ibid. 130.

69 Ibid.

of £5.[70] The legislation conformed to the recommendations of the Committee on Standards in Public Life in maintaining a limit on independent expenses, but raising it to £500 in the PPERA,[71] as per the Committee's proposals.

4.2.4 A Judge's Insight into the Differences with U.S. Campaign Finance Values

As is the also the case in respect of campaign regulation legislation in Greece, the relatively recent enactment of the PPERA means that no case regarding the violation of its provisions has been brought before any court of law in the U.K. Although allegations of violation of PPERA's spending limits during the general election of 2015 have led to the launch of investigations by the police in the U.K., no specific legal action has been launched at the time of this writing.

However, another aspect of the campaign regulatory regime that predates the PPERA has been brought before the English courts, before being challenged in the European Court of Human Rights, and should be mentioned here (in the absence also of more relevant cases). In 2005 a non-governmental organization based in London, Animal Defenders International (ADI), challenged the ban on political advertisement in broadcast media, after the broadcasting of one television advertisement directed against the keeping and exhibition of primates was refused by the competent authority, the Broadcast Advertising Clearance Centre. ADI sought before the High Court a declaration of incompatibility under section 4 of the Human Rights Act 1998 (the HRA) which incorporates into U.K. law the provisions of the ECHR. ADI argued that the ban on political advertising on television and radio imposed by the 2003 Communications Act was incompatible with Article 10 of the Convention. The applicant's (later appellant's) claim was dismissed by both the High Court and the House of Lords, so ADI, having exhausted all domestic remedies, brought the case before the European Court of Human Rights. After examining the applicable domestic law (the Communications Act 2003) and the practice of all European countries, the Court rejected the applicant's claim by the slimmest of majorities (9 to 8), concluding that the prohibition is not a disproportionate interference with the applicant's right to freedom of expression.[72]

More important from a comparative law point of view, however, is the decision of the House of Lords in the case. This is because in her opinion, Baroness Hale managed to capture the essence of the question not only in relation to U.K. law, but also to the U.S.

---

70 Ibid. 131.

71 PPERA, s 131.

72 *Animal Defenders International v. the United Kingdom*, ECHR 2013-II 203, 235-239, regarding the proportionality issue.

paradigm. Before proceeding to examining the legal framework regulating campaign finances in Greece, it is worth quoting the relevant passage in its entirety:

> My Lords,
> 47. There was an elephant in the committee room, always there but never mentioned, when we heard this case. It was the dominance of advertising, not only in elections but also in the formation of political opinion, in the United States of America. Enormous sums are spent, and therefore have to be raised, at election times: it is estimated that the disputed 2000 elections for President and Congress cost as much as US$3 billion. Attempts to regulate campaign spending are struck down in the name of the First Amendment: "Congress shall make no law ... abridging the freedom of speech, or of the press": see particularly *Buckley v. Valeo*, 424 US 1 (1976). *A fortiori* there is no limit to the amount that pressure groups can spend on getting their message across in the most powerful and pervasive media available.
> 48. In the United Kingdom, and elsewhere in Europe, we do not want our government or its policies to be decided by the highest spenders. Our democracy is based upon more than one person one vote. It is based on the view that each person has equal value. "Within the sphere of democratic politics, we confront each other as moral equals" (Ackerman and Ayres, *Voting with Dollars*, 2003, p 12). We want everyone to be able to make up their own minds on the important issues of the day. For this we need the free exchange of information and ideas. We have to accept that some people have greater resources than others with which to put their views across. But we want to avoid the grosser distortions which unrestricted access to the broadcast media will bring.
> 49. So this case is not just about permissible restrictions on freedom of expression. It is about striking the right balance between the two most important components of a democracy: freedom of expression and voter equality.[73]

4.3 The U.K. Campaign Finance System: Current Legislation and Typology

In the U.K., as seen above, the PPERA remains the applicable law of the land, which regulates private campaign finance and provides for the policy development fund. Two additional ways of public finance are also provided in regulations by the House of Commons (Short money) and the House of Lords (Cranborne money). Therefore, and as we will see in more detail below, the system in the U.K. can be characterized as a true

73 *R v. Secretary of State For Culture, Media and Sports* [2008] UKHL 15.

'mixed' one because it regulates relatively proportionately the distribution of money both from public and private resources, while political actors have been making concurrent use of both sources of finance to fund their activities.

4.3.1 Public Campaign Finance

Political parties in the U.K. may receive financial support from the state through mainly three schemes of funding. Each scheme is administered respectively by the House of Commons, the House of Lords and the Electoral Commission. Short money finance has been adopted in 1975 and has been amended in 2016 by a Resolution of the House of Commons.[74] This type of finance is granted to all opposition parties in the House of Commons that secured either two seats or one seat and more than 150,000 votes at the previous General Election. Short Money is not available to parties the Members of which have not sworn the oath. The scheme is provided to the opposition parties in order to, first, carry out their Parliamentary business,[75] second to cover their travel and associated expenses,[76] and, third, for covering the running costs of the Leader of the Opposition's office.[77]

Cranborne money is a channel for public financing of the opposition parties in the House of Lords and has been provided by a resolution of this body in 1996.[78] According to that resolution, this type of financing is provided to the two larger opposition parties in the House of Lords, under the condition that those parties provide the Accounting Officer of the House with an auditor's certificate which ensures that all the expenses to be reimbursed were incurred for the parliamentary function of the party. Since 1999 its recipients include also the Convenor of the cross-bench peers, i.e. peers who are not affiliated with any political party (and are not Lords Spiritual).

The third scheme of public finance is the Policy development fund which is provided under the PPERA. The grant is provided to all represented registered parties[79] for them to develop policies in their respective political manifestos and/or for their candidates' election.[80] The Electoral Commission develops and, following an approval provided by the Secretary of State, regulates this fund. More specifically, the Commission proposes the

74 HC Deb 26 May 1999, vol 332, cols 427-9 (see Appendix 4 for the text of the resolution). Note the resolution was altered by the Members Estimate Committee, see Appendix 4; HC Deb 23 March 2016 vol 607, cols 1714-1716.

75 The amount available is determined by the number of seats and votes actually won by a party at the previous general election.

76 The amount available is apportioned between qualifying parties in the same proportion as general funding.

77 A fixed annual budget is available.

78 Lords resolution 27 November 1996, see also HL Deb 27 November 1996, vol. 576, cols. 267-272.

79 A registered party is 'represented' if there are at least two Members of the House of Commons belonging to the party who have made and subscribed to the oath required by the Parliamentary Oaths Act 1866 (or the corresponding affirmation) and are not disqualified from sitting or voting in that House.

80 PPERA s 12 (1).

eligibility criteria and the allocation method of the funds to the eligible parties and submits a relevant recommendation to the Secretary of State.[81] The PPERA sets a maximum limit for the policy development grant at £2 million per financial year.[82]

4.3.2 Private Campaign Finance

On a general note, about private campaign finance in the U.K., it shall be observed that the PPERA, as already mentioned, does not economically constrain the amount of donations received by political parties; it does though impose limits on campaign expenditure.

Regulated 'donations' consist of: (i) gifts of money and property (including money or property transferred to a party for consideration of lower value); (ii) sponsorships to the party; (iii) subscriptions and affiliation fees; (iv) money spent (other than by or on behalf of the party) to pay expenses incurred by the party; and (v) loans, property, services and other facilities provided to the party on other than commercial terms.[83] The definition of a 'donation' applies to anything given or transferred to the party either directly or indirectly through a third person.[84] Sponsorships are distinguished on the fact that they are linked to the purpose of party assistance in order to cover certain 'defined expenses'.[85]

Parties are allowed to accept donations only from permissible donors and only in cases where the latters' identities are known.[86] Permissible donors do not include (i) foreign donors[87] and (ii) anonymous donors or donors with fictional identifies. For donations exceeding £7,500 a written declaration should be provided to the party by the donor,[88] including information about the identity of the donor and his residence; any money deposit without such declaration constitutes an offence.[89] Section 52 of the PPERA provides for exceptions to the notion of donations under section 50. The most notable exceptions are donations: (i) the value of which is less than £500;[90] (ii) which falls to be included in a return as to election expenses in respect of a candidate or candidates at

81 Ibid. s 12 (2-4).
82 Ibid. s 12 (8).
83 Ibid. s 50 (2).
84 Ibid. s 50 (8)(a).
85 Ibid. s 51 (1). Subsection (2) details such 'defined expenses' as 'expenses incurred in connection with: (a) any conference, meeting or other event organised by or on behalf of the party; (b) the preparation, production or dissemination of any publication by or on behalf of the party; or (c) any study or research by or on behalf of the party'.
86 Ibid. s 54 (1).
87 Ibid. s 54 (2).
88 Ibid. s 54A (1).
89 Ibid. s 54B.
90 Ibid. s 52 (2)(b). The amount was originally £200, but it was later increased by s 20 (1) of the Political Parties and Elections Act 2009.

a particular election;[91] (iii) consisted of the provision by an individual of his own services under the condition that those service are freely provided in his/her own time.[92]

Political parties bear the compliance responsibility with the above requirements.[93] They have 30 days to determine the status of each donation and take appropriate actions when the donation does not comply with the applicable formalities.[94] The PPERA also provides for sanctions in regard of accepted donations from an impermissible source, or where the identity of the donor is unknown, while it also sets the procedural framework under which these sanctions may be imposed.[95] Apart from the civil liability established under section 58, section 61 establishes also the criminal liability of any person knowingly entering into arrangements to facilitate donations by non-permissible donors, or furthering such arrangements, or knowingly supplying false information to a political party's treasurer, or withholding material information, about the amount or the source of any donation made to the party.[96] These provisions should be read in conjunction with section 66, which requires the treasurer of a party to declare that the party has not accepted any donations from an impermissible source.

The PPERA sets also the framework with respect to control donations to members associations[97] and individuals.[98] These donations are controlled if they are deployed by the recipients in connection to their "political activities", which may understood as any activity pertaining directly or indirectly to an election procedure.[99] The notions of donation and sponsorship[100] and the restrictions with regards to the permissibility of sources and acceptance of donations[101] are equivalent to those for political parties.

While the law does not provide limits with regards to donations, this is not the case with regard to expenditures, regulated by the PPERA and the Representation of the People Act 1983. Those acts introduce limits concerning: campaign expenditure, which refers to expenses incurred for election purposes by or on behalf of the party;[102] election (candidate) expenditure, which refers to the expenses incurred by a specific candidate for

91 PPERA s 52 (2)(a).
92 Ibid. s 52 (1)(g).
93 Ibid. s 56 (1).
94 Ibid. s 56 (2).
95 Ibid. ss 58-60.
96 Ibid. s 61.
97 A 'members association' as an organisation which is comprised wholly or mainly of members of the party, ibid. sch 7 (1)(6). According to the PPERA's Explanatory Notes, these are groups which lie outside the formal structure of the party for the purposes of controls on funding and which, therefore, will not have been included in the scheme proposed and adopted in accordance with s 26.
98 Ibid. s 71 referring to sch 7.
99 Ibid. sch 7 (1)(3).
100 Ibid. sch 7 (2)-(3).
101 Ibid. sch 7(6)-(9).
102 Ibid. s 72 (2). This definition is complemented by the provisions of sch 8. It should be noted that under sch 8 (3), the Electoral Commission will provide guidance with respect to the expenses qualifying as 'campaign expenditure'.

a relevant election period;[103] and controlled (third-party) expenditure, which refers to expenses incurred by or on behalf of a third party.[104] For campaign and election expenditure, political parties and candidates respectively have a duty to submit before the Electoral Commission spending returns and declarations.[105] Limits on campaign expenditure, namely on expenses incurred by a political party during a regulated period are introduced under Schedule 9 of the PPERA.[106] U.K. general elections usually have a regulated period of 365 days, ending on the day of the election. All the other elections have a regulated period of four months.[107]

Campaign expenditure is constrained in a two-fold manner: (i) the maximum amount of campaign expenditure for each political party is the amount derived from multiplying £30,000 by the number of constituencies contested in a certain part of Great Britain;[108] (ii) the minimum expenditure limits with respect to the constituencies for England is £810,000, £120,000 for Scotland and £60,000 for Wales.[109] The temporal scope of those limits is a calendar year prior to the election date, namely 365 days ending with the date of the election.[110]

With regard to election expenditure, which refers to expenses incurred by a candidate for its campaign for election during the regulated period, the Representation of the People Act 1983 provides only for maximum limitations. More specifically, the maximum amount for a candidate at a parliamentary general election is £7,150, with an additional 7p in county constituencies or 5p in borough constituencies for every entry in the register of electors.[111] Finally, controlled (third-party) expenditure which exceeds £20,000 in England or £10,000 in any of Scotland, Wales or Northern Ireland[112] requires the registration of the third party before the Commission as "recognized" and is subject to the same reporting obligations of donations[113] and campaign expenditure.[114]

The campaign finance system under the PPERA imposes a general reporting obligation on the economic situation of political parties as well as special obligations related to donations and expenditure both of political parties and candidates. First, the Electoral Commission assesses the economic situation of political parties and candidates

103 Representation of the People Act 1983 s 76 (1A).

104 PPERA s 85.

105 For campaign expenditure see ibid. s 82. For election expenditure see Representation of the People Act 1983 s 87A.

106 PPERA s 79 referring to sch 9.

107 Electoral Commission, 'Overview of Party Campaign Spending' 7 https://www.electoralcommission.org.uk/sites/default/files/pdf_file/to-campaign-spend-rp.pdf last accessed 12 November 2019.

108 PPERA sch 9 (3)(2).

109 Ibid. sch 9 (3)(3).

110 Ibid. sch 9 (3)(7)(a).

111 Representation of the People Act 1983 s 76 (2).

112 PPERA s 94 (5).

113 Ibid. ss 95A-95B.

114 Ibid. ss 96 and 98.

via the relevant annual reports it receives. Parties' treasurers should keep accounting records in order to ensure that the financial situation of the parties can be explicitly explained "with reasonable accuracy".[115] Additionally, they should prepare an annual account of the political party[116] and submit within four months of the end of the financial year a statement of accounts to the Commission.[117]

The treasurers are also under the obligation to submit reports to the Electoral Commission in relation to the donations received by the parties on a quarterly[118] and weekly basis.[119] A quarterly donations report shall record all impermissible donations, any permissible donation over £7,500, permissible donations and loans which are (or add up over) £7,500 from the same source in the same calendar year and those which are (or add up over) £1,500 and come from a source that has already been reported to the Commission at the same calendar year.[120] In particular, they are required to record, in respect of each recordable donation, the identity of the donor (including their name and address), the value of the donation and the circumstances in which the donation was made.[121] Where a party has received no donation, it is still required to file a relevant report.

The weekly reports are differentiated from the quarterly reports, since, firstly, they are submitted only during a parliamentary general election period[122] and secondly, because they include disclosable donations received, whether or not they are eventually accepted. Any registered party which does not intend to field candidates at a particular general election is exempted from the requirement to submit weekly donations reports.[123] Only donations of more than £7,500 made to a party need to be recorded in the weekly reports.[124] Section 65 requires the submission of quarterly donation reports within thirty days[125] and of weekly donation reports within seven days of the end of the period to which they relate,[126] and makes it an offence for the treasurer to fail to submit donation reports or to submit reports which do not comply with these requirements.[127]

Disclosure obligations before the Electoral Commission are also introduced for members' association and individuals. Donations of more than £7,500 in the case of a

115 Ibid. s 41 (1)-(2).
116 Ibid. s 42 (1).
117 Ibid. s 45 (1).
118 Ibid. s 62 (1).
119 Ibid. s 63 (1).
120 Ibid. s 62.
121 Ibid. sch 6.
122 See ibid. s 64 (6) for the definition of a 'general election period'.
123 Ibid. s 64 (1) and (2).
124 Ibid. s 63 (3).
125 Ibid. s 65 (1).
126 Ibid. s 65 (2).
127 Ibid. s 65 (3) and (4).

member's association and more than £1,500 in any other case shall be disclosed.[128] This obligation should be complied with within 30 days of the acceptance of any disclosable donation.[129] Failure to comply with the reporting obligations[130] as well as any omission to accompany donations with a declaration attesting the permissibility of its source,[131] constitute both criminal offences. It is also provided that disclosed donations will be included in a register of disclosable donations.[132]

Similar disclosure obligations are applicable to campaign expenditure. The treasurers should prepare a return after each campaign period, accompanied by a declaration of its accuracy, both to be submitted within three months of the end of the relevant campaign period.[133] However, in case the party's expenditure is higher than the amount of £250,000, the return should be also examined independently by a qualified auditor and be submitted within six months after the end of the relevant campaign.[134] Any failure to submit the return on time or knowingly or recklessly submitting false information is considered an offence.[135]All returns received by the Electoral Commission are to be open to public inspection.[136]

4.3.3 Assessment

Consisting of relatively proportionate co-existent provisions on both public and private campaign finance, the U.K. system is a true 'mixed' system. Distinguished for subjecting private donations to (very) strict disclosure requirements rather than to quantifiable limits, the U.K. system is based on a novel approach to campaign finance, with the focus being on transparency and control.

4.4 Supervision and Enforcement: The U.K. Electoral Commission

In the U.K. the Electoral Commission ('the Commission') constitutes a novel feature of the PPERA. After almost a century of unsuccessful efforts to regulate campaign finance in the U.K., the PPERA introduced a relevantly detailed framework closely connected to a new institutional set up in order to safeguard and supervise its application. Below, the structure and the competences of the Electoral Commission shall be analyzed, including

128 Ibid. sch 7 (10).
129 Ibid. sch 7 (11)(1)(b).
130 Ibid. sch 7 (12).
131 Ibid. sch 7 (13).
132 Ibid. sch (15).
133 Ibid. ss 80 and 82.
134 Ibid. s 81.
135 Ibid. s 83.
136 Ibid. s 84.

the changes brought about by The Political Parties and Elections Act 2009. An assessment of this mechanism will follow, highlighting its strengths and inefficiencies.

4.4.1 Structure

The Commission's structure is provided under Part I of the PPERA. The members of the Commission are known as Electoral Commissioners[137] and they should be nine or ten in number.[138] The appointment of both the Members and the Chairman of the Commission is performed by the Queen on an Address of the House of Commons.[139] A motion for such an Address may be exercised upon the fulfilment of three cumulative procedural conditions, namely: (i) a proposal of appointment in accordance with a procedure provided by the Speaker's Committee; (ii) a consultation of the registered leader of each registered party which has two or more Members in the House of Commons; and (iii) the consent of the Speaker of the House of Commons.[140] The Address should specify the period of incumbency of the candidate Electoral Commissioner or Chairman, which should not exceed ten years.[141]

One of the PPERA amendments in 2009 was the introduction of the notion of nominated Commissioners. From the total number of the Electoral Commissioners, at least four should be nominated Commissioners,[142] i.e. people proposed by leaders of qualifying parties.[143] The PPERA introduces two limitations in this procedure. Three of the nominated Commissioners should be put forward by the largest[144] three nominating[145] parties, but this procedure should not result in the appointment of two or more nominated Commissioners by the same party.[146] The Chairman of the Commission cannot be one of the nominated Commissioners.[147]

In general, the PPERA provides for the possibility of re-appointment of Commissioners following a procedure similar to that of the appointment.[148] It also

137 Ibid. s 1 (2).
138 Ibid. s 1 (3).
139 Ibid. s 3 (1).
140 Ibid. s 3 (2).
141 Ibid. s 3 (3).
142 Ibid. s 3A (1).
143 Qualifying party is a registered party with two or more Members of the House of Commons at the time of the person's appointment, ibid. s 3A (2).
144 The size is determined by the number of Members of the House of Commons belonging to each party, ibid. s 3A (7).
145 A nominating party is defined as a party whose registered leader either has proposed three persons as candidates to be considered for appointment as Commissioners, or has previously proposed candidates, one of whom was appointed as a nominated Commissioner and is expected to continue to hold office, ibid. s 3A (4).
146 Ibid. s 3A, (3) and (5).
147 Ibid. s 3A (6).
148 Ibid. s 3 (5)-(6).

provides for independence standards for the appointment; in particular the appointment might be blocked when the proposed candidate is a member of a registered party or has been employed by a registered party or at any time within the last five years[149] has performed such a role, or in the same timeframe has been named as a donor or a participant in recordable transactions under the PPERA.[150] Along the same lines, any functional or economic links with political parties occurred after the appointment of the Electoral Commissioner should result to his disqualification.[151] All these safeguards do not apply to nominated Commissioners.[152] Furthermore, a removal procedure is put in place, in cases of negligence, non-fulfilment of the appointment terms, conviction for criminal offence and bankruptcy or related economic failures by an Electoral Commissioner.[153] Ultimately, the Electoral Commissioner may willingly be relieved from his duties.[154]

A final remark in delineating the structure of this mechanism should be made in relation to its financial resources and economic control. The expenditure of the Commission shall be comprised of money from its own income and money provided by the Parliament (with some slight exceptions).[155] The Commission has annual reporting obligation of its income and expenditure before the Speakers' Committee, which examines the estimate and submits it before the House of Commons.[156] It also has an additional reporting obligation of a five-year activity plan, before the Speaker's Committee.[157] The latter is assisted in examining those reports by the Controller and Auditor General.[158]

4.4.2 *Powers*

The Commission is responsible to (i) regulate and distribute public funds; (ii) receive reports concerning the financial situation, the donations and the expenditure of candidates and political parties; and (iii) monitor and enforce the proper application of the PPERA.

The first of the aforementioned tasks concerns the policy development grant, which should contribute to the development of policies to be included in election manifestos,[159]

149 The time was originally ten years and was reduced to five by s 7 (1) of the Political Parties and Elections Act 2009.
150 PPERA s 3 (4).
151 Ibid. sch 1 (3)(3).
152 Ibid. s 3 (4A) and sch 1 (3A).
153 Ibid. sch 1 (3) (4)-(5).
154 Ibid. sch 1 (3)(7).
155 Ibid. sch 1 (14)(1).
156 Ibid. sch 1 (14)(2)-(6).
157 Ibid. sch 1 (15)(1).
158 Ibid. sch 1 (16)(1).
159 Ibid. s 12 (1).

and which has already analyzed previously in 4.3.1. The second main task of the Commission is to receive and assess reports related to the financial situation of political parties and candidates, and it has been also discussed in 4.3.2. Reporting obligations include donations and campaign expenditure as well. Distinguishing between the aforementioned, the PPERA does not constrain the amount of donations received by political parties; it does though, as seen, impose limits on campaign expenditure.

With regard to the Role of the Commission as an enforcer, it may be generally observed that its powers have been significantly strengthened with the amendments introduced by the Political Parties and Elections Act 2009. The PPERA conferred the Commission the general power to monitor compliance with the aforementioned expenses and donations.[160] The Commission not only restrains the parties' expenses and donations, but also has compliance powers for the same transactions concerning candidates under Representation and People Act 1983. The Political Parties and Elections Act 2009 armed the Commission with investigatory powers[161] and the power to impose civil sanctions in case of failure of respecting the commitments imposed by the PPERA.[162] The Commission can request from registered political parties, recognized third parties, permitted participants in a referendum campaign, regulated donees and candidates at an election to provide information (through a disclosure notice) to the Commission relating to their financial affairs, when it suspects a failure to comply with the Act.[163] Furthermore, the Commission has the power to interview witnesses.[164] Ultimately, it has the power to take action on its own in case of lack of cooperation by a party and, in certain circumstances, an authorized person with an inspection warrant may also enter the premises of a registered party, recognized third party or permitted participant to inspect their financial records.[165]

A legal challenge to the extent of the Electoral Commission's powers in regard of monitoring and enforcing compliance with the PPERA and electoral law in general was mounted within the context of the U.K. E.U. membership referendum (Brexit referendum) of 23 June 2016. Vote Leave, the designated lead campaigner in favor of Brexit, was fined by the Electoral Commission in relation to its campaign spending.[166] The same day the relevant notices had been served, the Commission published on its website a document entitled 'Report of an Investigation in respect of Vote Leave Limited, Mr Darren Grimes, BeLeave, Veterans for Britain, concerning Campaign Funding and Spending for the 2016 Referendum on the UK's Membership of the EU', which gave an account of the Commission's investigation and findings, culminating in its

160 Ibid. s 145.
161 Ibid. s 146.
162 Ibid. s 147.
163 Ibid. sch 19B (1).
164 Ibid. sch 19B (3)(2).
165 Ibid. sch 19B (2).
166 *Vote Leave Ltd v. The Electoral Commission* [2019].

determinations as to the offences for which Vote Leave was fined.[167] Vote Leave applied to the High Court on 8 October 2018 for permission to apply for judicial review of 'the making and publishing' of the report. The challenge was not to the Commission's decision that Vote Leave had committed the offences for which it was fined, but rather to the publication of the report, as Vote Leave maintained that the Commission had no power under the PPERA to publish such a report. After refusal of permission to apply for judicial review, Vote Leave applied for permission to appeal against the refusal. The case was brought before the Court of Appeal, which refused leave to appeal. The entire case was about the lack of express empowerment by the PPERA for making or publishing a report of this kind. The Court of Appeal read section 145 of the PPERA requiring the Electoral Commission to monitor and take reasonable steps to secure compliance with PPERA's provisions as empowering it to publish such reports as a reasonably step, especially for securing compliance.[168]

The enforcement action of the Commission has also been further strengthened through the provision of the power to impose civil sanctions under Schedule 19C.[169] These civil sanctions for violation of the Act include fines,[170] notices for compliance and restoration under which the Commission can require a party to take specific actions in order to comply with the law[171] and stop notices which require the cease of an action or an intended action.[172]

4.4.3 Assessment

4.4.3.1 Strengths

In general, it may be argued that the PPERA and its subsequent amendments have created a robust mechanism in order to ensure the effective supervision and compliance with the financing obligations of political actors.[173] The main strengths of the Electoral Commission can be summarized in three elements: information, transparency and deterrence.

The Electoral Commission has specific features which ensure its function as a well-informed mechanism regulating funding and expenditure. First, the remit of the

167 Electoral Commission, 'Report of an Investigation in respect of Vote Leave Limited, Mr Darren Grimes, BeLeave, Veterans for Britain, concerning Campaign Funding and Spending for the 2016 Referendum on the UK's Membership of the EU' (17 July 2018) https://www.electoralcommission.org.uk/who-we-are-and-what-we-do/our-enforcement-work/investigations/investigation-vote-leave-ltd-mr-darren-grimes-beleave-and-veterans-britain last accessed 11 May 2020.

168 *Vote Leave Ltd v. The Electoral Commission* [2019] §24.

169 PPERA sch 19C.

170 Ibid. sch 19C (1).

171 Ibid. sch 19C (5).

172 Ibid. sch 19C (10).

173 K.D. Ewing and N.S. Ghaleigh, 'The Cost of Giving and Receiving: Donations to Political Parties in the United Kingdom' (2007) 6 Election Law J. 56.

Commission is not restrained to funding of political parties but extends to the supervision and monitoring of the entire electoral process in the U.K., providing the Commission with a more in-depth and general view of how parties and candidates behave in the political scene.[174] Furthermore, the reduction of the years of absence from the political scene from ten to five with regard to the qualification requirements of the members of the Commission ensures that it will not be an "ill-informed" mechanism in terms of political exposure and reach and reduces its subjection to governmental pressure;[175] this perceived lack of experience in the original structure of the Electoral Commission was also the main reason for the introduction of nominated Commissioners. This temporal proximity with the engagement of its members in political life enhances the confidence between the regulator and the regulated parties, as well.[176]

In relation to transparency, one of the main strengths of the Commission may be found in the provision of reporting obligations for political parties, candidates and third parties. Before the PPERA, the financing of political parties was highly unregulated in the U.K., without the possibility of State intervention in case of violations.[177] Under the current legislative framework, as has also been pointed out by the Ministry of Finance, the Commission was effective in enforcing party finance and expenditure through the reporting obligations coupled with the publication of information on its website.[178] The combination of these two functions constitutes the major factor in ensuring transparency and accountability.[179] Those checks and controls conducted by the Commission, apart from their significant anti-corruption nature, secure also the establishment of a level playing field in the political scene. The published information encourages the public to actively participate in the electoral process and raises awareness about who finances whom. All in all, ensuring transparency is a major segment of the State prioritizing the safeguard of the electoral procedure's efficiency in the core democratic process.[180]

Last, compliance and deterrence can be regarded as one of the major achievements of the amendments of 2009. According to the observations of the European Commission,[181] the new framework enhanced the functions of the Electoral Commission through the

---

174 Justin Fisher, 'The political parties, elections and referendums act 2000' (2001) 38 Representation 11, 13-14; Ministry of Justice, Party Finance and Expenditure in the United Kingdom-The Government's Proposals (2008) 19 https://assets.publishing.service.gov.uk/government/uploads/system/uploads/attachment_data/file/238761/7329.pdf last accessed 12 November 2019.

175 Ibid. 18.

176 Committee on Standards in Public Life, 'Review of the Electoral Commission' (Cm 7006, 2007) 58.

177 Ewing and Ghaleigh (n 173) 56.

178 Ministry of Justice (n 174) 23.

179 Organization for Economic Co-operation and Development, *Financing Democracy: Funding of Election Campaigns and the Risk of Policy Capture* (2016) Organization for Economic Co-operation and Development Public Governance Reviews, 175.

180 Ewing and Ghaleigh (n 173) 59-60.

181 European Commission, 'United Kingdom: Annex 28 to the EU Anti-Corruption Report' COM (2014) 38 final 6.

provision of more flexible sanctions for non-serious violations and by also enabling the Commission to impose civil sanctions.[182] Only cases involving an element of *dolus* or other intentional violation restrict the Commission, which can then only refer the case for criminal prosecution.[183] Empirical studies of both the Electoral Commission and the OECD reach the same conclusion, namely that the outcome of enriching the Commission's powers acts as a deterrent mechanism for the political actors, ensuring a high level of compliance.[184] For the timeframe between 2010 and 2012, the Commission observed that, although no civil sanctions have been imposed and the Commission would try to resolve non-compliance without recourse to formal sanctions, the possibility of imposing civil sanctions remains as a mechanism to ensure future compliance and deterrence.[185] Additionally, the new investigatory powers of the Commission incite voluntary cooperation of the alleged infringers,[186] while the Commission's advice and guidance ensures also proactive compliance.[187]

4.4.3.2 Inefficiencies

The analysis above reveals that the role of the Electoral Commission presents a wide range of strengths in the regulation of campaign financing and expenses. However, certain structural and functional drawbacks of the mechanism shall be addressed, potentially resulting in fruitful proposals for further improvement.

Although it has been argued that the political experience of the nominated Electoral Commissioners can increase the effectiveness of the mechanism by enriching the Commission with an insight to the current political affairs of the country,[188] the strong links of such Commissioners with the political parties having nominated them may be also in contradiction with the Commission's fundamental premises. A brief recourse to the Committee on Standards in Public Life Fifth Report reveals that one of the Commission's main pillars of establishment should be complete neutrality, requiring the existence of a body which is entirely independent from the government and the political parties.[189] Furthermore, the vital importance of the Commission's independence was also highlighted. Independence should be reflected in its structure,

182 Before the introduction of the amendments in 2009, the imposition of civil sanctions was not possible, leaving the Electoral Commission with the dilemma either to refer the case to the criminal courts or not to take any formal action.

183 Electoral Commission, 'Use of New Investigatory Powers and Civil Sanctions' (2012) 2 https://www.electoralcommission.org.uk/__data/assets/pdf_file/0011/149627/Powers-and-sanctions-report-2012.pdf last accessed 12 November 2019.

184 Ibid. 5; OECD Financing Democracy (n 179) 180, Hayden Phillips, *The Review of the Funding of Political Parties, Strengthening Democracy: Fair and Sustainable Funding of Political Parties* (The Stationary Office 2007) 22.

185 Electoral Commission 2012 (n 183) 8.

186 Ibid. 3.

187 OECD Financing Democracy (n 179) 179.

188 Ministry of Justice (n 174) 26-27.

189 Committee on Standards in Public Life 1998 (n 13) 147.

namely that Commissioners 'should not, in the normal course of events, be people who have previously been involved in any substantial way in party politics'[190] and should not represent political parties, while independence should also be the main feature of the selection method of nominated Commissioners, though their acceptance by party leaders was strongly advised.[191]

Taking all these into consideration, the provision of the nominated Commissioners and the reduction of the timeframe of the Commissioners' absence from the political scene, seem to threaten their sought independence because of their retention of close links with their political parties. Consequently, the provision of nominated Commissioners who retain ties with their parties goes beyond the requirement of a well-informed body and might in turn reduce the confidence of the public in the Commission.

Another issue which leads to inefficiency at the enforcement level is the high standard of proof required in order to establish the existence of an offense. Although the Commission has been empowered with the competence to impose civil sanctions, the maintenance of the criminal standard of proof, which requires a case to be proved beyond any reasonable doubt,[192] sets a particularly high threshold, which impedes effective enforcement in case of violation. Furthermore, the proposed extension of the application of the criminal standard of proof, for example to the late submission of statutory reports, makes the Commission's work even more onerous.[193] It is proposed that the onus to meet the burden of proof should be eased, since there are significant safeguards still in force. An accused person can invoke exemption of liability under the 'reasonable excuse' ground and justify non-compliance with the Act, or invoke mitigating factors that can eliminate the imposition of sanctions.[194] As a result, the threshold of the applicable standard of proof should be lowered because any alleged infringer has a good

190 Ibid. 149.
191 Ibid.
192 As opposed to the civil standard of proof, on the balance of probabilities, Electoral Commission 2012 (n 183) 6.
193 Ibid.
194 Ibid. 7-8.

opportunity to prove its innocence. It must be noted, however, that the - extremely - limited case-law feedback spurred by cases in relation to Brexit campaigning seems to temper this assessment somehow. In the only appeal to a decision of the Electoral Commission that reached a court room, the Judge concluded that on the one hand the Electoral Commission failed to adhere to the criminal standard of proof required,[195] while on the other hand the Commission imposed the heaviest fine available to it for an infraction that was 'not conceivably the worst offence within the range of offences covered', as the Commission admitted itself that the appellant's actions appeared to be neither deliberate nor dishonest.[196] Not only was the £20,000 fine withdrawn by the court, but the Electoral Commission had to pay £235,000 in respect of the appellant's legal costs.[197]

In relation to the U.K. E.U. membership referendum of 23 June 2016, there has been some criticism levelled against the Electoral Commission for an alleged failure to regulate campaign financing adequately. Evidence, however, such as can be found in the cases the Commission investigated, does not appear to support such a criticism. Serious violations of the PPERA (those resulting in the imposition of fines of £1,000 or more) were few in comparison to the magnitude of campaigning (a little above ten in number, some involving multiple violations by the same offender), and in at least one case the Electoral Commission's decision to impose a fine was quashed on appeal before a court of justice, as we have seen above. Furthermore, if the assessment of the Commission's conduct in that case is in any way representative of its general approach to infractions in relationship to the referendum of 23 June 2016, it might be argued that it had erred on the side of severity. Moreover, many of the violations seem rather trivial; for example Unison, a trade union, was fined £1,000 for failure to provide a complete and accurate spending

195 The Electoral Commission failed to 'decide beyond reasonable doubt that BeLeave was not an unincorporated association', as the sitting Judge put it, see *Darren Grimes v. The Electoral Commission* [2019] §109. BeLeave was the name of the organization involved in the case (but not the appellant, who was only the person responsible and thus fined) and the whole case hinged on whether at the crucial time it was an unincorporated association or just a front for the appellant's activities; as an unincorporated association it would be considered a permitted participant in campaigning and entitled to much higher spending limit than a simple natural person (£700,000 versus £10,000; its actual spending was in the range of £675,000). BeLeave has been the recipient of money from Vote Leave, the lead designated campaigner in favor of Brexit, and also hired one of the its main contractors. This was perceived by the Electoral Commission as an attempt by Vote Leave to bypass its expenditure limit and was it fined for it, see supra n 167. One could venture the guess that, since BeLeave could not be held legally liable for this infraction, the Electoral Commission attempted to punish it by imposing the heaviest fine for an another unrelated and rather technical one.

196 Ibid. §112. It must be pointed out, however, that this assertion by the judge was in essence an *obiter dictum*, as having already found that the Electoral Commission failed to adhere to the criminal standard of proof, he had not to rule on the reasonableness of the sanction and avoided to do so.

197 Electoral Commission 17 July 2018 n 167 as updated on 7 May 2020.

report and £500 for the late payment of an invoice;[198] the only serious infractions seem to have been those of the lead designated campaigner for the leave outcome, Vote Leave (endorsed by Boris Johnson), which was found to have committed multiple offences under electoral law, and which after submitting an appeal against the Commission's decision, later dropped it and paid in full various fines of a total value of £61,000.[199] It should also be noted that from the two cases referred by the Commission to the Metropolitan Police for a criminal investigation, one, that of Leave.EU (endorsed by Nigel Farage), was dropped, as according to Scotland Yard, despite technical breaches of election law, there was insufficient evidence for a criminal investigation,[200] while the file of the other concerning one infraction attributed to Vote Leave has been handed to the Crown Prosecution Service, which although not having dropped the case has not taken any action until now.[201]

In conclusion, the Electoral Commission as the 'gatekeeper' of spending and financing of political actors presents a wide range of strengths and ensures compliance with what is a rather strict regulatory framework in the U.K. However, the above inefficiencies may necessitate some rethinking of its structural organization and further enhancement of its enforcement prerogatives of this body to secure its more uniform and efficient operation.

4.5 GRECO's Evaluation

4.5.1 GRECO's Approach to the Framework

GRECO focused on the implementation of the PPERA. Its reports addressed the public financing of political parties in the U.K. that comes in the form of both direct and indirect funding.

GRECO, first, focused on the following aspect of U.K. campaign finance legislation: (i) the policy development grant, to which all political parties with at least two MPs are entitled, with a maximum total of £2,000,000 for all beneficiaries;[202] (ii) the grants to

198 Electoral Commission, 'Campaigners and political parties fined for breaching political finance rules' (15 May 2018) https://www.electoralcommission.org.uk/campaigners-and-political-parties-fined-breaching-political-finance-rules last accessed 24 May 2021.

199 Electoral Commission, 'Media Statement: Vote Leave' (29 March 2019) https://www.electoralcommission.org.uk/media-statement-vote-leave last accessed 29 March 2020.

200 James Cusick, 'Johnson and Cummings under fire as police hand criminal evidence on Vote Leave to prosecution agency' *openDemocracy* (1 November 2019) https://www.opendemocracy.net/en/dark-money-investigations/johnson-and-cummings-under-fire-police-hand-criminal-evidence-vote-leave-prosecution-agency/ last accessed 29 March 2020. But see Chapter 4.5.2 below on GRECO's concern about reports indicating a general reluctance of the police to investigate and prosecute cases of electoral law violations.

201 BBC News, 'Brexit: Police hand Vote Leave file to Crown Prosecution Service' (2 November 2019) https://www.bbc.com/news/uk-politics-50276673 last accessed 29 March 2018.

202 PPERA, s 12.

opposition parties in both the House of Commons[203] and the House of Lords,[204] called, as already mentioned, 'Short Money' and 'Cranborne Money' respectively; (iii) the equivalent schemes for parties with seats in the Scottish Parliament and the Northern Ireland Assembly;[205] (iv) the indirect public funding coming mainly in the form of free political and election broadcasts;[206] (v) the free postage for a single electoral mailing to each elector in a candidate's constituency[207] and the free use of public meeting rooms to which candidates in Great Britain (but not in Northern Ireland) are entitled to.[208]

As far as contributions to political parties are concerned, GRECO noted that there are no limits at all, just transparency requirements for all donations exceeding a specified threshold through the submission of applicable reports to the Electoral Commission.[209] GRECO noticed how the PPERA uses the concept of 'permissible donor' to regulate contributions to political parties.[210] As for anonymous donations, GRECO's report noted that these cannot exceed a threshold of £200[211] and mentioned that after the PPERA was amended by the Electoral Administration Act 2006, transparency requirements analogous to the ones imposed on contributions were extended to loans to registered political parties.[212] GRECO, last, observed that transparency requirements analogous to those for donations to political parties exist for expenditures, not only by political parties and candidates,[213] but by recognized third parties as well.[214]

4.5.2 *GRECO Recommendations*

The GRECO Evaluation Report about the transparency of party funding in U.K. contains several recommendations, most of them being of a rather technical nature. First amongst these technical recommendations is the proposal to improve the format of the political parties' accounts and returns, so that such information becomes available to the public in

203 GRECO Eval III, U.K. Evaluation Report Theme II (2007) 7 §33.
204 Ibid. 7 §35.
205 Ibid. 7 §34.
206 See supra n 38.
207 GRECO Eval III, U.K. Evaluation Report Theme II (2007) 8 §38.
208 Ibid. §39.
209 Ibid. 8 §41.
210 See supra n 27.
211 £200 was the amount originally, and valid when the GRECO Evaluation Report was written; it was later increased by s 20 (1) of the Political Parties and Elections Act 2009. See PPERA s 52 (2). Moreover, in PPERA sch 7 (4) and sch 15 (4) it is mentioned under the heading 'Payments etc. not to be regarded as donations' that, amongst others, donations of a value of less than £500 shall be disregarded; these two schedules concern donations to members of registered parties or holders of certain elective offices and not registered or minor parties respectively (here too the original amount was £200, later increased to £500). In PPERA sch 16 (4), which concerns candidates at elections, the said limit is set at £50.
212 GRECO Eval III, U.K. Evaluation Report Theme II (2007) 9-10 §§49-50.
213 GRECO Eval III, U.K. Evaluation Report Theme II (2007), 15 §§74-75 and 16 §83 respectively.
214 Ibid. 11 §57 and 15 §77.

a more coherent, meaningful and comparable way.[215] Another, more important, recommendation concerns an increase of the transparency of political financing at the constituency level and in respect of parliamentary election candidates, since in those cases reporting has to take place only after the poll, which means that the required level of transparency is not as developed at the local as it is at the national level.[216] There are also recommendations about the reinforcement the regulating function of the Electoral Commission established by the PPERA and the adoption by the said commission of a more pro-active approach to the investigation of financing irregularities,[217] as well as about the introduction of more flexible sanctions in respect of less serious violations and the about provision of the Electoral Commission with the necessary powers to investigate such infractions, rather than submitting them to law-enforcement authorities.[218] Although the recommendation of research about the future investigation and prosecution by the police of political financing offences seems also of comparatively minor importance, it should be taken into special consideration, particularly because the reason of GRECO's concern was the existence of reports indicating a general reluctance of the police to investigate and prosecute such cases.[219]

Clearly, though, the most important recommendation, at least from a strictly legal point of view, is that which concerns the extension of the transparency provisions about loans to individual candidates and third parties.[220] As already mentioned before, the obligation of political parties to report all loans was established with the adoption of the Electoral Administration Act 2006, which amended the PPERA. Until that time, political parties were required to report loans as donations, but only when these were granted on other than commercial terms. Although this requirement was absorbed in the wider obligation to report all loans by political parties, this has not happened in the case of individual candidates and third parties, which means that by applying to them the previous regime, there is the possibility of bypassing the restrictions imposed after the introduction of the Electoral Administration Act 2006. Furthermore, as also mentioned in one of the other recommendations (the one about increasing transparency of political financing at the constituency level and in respect of parliamentary election candidates), the reporting requirements below the national level are more relaxed as far as their timing is concerned. Thus, GRECO recommended that election candidates and third parties are subjected to the same transparency standards in respect to loans comparable to the ones applying to political parties.

215 Ibid. 24 §125.
216 Ibid. 25 §127.
217 Ibid. 25-26 §128.
218 Ibid. 27 §131.
219 Ibid. 27-28 §132. As it was succinctly put in the Evaluation Report, it was a problem more of enforcement of the legislation than of the legislation itself.
220 Ibid. 24-25 §126.

According to GRECO's initial[221] and Second Compliance Reports,[222] all recommendations, with the exception of the last two, have been implemented satisfactorily.[223] That conclusion was reached despite the fact that the new accounting standards by the Electoral Commission in response to the Evaluation Report's first recommendation are to be followed on a voluntary basis.[224]

At the outset, GRECO addressed considerably more recommendations to the U.K. compared to the U.S. This is an indication that the U.K. approach is viewed as far from perfect and that improvements are required to increase its efficiency in dealing with political corruption. There are two main areas of concern, GRECO focused on: transparency and enforcement. The U.K. campaign finance system seemed not to favor full or clear transparency in terms of the several disclosure requirements it introduces, at least for individual candidates and third parties, while enforcement seems to have fallen behind in terms of the actual number of investigated cases. GRECO's recommendations along these lines were thought to have been complied with, although certain of the changes introduced – those related to the accounting standards adopted for disclosure of parties' finances – were not mandatory; this reflects also the purely advisory character of GRECO's review of its Member States' campaign finance systems.

221 Eval III, U.K. Compliance Report (2009).

222 Eval III, U.K. Second Compliance Report (2012).

223 It must be noted that the first recommendation (improvement of the format of the political parties' accounts and returns) had not been implemented by the time of the initial Compliance Report.

224 Eval III, U.K. Second Compliance Report (2012) 5 §23.

Chapter 5 Campaign Finance Regulation in Greece

5.1 Historical Background, Main Characteristics and Constitutional Aspects

The current legal framework concerning the funding of political parties and candidates in Greece comprises of Law 3023/2002,[1] as amended and currently in force.[2] It is the 'third generation'[3] piece of legislation regulating the finances of political parties. Its enactment was deemed necessary for the legislation regulating campaign finance matters to conform to the new provisions of the relevant Article (Article 29)[4] of the Constitution, which had been amended at the 2001 Amendment. The amended article turned public financing of the political parties into a constitutional right (until then public financing of the parties was considered to be solely and entirely subject to the discretion of the common legislator). Therefore, it was considered best at the time to enact a new law rather than amend the previous one, even though less than 6 years had passed since the adoption of the latter in 1996.[5]

Law 3023/2002, which regulates campaign finance in Greece is based on the principles of (limited) public funding of political parties and parliamentary scrutiny of parties' finances in general.[6] As can be deduced from these principles, and considering the adoption of the Law as a *sui generis* measure of legislative harmonization with the constitution at the level of public campaign financing, the matter of contributions to political parties and candidates, although regulated by Law 3023/2002, was not amongst its primary parameters.

---

1 Officially: 'Financing of the Political Parties by the State, Income and Expenses, Promotion, Publicity and Regulation of the Finances of Political Parties and Candidates for Parliament' (ΦΕΚ Α΄ 146, 2002, that is #146 of Volume 1 of the Official Journal of the Government of 2002).

2 According to Greek legislative practice, the usual way to amend pieces of legislation is to include amendments, especially minor ones, as articles at the end of other pieces of legislation. Therefore, it is unadvisable to use the piece of legislation in which the amendment was included to refer to it, in order to avoid confusion; rather, the usual method is to refer to the amended (original) piece of legislation as was in force at a specific moment.

3 The first generation being Law 1443/1984 (ΦΕΚ Α΄ 73, 1984) and the second being Law 2429/1996 (ΦΕΚ Α΄ 155, 1996).

4 Article 29 para 2 of the Constitution starts as follows: 'The parties are entitled to receive financial support by the State for their election and regular expenses.'

5 See supra n 3.

6 Γεώργιος Γεραπετρίτης, 'Χρηματοδότηση των Πολιτικών Κομμάτων και Πολιτικός Ανταγωνισμός στην Ελλάδα' (2013) 8 ΕφΔΔ 270, 270-271.

Law 3023/2002 establishes a public funding scheme of political parties in three different forms: (i) regular subsidies; (ii) election subsidies and (iii) research and educational subsidies.

The subsidies are calculated on the basis of net government revenue of the previous year: (i) 0.05% of previous year's net government revenue is allocated to be distributed amongst the parties entitled to financial support as regular support on years when there is no electoral contest for the national or the European Parliament; (ii) 0.008% of previous year's net revenue is allocated on election years for electoral expenses (and can be increased up to 0.015% in case of two or more elections in the same year); and (iii) 0.01% of the previous year's net government revenue is allocated to political parties for research and educational purposes (provided the recipient party is involved in research and/or educational activities).[7]

Furthermore, Law 3023/2002 regulates the promotion of the parties' political agenda by television and radio during the period prior to each election,[8] by obliging television and radio stations to broadcast party created political advertising free of charge (the exact total duration of which is to be determined each time by ministerial decree; this decree also determines the total duration of time to be devoted by television and radio media to cover the activities of parties during the same period).[9] State subsidies and free television and radio promotion are the main elements of the public financing scheme of Law 3023/2002.

Besides establishing a public funding scheme for political parties, Law 3023/2002 regulates contributions to individual candidates for the national or the European Parliament. The restrictions placed on such contributions are many and concern (i) permissible donors; (ii) the maximum contributions allowed and (iii) the way the funds are disbursed to the recipients. Specifically, the contributors must be natural persons having Greek nationality. Natural persons of other nationalities, as well as any legal persons of any form, are not allowed to contribute either to political parties or to individual candidates.[10] The same applies to Greek nationals who are owners or editors-in-chief of newspapers or magazines or owners of television or radio stations, as well as their wives and descendants.[11]

---

7 Law 3023/2002 Article 1 paras 3-5. The original percentages were 0.102% regular support and 0.022%for electoral expenses regardless of the number of elections held. The current percentages, as well as the subsidies for research purposes, were introduced by Article 1 of Law 4304/2014, officially: 'Financing of the Political Parties by the State, Income and Expenses, Promotion, Publicity and Regulation of the Finances of Political Parties and Candidates for the National and European Parliament' (ΦΕΚ Α΄ 234, 2014).

8 This period, which starts the day the Decree dissolving the Parliament is published, or twelve days before its term expires, can last – given the fact elections are always on Sundays – from to 26 to 34 days. In practice it is very rare for the term of Parliament to reach its end. The first, last and only time this has happened after 1974 was in the case of the 1985-1989 term.

9 Law 3023/2002 Article 10.

10 Ibid. Article 7, para 6, and Article 7B, para 4 respectively.

11 Ibid.

The maximum amount of contributions by a single contributor cannot exceed €20,000 per year to a political party and €5,000 per year to a candidate.[12] Each contribution has to be traceable back to the contributor and if it exceeds €500, it has to be deposited to special bank accounts kept by the parties and candidates according to the provisions of Law 3023/2002. There is a provision for small contributions under €50 to a political party, which can be made without disclosing the identity of the contributor, but there is an aggregate limit: the sum of such donations received by each party cannot exceed €100,000 or 5% of last year's regular financial support by the state, whichever is less, while for smaller political parties not entitled to financial support the amount cannot exceed €20,000 per year.[13] No such exception exists for the candidates.

As far as expenditures are concerned, Law 3023/2002 restricts expenditures by both political parties and candidates for the national or the European Parliament during the period prior to the election. The limit for parties is 20% of the sum of the entire amount allocated as regular financial support to all political parties over the previous year.[14] In this respect, the legislator seems to attempt to level the field for all parties participating in an election: Larger parties having won a considerable part of the popular vote, and thus being entitled to more extensive subsidies, may find themselves unable to spend all of the funds received within the period before the election, while parties entitled to limited or no subsidies at all may match the expenditures of larger parties by soliciting contributions from multiple individuals under the limits prescribed for contributions. It has been argued, however, that the whole framework promotes the interests of the established political formations, since – notwithstanding the limits on expenditures – the combination of public funding based on electoral support with the extensive restrictions in contributions makes the financial survival of new parties highly unlikely.[15] The limit for candidates for the national Parliament is determined by a formula introducing proportionality to the system and based on the number of seats each electoral district elects to the Parliament, with the minimum being €15,000 for single-seat districts.[16] The limit for candidates for the European Parliament is set at €135,000.[17]

Law 3023/2002 seems to ignore independent expenditures. There is no provision concerning expenditures that do not originate directly from a political party candidate or an independent candidate. To be fair to those who drafted the law, there has been no known practice of independent expenditures in Greek politics, with the exception of targeted support to and coverage of the activities of parties and/or candidates by the media. Such support and/or coverage is now regulated under Law 3023/2002, not only

12 Ibid. Article 8, paras 1 and 2.
13 Ibid. Article 7, para 4.
14 Ibid. Article 13.
15 Γεραπετρίτης n 6 280.
16 Law 3023/2002 Article 14, para 1.
17 Ibid. Article 14, para 4.

in that it provides for the free of charge transmission of messages by political parties, but also because it establishes as compulsory the equal treatment of all candidates by the press as far as costs for ads are concerned.[18] Furthermore, in the relevant provisions regulating contributions to candidates, there is the specific requirement that all deposits to the specially designated bank accounts must have been previously accepted and confirmed by the recipient.[19] From this – limited admittedly – evidence it may be argued that the concept of independent expenditures, is not only alien to Law 3203/2008, but also incompatible to its spirit. Of course, in the absence of any legislative initiative to fill the *lacuna*, saying that there is such an incompatibility is of very limited value.

It may be inferred from the above that the principle of equality lies at the basis of Greek campaign finance legislation. The legislature struggled to introduce a scheme that would create a level playing field between political parties and candidates alike for general elections. Specific regulation of contributions to and expenditures by political parties and individual candidates alike sets the barrier relatively low from a *stricto sensu* monetary perspective, in the sense that the limits imposed themselves are relatively low; the framework thus may be criticized as creating a loophole for circumvention of the system. In fact, the relevant limits may be unrealistic given the actual amounts a party needs to spend to reach the 3% of the national vote threshold required to enter the Parliament and a single candidate to get a seat in the Parliament, especially in the larger electoral districts. This has been argued to cause the creation of illegitimate interests and shady relationships between Greek political parties and politicians and big Greek and foreign corporations.

Greek courts seem not to have concerned itself seriously with the matter of political contributions and expenditures (especially independent expenditures). No final decisions based on Law 3023/2002 have been published by Greek courts of law regarding such issues. As a result, it is difficult to speak about jurisprudence on the matter. Furthermore, all relevant theoretical analyses of Law 3023/2002 are mostly focused on the public funding scheme and the issues arising out of its application.[20] There is, however, a recent issue that has concerned legal theory and has been brought before a court of law, which while not a matter of combat against corruption *stricto sensu*, is worth a short examination, since it may be indicative of the treatment reserved for constitutional issues arising out of the Law's provisions. It concerns Article 7A of the Law and its constitutionality.

---

18 Ibid. Article 12, para 1.

19 Article 7B, para 3 of Law 3023/2002

20 For example, Γεραπετρίτης n 6; Αθανάσιος Γ. Ξηρός, *Ζητήματα Δικαίου των Πολιτικών Κομμάτων* (Αντ. Ν. Σάκκουλας 2010); Αθανάσιος Γ. Ξηρός, *Η Ίδρυση, η Συμμετοχή στις Εκλογές και τα Οικονομικά των Πολιτικών Κομμάτων στο Σύνταγμα, στη Νομοθεσία και τη Νομολογία* (Εκδόσεις Σάκκουλα 2014).

5.2 Campaign Finance Regulation as a Tool in Defending Democratic Values

5.2.1 *Legal Basis*

Article 7A of Law 3023/2002 provides for the suspension of public financing of a political party in case its leader or other members are involved in criminal activities. Specifically, if the leader of a party, or at least one fifth of the members of the national or the European Parliament belonging to the party, or one fifth of its main decision-making organ have been prosecuted and remanded in custody pending the trial for conspiracy to commit a felony, if such crimes have been carried out within the framework of political activities of their party or in its name, then a procedure can be set in motion by which, the financial support the said party is entitled to, can be suspended.

This article has been criticized on many grounds.[21] It has been characterized as unconstitutional, because it is claimed to allow the limitation of a constitutional right, while the relevant Article of the Constitution does not provide for any limitations.[22] It also seems to violate the presumption of innocence of the accused, since it requires only criminal prosecution and not the final conviction of the persons involved in the alleged criminal activity.[23] Finally, given the factual circumstances that led to the adoption of the specific provisions,[24] the latter seem also to lack the adequate general and impersonal character required from a rule of law perspective, since the provision seems to have been tailored to conform to a certain set of facts, that at the time had been at the forefront of public discourse.[25] This practically demonstrates the link the legislature wants to create between of broader public interest and social interest with public political funding: Political parties whose members are accused of criminal activity cannot benefit from the taxpayers' money to finance their activities. It should also be mentioned that the one fifth requirement leaves out of the picture the larger mainstream parties, since the numbers of their members of Parliament make unlikely the possibility of one fifth of them being criminally prosecuted (one would certainly hope that the state would have intervened before a couple of dozen amongst the

21 Αθανάσιος Γ. Ξηρός, 'Αποκλεισμός Πολιτικού Κόμματος από την Κρατική Χρηματοδότηση και Αναστολή στην Καταβολή της' (2014) 9 ΕφΔΔ 222.

22 Ibid. 235-237.

23 Ibid. 233-234. The requirement of a conviction would offer the increased guarantees of a judicial decision (preferably a final one) that could to a degree excuse the limitation of a constitutional right.

24 As can be deduced by its numbering, Article 7A was not part of the original legislation; it was introduced as an amendment to Law 3023/2002 and inserted between Articles 7 and 8 on November 1 of 2013 (by Article 23 of Law 4203/2013, ΦΕΚ Α΄ 235, 2013), after the leader of a specific political party and two of the members of the national Parliament belonging to it had been prosecuted and remanded in custody for conspiring to commit several felonies.

25 Ξηρός Αποκλεισμός (2014) n 21 237-238.

members of the Parliament belonging to the leading party would have managed to form a conspiracy to commit felonies).[26]

5.2.2 *Proceedings before the Council of State*

The introduction of Article 7A of Law 3023/2002 led to the suspension of public funding to a political party, after the publication of a common ministerial decree by the Ministers of Finance, the Interior and Justice.[27] The political party affected was the newly – at the time – emerged radical right 'Golden Dawn', the activity of which had become the subject of considerable controversy in Greece and Europe in general; they filed an 'application for annulment'[28] of the decree and indirectly challenged the constitutionality of Article 7A, on which the decree was based, before the Council of State, the Greek Supreme Administrative Court.

The arguments put forward by the petitioner, however, were all rejected by the Court in its decision 518/2015.[29] In paragraph 7 the Council of State examined and rejected the allegation that the provision lacked the adequate general and impersonal character required from a rule of law perspective, judging that the application of the relevant provisions in all similar future cases satisfied the Court's requirements, notwithstanding the unique character of the alleged actions of the petitioning party. In paragraph 9 the Court rejected the claim that Article 29 of the Constitution allowed no limitations to the right of public funding of a political party, arguing that the relevant provisions of Article 7A should be construed not as instituting a limitation, but rather as setting a set of requirements for eligibility, similar for example to those concerning the minimum electoral influence necessary to establish the right to public funding. In paragraph 10 the allegation that the suspension was disproportional was rejected, as the Court deemed that its limited duration and the fact that other privileges of the petitioning party have not been affected, are proportional to the objective of the avoidance of

26 Ibid. 227.

27 Common Ministerial Decree 51776/23.12.2013 (ΦΕΚ Β΄ 3275, 2013).

28 The translation of most Greek Administrative Law terms follows that of the relevant chapters of Konstantinos Kerameus and Phaedon J. Kozyris (eds.), *Introduction to Greek Law* (Kluwer-Sakkoulas 1988).

29 Strangely enough, considering the importance and the notoriety of the case, not to mention its political interest, the entire decision has not been published in any legal journal; only syllabi have appeared in volumes (2015) 8 ΘΠΔ 857 and (2015) 63 NoB 1319-1320. All references to it from this point on are to paragraphs of the slip decision from the archive of the Council of the State, which have been consulted for the purposes of this study.

public funding of criminal activities and that, though the measure hindered to a degree the activities of the party, it did so in a lawfully modest and proportionate way. Furthermore, the Court judged that due to the temporary character of the suspension, no property rights protected by Article 1 of the First Additional Protocol of the European Convention of Human Rights (ECHR)[30] have been infringed (Paragraph 12) and that the measure of suspension is not forceful enough as to constitute a criminal sanction according to Article 6 of the European Convention of Human Rights.

The decision of the Council of the State sidestepped some of the major issues brought forward by legal theory, including the most basic and important of all: How is it possible to limit a constitutional right when the Constitution makes no provision to allow such a limitation? Perhaps, the Court's decision was in the same vein as that of the legislature and the executive and betrayed a similarly spasmodic reaction to the phenomenon of a political party abusing its privileges to subvert the Constitution. Or it was taken in fear of what has presciently been described as the danger of an unmitigated constitutional uncertainty during a period of extreme institutional and financial crisis dividing the Greek society and the political system, should the provisions of Article 7A be found unconstitutional.[31]

5.3 Legitimate Public Funding, Disclosure of Contributions and the Right to Privacy in Greece

The issues which have concerned Greek legal theory and jurisprudence regarding the finances of political parties seem entirely different from those faced by the U.S. and U.K. Courts. It may be that the history of such regulation is rather short, the first relevant law being published only about 35 years ago. Legislative measures about contributions and expenditures seem to be generally respected, or at least avoided in ways both effective and undetectable. Instead of dealing with those issues, the legal system seems to focus and exhaust itself on the public funding scheme set by Law 3023/2002. As a result, any comparison with the U.S. and the U.K. becomes challenging, compounded by the prolonged financial crisis in Greece, which has affected its institutions across the board.

As mentioned above, Greek jurisprudence involving constitutional rights and campaign finance regulation is in fact very limited. Nevertheless, there have been a

30 The text of Article 1 of the First Additional Protocol of the European Convention of Human Rights has as follows: 'Every natural or legal person is entitled to the peaceful enjoyment of his possessions. No one shall be deprived of his possessions except in the public interest and subject to the conditions provided for by law and by the general principles of international law. The preceding provisions shall not, however, in any way impair the right of a State to enforce such laws as it deems necessary to control the use of property in accordance with the general interest or to secure the payment of taxes or other contributions or penalties.'

31 Ξηρός Αποκλεισμός (2014) n 21 240.

couple of instances were judicial and regulatory panels were called to review the applicable legislation and concluded in some very interesting findings. The right to freedom of expression has never been contested before a Greek court of law in their rather meager case law involving campaign finance regulation. In the sole case of importance before a Greek Court of Law, the one concerning the suspension of public funding to a political party due to the illegal activities of its leader and of considerable number of its members of Parliament discussed above,[32] the arguments (which as may be recalled were all rejected) about the unconstitutionality of Law 3023/2002 (the latter being legal basis of the administrative act the applicant political party sought to have annulled), included: (i) the inadequately general and impersonal character of the relevant provisions;[33] (ii) the violation of the party's constitutional right to the funding;[34] (iii) the violation of the party's right to property as protected by Article 1 of Additional Protocol 1 to the ECHR;[35] (iv) the breach of the right to free elections as protected by Article 3 of the aforementioned Protocol;[36] as well as the violation of the party's members presumption of innocence;[37] nowhere amongst those was there even a reference to the potential violation of the right to free speech.

Of special constitutional importance has become the constitutionality of the provisions of Law 3023/2002 about the disclosure of the identity of contributors to political parties of amounts above €5,000.[38] The matter became of some considerable public interest due to the great importance many political parties, especially on the left, attach to protecting the anonymity of their members, voters and contributors, a remnant of politically and constitutionally troubled times, when one's political affiliation with parties considered as subversive could result in administrative and even criminal sanctions.[39] A case concerning the constitutionality of the disclosure provisions was brought before the Hellenic Data Protection Authority, an independent controlling public authority, when the Control Committee, responsible for collecting and

32 Decision 518/2015 of the Council of State, see supra n 28.

33 As protected by Article 4 para 1 (equality before the law) in conjunction with Article 26 (separation of powers) of the Constitution, rejected in paragraph 7 of Decision 518/2015 of the Council of State.

34 As protected by Article 29 para 2 of the Constitution, rejected in paragraph 9 of Decision 518/2015 of the Council of State.

35 As protected by Article 1 of Additional Protocol 1 of the European Convention of Human Rights, rejected in paragraph 12 of Decision 518/2015 of the Council of State.

36 As protected by Article 3 of Additional Protocol 1 of the European Convention of Human Rights, rejected in paragraph 13 of Decision 518/2015 of the Council of State. The text of Article 3 of the First Additional Protocol of the European Convention of Human Rights has as follows: 'The High Contracting Parties undertake to hold free elections at reasonable intervals by secret ballot, under conditions which will ensure the free expression of the opinion of the people in the choice of the legislature.'

37 As protected by Article 6 of the European Convention of Human Rights, rejected in paragraph 14 of Decision 518/2015 of the Council of State.

38 See supra n 11.

39 During the 20th century and before the establishment of the Third Hellenic Republic in 1974, becoming known as a supporter of such a party was enough for one to be liable to administrative sanctions (a common one being forced displacement) and in certain cases criminal prosecution.

publishing the data of the contributors as the competent regulatory body under Article 21 of Law 3023/2002, asked for an advisory opinion of the Data Protection Authority, after a political party refused to provide the Committee with the identities of contributors of amounts above €5,000, citing the unconstitutionality of the relevant provisions.

5.3.1 *The Hellenic Data Protection Authority*

The Hellenic Data Protection Authority was established under Chapter D (Articles 15-20) of Law 2472/1997.[40] Since its inception, it has been one of the most genuine paradigms of a truly independent public authority in Greece, bearing extensive powers and its members enjoying full independence, both personally and functionally.[41] The Law itself, adopted fourteen years after an expert commission had submitted the first bill, was long overdue, as Greece had already signed since 1981 and the Parliament ratified since 1992 Council of Europe's European Convention on the Protection of Individuals with regard to Automatic Processing of Personal Data,[42] without at the time having any legislation in place - a requirement of the Convention.[43] The enactment of the EU Data Protection Directive 95/46/EC provided additional pressure and impetus to the adoption of a legislative regulatory framework and, although Greece was the last EU member-state to adopt such legislation, it succeeded in implementing the Directive first, well ahead of schedule and before any other EU member-states transposed the Directive.[44] It should be noted that the establishment of an independent regulatory authority was not amongst the provisions of the European Convention on the Protection of Individuals with regard to Automatic Processing of Personal Data, at least until the adoption of the Additional Protocol Regarding Supervisory Authorities and Transborder Data Flows,[45] which Greece anyway has still not yet ratified.

5.3.2 *Legal Basis*

Law 2472/1997 comprises of a nexus of provisions based on three pillars: (i) a set rules defining the legal requirements of data processing balancing in a binding way the conflicting rights and interests; (ii) the recognition of rights to protect the legitimate interests of data subjects and (iii) the introduction of a supervising regime to oversee

40 Officially: 'Protection of Individuals from the Processing of Personal Data' (ΦΕΚ Α΄ 50, 1997).
41 Λίλιαν Μήτρου, *Η Αρχή Προστασίας Προσωπικών Δεδομένων* (Αντ. Ν. Σάκκουλας 1999) 34-35.
42 ETS no. 108, ratified by Law 2068/1992 (ΦΕΚ Α΄ 118, 1992).
43 L. Mitrou, 'A Data Protection Law for Greece: A Few Introductory Remarks' (1997) 50 RHDI 645.
44 Ibid.
45 ETS no. 181.

the application of the Law.[46] Its provisions are applied in all cases of data collection and processing and not just on automatic processing.

Building on the foundations laid down by Law 2472/1997 and providing its basic principle of informational self-determination the enhanced legal status of a constitutional provision, is Article 9A of the Constitution,[47] adopted in the Constitution's 2001 amendment.[48]

The new article combined the protection of the right to privacy and the restriction of the processing of personal data afforded until then by Article 9 (Inviolability of home and of private life), Article 2 paragraph 1 (Respect and protection of the value of human being), Article 5 paragraph 1 (Free development of personality) and Article 19 (Secrecy of correspondence),[49] aiming at expanding these in an attempt to protect the individual and especially private and family life from novel and emergent threats to privacy.[50] In practice, however, the data of greatest value to third parties (be that the state or private persons) is that pertaining to the individual's participation in the economic and political life of the country which can – evidently – be more readily exploited, financially or otherwise.[51] In this respect, the right of informational self-determination established in Article 9A should be viewed as the result and refinement of the right to the free development of the personality and the free participation in the social, economic and political life enshrined in Article 5 paragraph 1 of the Constitution, in the sense that a person's control over their own personal information is an aspect of their broader right to develop their personality and participate in the eco-social framework of the country; in fact this broad right to the free development of an individual's personality is frequently used as the ultimate constitutional protection afforded to different types of activity in Greece by Courts.[52]

5.3.2 *The Case*

The case brought before the Hellenic Data Protection Authority concerned the alleged unconstitutionality of the disclosure provisions of the campaign finance regime (Law 3023/2002) and was novel in two ways. Not only was it the first challenge to the

46 Μήτρου n 41 16.

47 The text of Article 9A of the Constitution has as follows: 'All persons have the right to be protected from the collection, processing and use, especially by electronic means, of their personal data, as specified by law. The protection of personal data is ensured by an independent authority, which is constituted and operates as specified by law.'

48 Resolution of 6 April 2001 of the VIIth Revisionary Parliament (ΦΕΚ Α΄ 84, 2001).

49 Explanatory memorandum of the bill of Law 2472/1997, 2 §3.

50 Κώστας Χρυσόγονος, *Ατομικά και Κοινωνικά Δικαιώματα* (Γ΄ έκδοση, Νομική Βιβλιοθήκη 2006) 210.

51 Ibid.

52 The text of Article 5 para 1 of the Constitution has as follows: 'All persons shall have the right to develop freely their personality and to participate in the social, economic and political life of the country, insofar as they do not infringe the rights of others or violate the Constitution and the good usages.'

constitutionality of the disclosure requirements, which constitute a vital ingredient of the efficacy of campaign finance regulation, it was also the first major case concerning the issue of political opinions and affiliation and their protection under the regime established by Law 2472/1997 and Article 9A of the Constitution. In the past there has been only one other case involving the protection of the individual's political affiliations and it was rather limited in its scope and impact,[53] a result perhaps of the great restrain that sensitive area has been dealt with.

In its request for an advisory opinion of the Authority, the Control Committee responsible under Article 21 of Law 3023/2002 for collecting and publishing the data of the contributors, submitted a letter of the political party refusing to comply with the obligation to provide the identities of contributors over the threshold of €5,000, in which it explained the reasons for its refusal. According to the letter, the refusing party claimed that the identities of the donors remain at the disposal of the Control Committee, as long as they do not become public at the Committee's website. The relevant data is of sensitive nature, as they can be used to associate an individual with the party and thus expose the individual's political affiliations and convictions.[54] Furthermore, the rights to the free development of the personality and the free participation in the social, economic and political life of the country include the individual's freedom to contribute financially to political parties.[55] Both of the above rights are also connected to the secrecy of the vote, the right to which is protected by the Constitution and the European Convention of Human Rights.[56] Collecting, processing and making public the data requested by the Control Committee would infringe all those rights in an excessive way, incompatible with the principle of proportionality. The Authority, in its opinion examined the following three issues:(i) Whether making public the identities of the contributors of a political party constituted processing of sensitive personal data; (ii) whether the disclosure provisions of Article 21 of Law 3023/2002 can be considered to fall within

53 It concerned an advisory opinion of the Authority on the permissibility of the use of the public voting registries by a political party which sought to hold an election for its leadership open to all voters and not just its members. The Authority had ruled at that time that, since voting registries are pubic documents and contain non-sensitive personal data, anyone shall have access to them and can use them; what is not allowed is any kind of processing that would create a new file of sensitive data, for example a new register of who has voted in the internal proceedings of a specific political party (or even crossing out the names of those who had voted in copies of the public registers), since such a register could reveal sensitive information about the political convictions of the persons who participated as well as those who did not. The Authority decided to allow the *ad hoc* creation of lists consisting only of those who voted in order to prevent double-voting , provided that these lists would be destroyed immediately after the election, without being subjected to any kind of processing (such as photocopying or scanning); see Decision 26/2006 of the Hellenic Data Protection Authority, available on its website. A laudable – in its attempt to strike a balance between conflicting interests – decision, which however seemed difficult in practice to adhere to, as the Authority did not use any means to ensure that the lists of voters in the party's internal election would be in fact immediately destroyed.

54 Advisory Opinion 1/2018 of the Hellenic Data Protection Authority 2.

55 Ibid.

56 Ibid.

the data protection framework established by the Constitution, the transnational legal rules binding on Greece and the relevant national legislation; and (iii) whether reasons of public interest can justify the restrictions on data protection by the disclosure provisions of Article 21 of Law 3023/2002.

5.3.4 *The Decision*

For its assessment, the Hellenic Data Protection Authority took into consideration the right to the free development of the personality and the free participation in the social, economic and political life of the country as protected under Article 5 of the Constitution, the right to protection of personal data as protected under Article 9A of the Constitution, Article 8 of the Charter of Fundamental Rights of the European Union,[57] Article 8 of the European Convention of Human Rights,[58] and the right of political parties to financial support established under Article 29 paragraph 2 of the Constitution,[59] noting that the statute called for in the last Article is Law 3023/2002 and the special body provided therein is the Control Committee of Article 21 of the said Law.[60]

Examining the first issue, the Hellenic Data Protection Authority accepted the refusing party's assertion that political convictions belong to the category of sensitive personal data, according to Article 2 of Law 2472/1997, as well as that making the identities of contributors public at a website constitutes processing of sensitive personal

57 The text of Article 8 of the Charter of Fundamental Rights of the European Union has as follows: 'Protection of personal data 1. Everyone has the right to the protection of personal data concerning him or her. 2. Such data must be processed fairly for specified purposes and on the basis of the consent of the person concerned or some other legitimate basis laid down by law. Everyone has the right of access to data which has been collected concerning him or her, and the right to have it rectified. 3. Compliance with these rules shall be subject to control by an independent authority.'

58 The text of Article 8 of the European Convention of Human Rights has as follows: 'Right to respect for private and family life 1. Everyone has the right to respect for his private and family life, his home and his correspondence. 2. There shall be no interference by a public authority with the exercise of this right except such as is in accordance with the law and is necessary in a democratic society in the interests of national security, public safety or the economic well-being of the country, for the prevention of disorder or crime, for the protection of health or morals, or for the protection of the rights and freedoms of others.'

59 The text of Article 29 para 2 of the Constitution has as follows: 'Political parties are entitled to receive financial support by the State for their electoral and operating expenses, as specified by law. A statute shall specify the guarantees of transparency concerning electoral expenses and, in general, the financial management of political parties, of Members of Parliament, parliamentary candidates and candidates for all degrees of local government. A statute shall impose the maximum limit of electoral expenses, may prohibit certain forms of pre-electoral promotion and shall specify the conditions under which violation of the relevant provisions constitutes a ground for the forfeiture of parliamentary office on the initiative of the special body of the following section. The audit of the electoral expenses of political parties and parliamentary candidates is carried out by a special body which is constituted also with the participation of senior judicial functionaries, as specified by law. A law may also extend these regulations to candidates for other offices held through election.'

60 Advisory Opinion 1/2018 of the Hellenic Data Protection Authority 3-4.

data in the meaning of said Law.[61] Although the nature and purpose of the provisions of Article 21 of Law 3023/2002 is not amongst those that according to Article 7 of Law 2472/1997 would allow an exception from the general prohibition of processing sensitive personal data, Article 8 § 4 of EU Data Protection Directive 95/46/EC[62] allows the member states to introduce additional exemptions, not necessarily at the same time and in the same piece of legislation that transposes the Directive.[63] Therefore, the Authority concluded that under the prism of Article 29 paragraph 2 of the Constitution, which raises the transparency of campaign finance regulation to a constitutional principle and constitutes a hierarchically superior legal basis, the provisions of Article 21 of Law 3023/2002 can be found to be justified for reasons of substantial public interest.[64]

Having reached the above conclusion, the Authority examined the final issue, whether the restrictions imposed by the provisions of Article 21 of Law 3023/2002 were proportionate to the aims of the said legislative framework. The amount above which the identities of donors have to be disclosed is left at the discretion of the common legislature. The amount of €5,000, which currently applies, was found reasonable and not low enough to constitute an excessive restraint of the right to personal data protection.[65] However, the Authority found in the end that the period of 10 years, over which the disclosed data remain available on the Control Committee's website, is excessive and disproportionate for such sensitive information; it proceeded with recommending a reduction of said period to two years, highlighting the risk of published identity data being subject to indexation by external search.[66]

Considering that the normal election cycle is typically four years,[67] and that the public can be considered to have a legitimate expectation to be aware of a political party's contributors since at least the latest election, one has the feeling that the Hellenic Data Protection Authority has erred on the side of caution by promoting a period of just two years. Perhaps this was the result of concerns over the sensitivity of the matter at hand; any such concerns were in fact unfounded: the real issue at hand – from the point of view of those political parties on the left objecting to the disclosure of the donors' identities – was the disclosure itself, not its duration. If this part of the decision sought to please somebody, it managed to do that not with those political parties that would object to the disclosure of their contributors' identities as a matter of principle, but rather with

61 Ibid. 4.

62 The text of Article 8 § 4 of EU Data Protection Directive 95/46/EC has as follows: 'Subject to the provision of suitable safeguards, Member States may, for reasons of substantial public interest, lay down exemptions in addition to those laid down in paragraph 2 either by national law or by decision of the supervisory authority.'

63 Advisory Opinion 1/2018 of the Hellenic Data Protection Authority 4-5.

64 Ibid. 5.

65 Ibid. One might detect some faint echo of the *Bowman* decision here.

66 Ibid. 5-6.

67 Though it hardly ever lasts so long, see supra n 8.

those that would feel uncomfortably because of the very identities of their contributors. In any case, it should be recalled that the Hellenic Data Protection Authority is not a judicial body (although its decisions show elaborate legal reasoning, sometimes superior to that expected from lower domestic courts of law) and its decisions and opinions are not binding on Greek courts of law.

5.4 The Greek Campaign Finance System: Current Legislation in Detail and Typology

As seen above, campaign finance in Greece is regulated under Law 3023/2002 which has been amended several times.[68] The regulatory framework gives preponderance to public campaign finance, since empirical studies indicate that the major flux of money in Greek politics (90% of funds) stems from public resources. Therefore, the system can be characterized as a 'public' one with certain private campaign finance elements. Despite the fact that the system's main focus is funds from the state budget that should become available to qualifying political parties, recent legislative amendments have enlarged the material scope of regulation, by including provisions with regards to campaign finance by private resources as well.[69]

5.4.1 Public Campaign Finance

Under the Greek framework, the public campaign finance is distinguished into three categories: (i) ordinary public finding; (ii) electoral public funding and (iii) public financing for research and training purposes.[70] Ordinary public finance is defined by law as the economic contribution provided annually by the state to political parties or coalitions of parties to assist them with covering their operational expenses.[71] Electoral public finance is provided by the state to political parties in order to cover expenses incurred for electoral campaigning purposes,[72] while the third form of public finance is granted only to eligible political parties for them to establish and operate research and study centres as well as for covering the organization of training programs for their executives.[73]

---

68 More specifically it has been amended to a greater or lesser extent by Laws 3731/2008, 4203/2013, 4304/2014, 4255/2014, 4325/2015, 4472/2017, 4475/2017, 4483/2017, 4509/2017 and 4604/2019.

69 This extension of the scope was realized mainly after the amendments of 2017 and 2018.

70 Law 3023/2002 Article 1 para 1 (β).

71 Ibid. Article 1 para 1 (βα).

72 Ibid. Article 1 para 1 (ββ).

73 Ibid. Article 1 para 1 (βγ).

Public finance is solely provided to political parties which are represented in the Greek or in the European Parliaments based on the results of the last elections[74] and to those parties that have participated in the last national elections in at least the 70% of electoral districts of the country and have exceeded a national threshold of 1.5% of all valid votes,[75] while at European level, state funding is provided to political parties which have exceeded the national threshold of 1.5% of valid votes[76] (since the entire country is considered a single electoral district for the purposes of electing the members of the European Parliament). Public finance ought to only partly cover the expenses incurred by political parties;[77] for every category of public finance the law provides a specific rate of the annual State budget that should be dispensed for those purposes.[78]

The allocation of those resources also depends on the category of public funding. 80% of ordinary public finance is granted to the political parties which are represented in national Parliament, 10% to the political parties represented in European Parliament and the final 10% to all political parties entitled to state subsidies.[79]

Concerning the electoral public finance, when national elections take place, the parties represented in national Parliament are beneficiaries of 50% of the total amount and the parties are represented in European Parliament are granted 10%, while these percentages are reversed in the case of elections for the European Parliament; in any case, the final 40% is divided amongst all parties entitled to state subsidies.[80] The law also provides that when criminal proceedings are initiated against the heads or the actual administrators of political parties or against the one fifth of the party's Parliament members, then all state fund shall be suspended, following a decision of the Parliament by roll-call vote and with simple majority of the total number of its Members.[81]

5.4.2 *Private Campaign Finance*

Regulation of private campaign finance is a relevantly nascent provision in the Greek legal system. After the legislative amendment of 19 May 2017, a provision was introduced defining private campaign finance as the economic support provided by a natural person to political recipients.[82] The system of private campaign finance regulation in Greece has been significantly revised in the last amendments between 2014 and 2017.

74 Ibid. Article 1 para 1 (στα) and (στγ) respectively.
75 Ibid. Article 1 para 1 (στβ).
76 Ibid. Article 1 para 1 (στδ).
77 Law 3023/2002 Article 1 para 2.
78 See supra n 7.
79 Law 3023/2002 Article 3 para 1.
80 Ibid. Article 3 para 2.
81 Ibid. Article 7 para 1; see also the relevant jurisprudence under Section 5.2
82 Law 3023/2002 Article 1 para 1 (γ) as amended by article 36 para 1 of Law 4472/2017.

The law sets limits to private finance both for political parties and candidates. As mentioned above, each natural person can provide to political parties no more than €20,000 per year[83] and not more than €5,000 for candidates and/or elected representatives in the Greek and European Parliament.[84] In case of violation of those provisions, there are criminal sanctions to be imposed: the contributor shall be punished by a term of imprisonment of up to one year and a financial penalty.[85]

The most common way of providing private financing to parties or candidates is by wiring or depositing funds to the special bank accounts kept by political parties.[86] Funds can be wired or deposited only after the identification of the depositor, for which the bank is responsible.[87] However, private funding through alternative methods is allowed, conditioned though upon the full identification of the contributor,[88] although this applies only for amounts up to €500.[89] The law also provides for certain formalities that should be followed and upper limits with regards to vouchers issued by a political party and used as a means of funding.[90]

The following individuals are prohibited from engaging into private political funding: (i) natural persons who do not have the Greek nationality; (ii) legal persons governed by public or private law; (iii) local authorities of every type and (iv) natural persons who are owners or publishers of daily or periodical newspapers at local or national level or are owners of radio or television stations in general, as well as their spouses and descendants.[91] Furthermore, the law provides for an outright prohibition for loans to political parties with collateral in the form of (a) future state funding or (b) more than 50% of the current year state funding. For every new or amended loan contract, including refinance agreements, the political parties shall notify the content of the contract both to the Control Committee and to the Bank of Greece.[92]

The Greek system empowers the Control Committee to apply checks and controls (among other measures)[93] to political parties and candidates, in respect both of the

83 Ibid. Article 8 para 1.

84 Ibid. Article 8 para 2.

85 Ibid. Article 8 para 3.

86 Ibid. Article 7 para 1. Similar limits and restrictions are provided under article 7B of said Law in relation to candidates and / or elected representatives of the Hellenic Parliament and the European Parliament.

87 Ibid. Article 7 para 5.

88 Ibid. Article 7 para 1.

89 Ibid. Article 7 para 3.

90 Ibid. Article 7 para 4. The upper limits are €75,000 per year for parties which receive ordinary state funding and €20,000 for those parties which do not receive such funding.

91 Ibid. Article 7 para 6. See also Section 5.1 of this Chapter.

92 Ibid. Article 7 para 7.

93 The law provides for a long list of controlled people, which includes political parties which are eligible for public finance, candidates at regional, national and European level, as well as media and advertising companies. Ibid. Article 1 para 1 (ιδ).

contributions they received from private and public sources[94] as well as of their expenditure.[95] Apart from the aforementioned limitations concerning the contributions, the law limits expenditure of political parties to the 20% of the amount received as ordinary public finance, while for candidates their maximum permitted expenditure is linked with the available seats in their respective electoral district.[96]

Last, the law sets a number of reporting and transparency obligations. Money transfers are always conducted via specific bank accounts[97] which need to be disclosed to the Control Committee; political parties have the right to perform payments to third-parties without using those accounts, when such payments do not exceed €20,000 and are supported by adequate evidentiary documentation.[98] Political parties shall keep records both for contributions and expenditures; a separate record for electoral contributions and expenses shall also be maintained.[99] Their accounting books are audited annually based on the balance sheets and reports that the parties make available on their own responsibility.[100] Political parties which receive public finance should publish reports (balance sheets for the ordinary finance) on their official website.[101] They are also obliged to keep their accounting and tax records for a period of ten (10) years.[102] Finally, the Law requires from the controlled persons to submit before the Control Committee a wide array of documents (including balance sheets, accounting records, statement of accounts, receipts etc.) evidencing all the economic transactions they have been engaged in.[103]

---

94 The Law defines those contributions as 'income' of the political parties, which includes financial support from any source; in particular this consists of regular and extraordinary contributions by members, deputies, supporters, voters and friends, donations, loans, dividends, interest, exploitation of their movable or immovable property or any other activity during the parliamentary term and during the election campaign, as well as public campaign finance. Ibid. Article 1 para 1 (ζ).

95 Expenditure of political parties and party alliances: all types and origins of political parties and party alliances disbursed for the purpose of meeting all their needs during the parliamentary term and the election campaign period, Ibid. Article 1 para 1 (θ). See also section 5.1 of this Chapter.

96 Law 3023/2002 Articles 13-14. The basic amount is €15,000 for single-seat districts, to which €7,500 is added for every seat above that number up to (and including) seven seats and €1,500 for every other seat of the district. The amounts are increased by 50% in the cases of the Cyclades and Dodecanese districts, which comprise of multiple small islands. It should be noted that the current amounts were amended by Article 112 of Law 4604/2019 (ΦΕΚ Α΄ 50, 2019), and the first time they were implemented for the national election of July 2019, the adjustments for Cyclades and Dodecanese were wrongly applied, the adjustment being calculated only on the basic amount of €15,000 and not the entire amount, as Article 14 of Law 3023/2002 as amended provides; see Ministerial Decree of the Minister of the Interior 46111/2019 (ΦΕΚ Β΄ 2439, 2019).

97 Maximum three bank accounts for each political party or alliance and one account for each candidates; see Law 3023/2002 Article 5 para 1 and Article 6 para 1 respectively.

98 Ibid. Article 5 para 1.

99 Ibid. Article 16 para 1.

100 Ibid. Article 16 para 2.

101 Ibid. Article 16 paras 5-6.

102 Ibid. Article 16 para 7.

103 Ibid. Article 16 para 1 (γ).

5.4.3 Assessment

As witnessed above, the Greek political finance system is largely based on the regulation of public funding that dominates campaign finance in this jurisdiction. The regulation of – the in reality non-extensive – private campaign finance is based on recent legislative amendments. All these, coupled with the total prohibition of corporate financing to parties and candidates and the long standing tradition of public campaign finance in the country[104] are elements allowing us to categorize the Greek System as a public campaign finance system with certain private campaign finance elements.

5.5 Supervision and Enforcement: The Greek Control Committee

The Greek Control Committee was introduced by Law 3023/2002;[105] this legislation is practically an executive law of Article 29§2 of the Greek Constitution, which empowered the common legislature to regulate the financing of political parties by introducing relevant legislation. The Constitutional clause coupled with the executive law aim to ensure transparency in the financing of political parties, and ultimately protect and enhance the democratic efficiency of the Greek parliamentary democracy. After the amendment of Law 3023/2002 by Law 4304/2014,[106] The Greek Control Committee was consolidated with the Control Committee established in Law 3213/2003[107] as amended by Law 4281/2014,[108] and specifically Article 225 of the latter, and remains responsible for guaranteeing the proper financing of political actors in Greece.

The structural organization of this institution and its competences are analyzed below. Following this description, the strengths and the drawbacks of the Committee's functions are assessed so to better understand whether this institutional pillar ensures effectively compliance with the regulation of financing of political parties.

5.5.1 Structure

The Greek Control Committee is a special institution originally composed of nine members and nine surrogates,[109] with high level of expertise in legal, auditing and

104 The post-military dictatorship Third Greek Democracy in 1974 and the pro-democratic values it introduced played a fundamental role in the introduction of public campaign finance norms.

105 Article 10 of Law 3023/2002

106 Law 4304/2014 (ΦΕΚ Α' 234, 2014).

107 Law 3213/2003, officially: 'Asset Declaration and Control of Members of Parliament, Public Officials and Civil servants, Mass Media Owners and Other Categories of Persons' (ΦΕΚ Α' 309, 2003).

108 Law 4281/2014, officially: 'Measures for the Support and Development of the Greek Economy, Organizational Issues of the Ministry of Finance, and Other Provisions' (ΦΕΚ Α' 160, 2014).

109 Law 3213/2003 Article 3A para 1.

financial affairs. Those qualifications are necessary for the Committee's members to successfully complete their duties in absolute independence.[110] The Head of the Committee is a member of the Parliament appointed as the Parliament's Head of the Special Permanent Committee on Institutions and Transparency. The rest of the Committee consists of a Judge from the Supreme Court of Greece, a Counselor from the Council of State and a Counselor from the Court of Audit, the Vice-Governor of the Bank of Greece, the Head of the Hellenic Anti-Money Laundering and Anti-Terrorism Financing Authority, the Greek Ombudsman and two members of the Greek Parliament from the two major parties.[111] After a recent amendment of the relevant provisions by Law 4571/2018,[112] two more members (and their surrogates) were added, one more Counselor from the Council of State as well as the Deputy Prosecutor of Supreme Court of Greece.

The Committee's members are appointed by a decision of the President of the Parliament. The Judges serve in the Committee on a two-year term, with a possible extension for another two years, while the Vice-Governor of the Bank of Greece serves on a four-year term. In case of general elections, the parliament Committee members are appointed a month after the selection of the new Board of the Parliament, which consists of the President of the Parliament and the Vice President, 9 Vice-Chairmen, 3 Deans and 6 Secretaries, its main characteristic being its multi-partisan constitution. When a member leaves, his surrogate carries out their duties until the appointment of the new member.[113] The work of the Committee is further supported by a Secretary[114] and a special (directorate equivalent for administration purposes) scientific, administrative and other auxiliary staff.[115]

5.5.2 Powers

The statutory purpose of the Committee's function is the control of financing of political parties and candidates. In order to pursue this objective, the Committee is empowered to collect a wide range of information and (until 2017) impose administrative fines for compliance. Furthermore, it also has an advisory role in campaign finance litigation, while it is also assigned with certain reporting obligations.

The Committee is competent to collect and access information from various sources. This information concerns, *inter alia*, certain transactions or other activity of natural and legal entities and other relevant data with regards to the public and private funding of

110 Ibid.
111 Ibid. Article 3A para 2.
112 Article 5 of Law 4571/2018 (ΦΕΚ Α΄ 186, 2018) amended the relevant article 3A of Law 3213/2003.
113 Law 3213/2003 Article 3A para 5.
114 Ibid. Article 3A para 3.
115 Ibid. Article 3A para 6.

political campaigns. The Committee can review any kind of information which is related to the trueness of financial statements. It has also access to the TIRESIAS system[116] and to relevant documents produced by other public authorities. Any kind of privacy or relevant under Greek or EU legislation may be derogated from when needed in the context of the Committee's functions.[117] Furthermore, it can seek and receive testimonials from individuals and request audits of all relevant financial books and declarations. In all the above tasks, the Committee is supported by a public Prosecutor who must launch judicial or extra-judicial procedures that need to be carried out in the context of the Committee's powers e.g. the issuance of a warrant, where required,[118] as well as the technical knowledge of special scientific personnel from private or public authorities.[119]

When notified of a claim of campaign finance regulation violation, the Committee should examine all case details and take a decision by majority, including the minority's opinion as well.[120] Notably, it can no more impose administrative sanctions,[121] as it used to be competent to do – until 2017 and before the 2018 legislation amending law 3023/2018 – during the pre-election period when it recorded and evaluated the financing of the candidates. After the audit, the Committee decides to (i) close the case or (ii) forward that to the public Prosecutor.[122] The audit procedure is highly confidential and shall be carried out with objectivity and impartiality.[123]

In some cases, the Committee has to support certain judiciary's functions relating to political personnel: (i) a referral duty of cases concerning the disqualification of members of the Parliament to the Special Court provided by Article 21 of the Greek Constitution;[124] (ii) the provision of a justified opinion in case the Parliament conducts

116 The progressive development of the Greek economy and the banking system have led to the Greek Banks demand for access to reliable and accurate credit related data. Over the years, the importance of such data has become clear; it protects credit financial institutions and reduces the risk from insolvency. Therefore, it benefits both the clients and the banks. As a result, nearly all Greek Banks confunctioned to create 'Tiresias', a company entrusted with the development and management of a reliable Credit Profile Databank. Tiresias was formally founded on September 1977 as a non-profit organisation, and has been operating as a joint stock (SA) company, yet fully maintaining the philosophy of a genuine non-profit organisation while securing the necessary preconditions for its further development. Today, Tiresias specialises in the collection and supply of credit profile data on corporate entities and private individuals and the operation of a risk consolidation system regarding consumer credit. Additionally, the company develops interbanking information systems and provides information and communication services to all concerned parties. Tiresias, 'The Company' http://www.tiresias.gr/en/company.html last accessed 24 November 2019.

117 Law 3213/2003 Article 3B paras 1 and 2.

118 Law 3023/2002 Article 21 para 2 (ζ) and (ιβ).

119 Law 3213/2003 Article 3B para 3.

120 Law 3023/2002 Article 21 para 2 (α) and (ια).

121 The relevant clause in Article 21 para 2 (β) of Law 3023/2002 was repealed by Article 65 para 6 of Law 4509/2017 (ΦΕΚ Α' 201, 2017).

122 Law 3213/2003 Article 3B para 4.

123 Ibid. Article 3B para 5.

124 Ibid. Article 21 para 2 (ιε).

a criminal examination or prosecution against active or former members of the government or undersecretaries according to Article 86 of the Constitution.[125]

In the end of every year, the Committee publishes a report of investigated and potential violations as well as the relevant actions undertaken thereof.[126] It has also significant disclosure obligations, complied with through publication in its own website.[127] The information published concerns a wide spectrum of its work, such as the public funding of political parties, the loans and the donations given to the beneficiary political organizations and politicians, the annual budgets and the balance sheets of the parties, the campaign expenses and the decisions issued in auditing cases.[128]

5.5.3 Assessment

5.5.3.1 Strengths

Judging from the outline of the establishment and the function of the Committee above, it may be generally observed that the Committee enhances the implementation of the law regulating financing of political parties and election campaigns. The two main strengths that can be highlighted are: (i) the guarantee of institutional supervision in the proper implementation of the law and (ii) its monitoring ensures that public and private campaign financing is distributed properly.

Looking at the rationale of establishing an institution assigned with the duties to enforce the law of campaign and party financing, it is clear that the law attempts to impede corruption, promote fair competition and limit public spending, in the context of the broader aim of enhancing public confidence in the political system and protecting the functions of the democratic system. The Committee does contribute to the elimination of practices that could rebalance excessively the influence of some political parties and thus undermine democracy. Beyond ensuring a proper level of compliance, the Committee has also a proactive role by performing its enforcement and reporting duties. It also provides for legal certainty for the regulated candidates and political parties as to the correct interpretation of the law regulating their various obligations concerning their financing.

In addition, the Committee safeguards political pluralism by ensuring a fair and consistent way of political financing. With regards to public funding, the Committee ensures that money is distributed in a legitimate and constitutionally consistent manner.[129] It has been argued that the law regulating public funding is inefficient since it provides for financial support only to parties with a certain quantifiable percentage of

---

125 Ibid. Article 21 para 2 (ιστ).
126 Ibid. Article 21 para 2 (ι).
127 Επιτροπή Ελέγχου epitropielegxou.parliament.gr last accessed 24 November 2019.
128 Law 3213/2003 Article 21 para 2 (ιδ).
129 See supra n 4.

parliamentary representation. Therefore, beneficiary parties of public funding are solely those exercising some influence to the voters.[130] While the Committee does not have any power to amend the legislation, at least its enforcement powers ensures that even such an ill-placed legislation is properly implemented and political parties receive the public finding corresponding to their popularity as expressed in the most recent electoral procedure each time. The absence of an enforcement mechanism in a dysfunctional legal background would have deteriorated the situation leading to even worse violations and increased number of deviations.

Furthermore, the Committee contributes in ensuring that public and private funding regulation is respected by the political parties. Without auditing, a party could receive excessive amounts of funds, stemming from both the public and/or the private sector, and acquiring an illegitimate advantage over competing parties. In the first case, different public services would be deprived from valuable resources, if excessive spending was devoted for the funding of political parties and candidates. In the latter case, specific parties or candidates would be easily manipulated by individuals with special interests. The private sector may finance its favorite parties, but it should not be neglected that the private sector is very often self-serving, with its interests often differing from or even contradicting public interest and prosperity. While all parties represent special groups of votes focusing on specific policies, uncontrollable financing by the private sector will lead to biased decisions and malfunction of the democratic institutions.[131]

Ultimately, the importance of money in politics is related not only to its sources but also to its spending. Ensuring transparency through published reports, the Committee keeps public awareness on how the money is spent in politics. Furthermore, it safeguards that money is reasonably spent and not beyond serving the purposes for which it is provided.

5.5.3.2 Inefficiencies

Coupling the protection of substantive law with institutional supervision is something that can be positively assessed in any field of law. However, adequate institutional supervision is conditioned upon a basic prerequisite, namely the proper composition and function of the institution in charge. The Committee presents significant inefficiencies at both structural and functional levels, creating the need for further improvement of its structure and functions.

---

130 Αθανάσιος Γ. Ξηρός, 'Κριθέντα και Ανοικτά Ζητήματα στην Κρατική Χρηματοδότηση των Πολιτικών Κομμάτων υπό το Φως των Προσφάτων Νομολογιακών Εξελίξεων' in Ελίζα Αλεξανδρίδου, Φιλοκτήμων Αρναούτογλου και Φίλιππος Βασιλογιάννης, *Σύνταγμα, Δημοκρατία και Πολιτειακοί Θεσμοί - Μνήμη Γιώργου Παπαδημητρίου ΙΙ* (Εκδόσεις Σάκκουλα 2013) 727.

131 As mentioned in the explanatory memorandum of Law 4304/2014 (which revised Law 3023/2002), over-funding from the private sector may 'change the principles of exercising the public power'.

The core structural issue to be examined lays on the allegation that the Committee's composition is deprived of the fundamental prerogatives of its establishing law, namely, independence and impartiality. Looking at the appointment of the Committee members the strong structural linkage of the Committee with the political world is easily detectable.

More specifically, the Head of the Committee is the Head of the Special Permanent Committee on Institutions and Transparency of the Parliament; the latter is always a member of the governing political party. Moreover, two members of the Committee are members of the Parliament coming from the major parties. This means that three of the nine (later increased to eleven)[132] members come from the two major political parties of the current Parliament. Additionally, two other members of the Committee may not come from political parties, but are mainly appointed by political 'institutions'. For instance, the Greek Ombudsman used to be elected by the Government, but following strong criticism, he is now appointed by the Board of the Parliament.[133] Even this could be seen as problematic, since there is no independence in the relevant appointment. Also, the Vice-Governor of the Bank of Greece is appointed after a proposal made by the Government.[134] As a result, a considerable number of the members of the Committee (five out of eleven members; originally it was a majority of the members, five out of nine) present strong or at least considerable linkage with the legislature, something that can meaningfully underscore the independence and impartiality of the mechanism. Establishing a mechanism with those values requires a clear distinction between the regulator and the regulated person, thus a separation of politicians from regulators.[135] On the other hand, while experience in politics can be an important aspect in enhancing the function of the mechanism, such a concern should not be the primary criterion when establishing the core foundations of the mechanism.

With regards to the enforcement practice of the Committee, it may be generally observed that the Committee has not adopted so far drastic measures in regulating political funding. Its recent 2016 annual report shows that the Committee did not proceed with imposing fines for various investigated violations, although it had the power to do so. This report also reveals the lack of the Committee's eagerness to impose administrative sanctions.[136] Recent legislative amendments[137] have harmed even more the Committee's effectiveness, depriving entirely the Committee of its power to impose fines.

---

132 See supra n 112.

133 'Ο Θεσμός του Συνηγόρου του Πολίτη στην Ελλάδα' greeklaws.com/pubs/uploads/259.pdf last accessed 24 November 2019.

134 Statute of the Bank of Greece, Article 29.

135 Criticism is caused due to the fact that parliament members and political parties are under audit control while they have at the same time the majority voting at the auditing procedure, as mentioned in the explanatory memorandum of Law 4304/2014, supra n 131, 1.

136 Greek Control Committee, 'Activity Report for the Year 2016' (2017).

137 Law 4509/2017.

Another concern at the enforcement level may be found in the reduced accuracy of the regulation. In several occasions, the Committee relies on the examination of information provided by the parties, while external auditing is rarely realized.[138] The Committee may solely examine the documents found or limit the real auditing in case a complaint comes to it. Furthermore, non-reported contributions and expenses escape the Committee's oversight if they concern donations of equipment, supplies and gifts that could easily not be recorded. Such inefficiencies stress the need for establishing a better recording system capable to evaluate the real property and assets of the political parties,[139] while also ensuring the completeness of regulation catching all kinds of political funding and expenditure.[140]

5.6 GRECO's Evaluation

5.6.1 GRECO's Approach to the Framework

The provisions regarding the funding of political parties and individual candidates in Greece are enshrined in Law 3023/2002, as already mentioned. Law 3023/2002 transformed into law the right of the political parties to public funding established by the 2001 amendment of the Constitution. GRECO commenced its Report by making a distinction between types of funding available to political parties and quoting the relevant parts of the legislation as valid at the time of its report. It went on to mention the regulatory framework regarding the income of and the contributions to political parties focusing on the restrictions in relation to the person of the contributor,[141] as well as on the aggregate monetary limits to donations to political parties or coalition of parties and to candidates for the Greek or the European Parliament.[142]

The Report mentions that political parties are also entitled to membership fees, the amount of which has no limit, and contributions from their elected representatives, subject to an agreement between the parties and the representatives themselves.[143] The original regime also made provision for income from companies and privately held legal entities owned by a political party or persons authorized by it to this purpose, as long as their shares were registered, as an exception to the general rule prohibiting all

138 A typical case confirming this note is that administrative sanctions were imposed only according to the documents provided by the parties, as mentioned in the explanatory memorandum of Law 4304/2014, supra n 131, 1.

139 As mentioned in the explanatory memorandum of Law 4304/2014, supra n 131, 6.

140 For this reason, GRECO made a series of proposals so that transparency, direct information and strengthening of auditing mechanisms are supported in Greece. Greece has entered the GRECO committee of the Council of Europe in 1999. See also below the last section of this Chapter.

141 GRECO Eval III, Greece Evaluation Report Theme II (2009) 9 §34.

142 Ibid. §36.

143 Usually amounting to 10% or 20% of their yearly allowances.

contributions from legal persons or entities. As Law 3023/2002 originally stood, parties had to disclose to the Control Committee the names of all donors of amounts above €600 and individual candidates of those of above €150.[144] However, there was no provision requiring public disclosure of these data. After its most extensive amendment, that by Law 4304/2014,[145] the relevant provisions of Law 3023/2002 changed, so that political parties have now to report all donations (with the exception of minor donations by means of coupons, which we shall address further below), and for additional reliability of the data the tax registration number of the donors has to be included too,[146] but individual candidates are no more under a similar obligation, as the relevant Article was repealed.[147] As is also the case with PPERA after adoption of the Electoral Administration Act 2006, donors have no reporting obligations.[148]

Regarding expenses incurred for political campaigning purposes, the Report focuses on the extensive restrictions on campaign spending during the election period. As discussed, for parties, it cannot exceed 20% of last year's regular financial support to all political parties (the main part of public funding, aimed at covering the parties' operational costs).[149] For individual candidates standing for elections to the national Parliament, the limit is determined by a formula based on the number of members each electoral district elects to the Parliament,[150] while for the candidates standing for the 12 seats of the parliament which do not correspond to a specific electoral district, but are awarded according to the percentage of the votes each party received throughout the entire country, the limit is equated to that of candidates standing in the first electoral district of Athens.[151]

Originally the same method was applied to determine the spending limit of candidates for the European Parliament, but later the limit was changed, as already mentioned above

144 Law 3023/2002 Articles 16 para 2 and 20 para 2 respectively.

145 Supra n 7.

146 Current Article 16 para 3 as amended by Article 12 of Law 4304/2014.

147 Article 16 of Law 3023/2002 was repealed by Article 20 para 1 of Law 4304/2014.

148 GRECO Eval III, Greece Evaluation Report Theme II (2009) 13 §60.

149 Law 3023/2002 Article 13.

150 For how the current limit for specific districts is calculated, see supra n 96.

151 Article 4(4) of Law 3023/2002. It should be noted that the author(s) of GRECO's Evaluation Report failed to understand the specifics of this provision or, at least, failed to communicate properly their findings. Specifically, they state: '*The maximum amount of electoral expenses allowed to each candidate to the parliamentary elections or the elections to the European Parliament is determined each time on the basis of the amount applicable for the candidates for election in the A' Electoral Region of Athens*', GRECO Eval III, Greece Evaluation Report Theme II (2009) 11 §49. What has been translated above as *A' Electoral Region of Athens* (Electoral District may have been a more accurate term) is in fact one of the five (at the time) constituencies of Attica. But the flagrant mistake is that the limit is equated to that of candidates standing in the first electoral district of Athens not for every candidate of the national election, but only for those standing for these 12 seats, which do not correspond to a specific district.

and in the GRECO report to a fixed one of €135,000.[152] There is also an additional cap on expenses by individual candidates for publishing advertisements in the press, which cannot exceed 20% of the highest permitted limit for campaign expenditures by such candidates.[153]

The original reporting obligations, concerning mainly election campaigns, were many and somewhat complicated; GRECO's Evaluation Report seems, however, to have slightly misconstrued certain relevant provisions of Law 3023/2002.[154]

5.6.2 Recommendations

The Evaluation Report of GRECO found several shortcomings in Greece's campaign finance regulation regime. In total, it issued 16 recommendations, almost double the number of recommendations addressed to the U.S. and the U.K. combined. In order to avoid confusion, they will be numbered as in the Evaluation Report (from i to xvi), even if some of them are not closely examined.

Recommendation (i) concerned the duration of the period before the election, when most of the reporting obligations apply. Its brief duration, originally of about a month,[155] encourages circumvention for many of the limits imposed by collecting funds and spending them before the official campaigning period has begun. Therefore, GRECO recommended extending the duration of the reporting period.[156] Recommendation (ii) was about donations through anonymous coupons, a practice allowed by Greek legislation whereby parties issue vouchers for purchase by any individual as contributions to the parties, as well as about the use of cash for contributions to parties or candidates.[157] Recommendation (iii) concerned loans to political parties and candidates; although these had to be reported as a source of income and as an expense when reimbursed, they were not subject to supervision when written-off by the lender: this discrepancy created the possibility of circumventing the restrictions on

152 GRECO Eval III, Greece Evaluation Report Theme II (2009) 11 §49. The new limit was set by Article 14 of Law 4255/2014, officially: 'Election of the Members of the European Parliament and Other Provisions' ΦΕΚ Α΄ 89, 2014.

153 Law 3203/2002 Article 14 para 5.

154 For example, it is stated that '[P]*arties and coalitions that took part in national or European elections, whether they received electoral public funding or not, have to publish in the Government Gazette within a period of two months after the election date, the report on their electoral income and expenditure (Article 18 (2) and 19 (1), Law 302/2002*', GRECO Eval III, Greece Evaluation Report Theme II (2009) 13 §61. The actual provisions of these two articles were that parties and coalitions that took part in national or European elections, whether they received electoral public funding or not, have to publish within a period of two months after the election date, the report on their electoral income and expenditure in two daily newspapers published in Athens; the details and data to be included in such a report are defined by Ministerial Decree published in the official Gazette of the Government.

155 See supra note 8.

156 GRECO Eval III, Greece Evaluation Report Theme II (2009), p. 22 §112.

157 Ibid. 22-23 §113.

contributions, both as regards the limits of allowed donations and as regards the prohibition of donations by legal persons and entities.[158] Recommendation (iv) concerned issues with donations-in-kind,[159] while recommendation (v) was about taking into consideration the value of services by public officials who are seconded to assist members of the national or European parliament in carrying-out their duties, but their salaries are paid by the departments from which they have been seconded.[160] Recommendation (vi) aimed at the transparency and the consolidation with party accounts of the accounts of entities related to political parties, like research centers and foundations, which can receive public and private funding or make expenditures on their own, and their activities can benefit the party each is affiliated with.[161] Recommendation (vii) suggested the introduction of an obligation of timely publishing of private donations to political parties and candidates above a certain threshold, since otherwise they only had to publish their yearly balance sheet.[162] Recommendation (viii) concerned mainly the candidates standing for local or regional elections, but also suggested publication requirements for all candidates, including candidates to the national or the European parliament.[163] Recommendation (ix) was about facilitating public access to published information on the financing of political parties, as the publishing had to take place only in daily newspapers.[164] Recommendations (x), (xi) and (xii) concerned independent auditing of political parties, strengthening the independence of the Control Committee and increasing the monitoring of parties' financial accounts and documents by it.[165] Recommendation (xiii) addressed the access to the Control Committee's reports and the introduction of provision for dissenting or minority opinions by members of the Committee to be included in them.[166] Recommendation (xiv) was about the retention of financial documentation by parties and candidates and the re-opening of cases and recommendation (xv) about the monitoring of political level at sub-national level.[167] Finally, recommendation (xvi) concerned the reporting of suspected violations of the political funding regime to the law-enforcement authorities and the operation of the sanctions imposing mechanism.[168]

Greece's record of compliance with GRECO's 16 recommendations was initially poor, resulting in five different compliance reports, including three interim ones, and a re-

158 Ibid. 23 §114.
159 Ibid. §115.
160 Ibid. 23-24 §116.
161 Ibid. 24 §117.
162 Ibid. §118.
163 Ibid. 24-25 §119.
164 Ibid. 25 §120. In this paragraph the misunderstanding by the Evaluation Report's author(s) of the role of the Gazette of the Government becomes evident once more.
165 Ibid. 25 §121, 25-26 §123 and 26 §124 respectively.
166 Ibid. 26-27 §125.
167 Ibid. 26 §126 and §127 respectively.
168 Ibid. 27-28 §129.

assessment of compliance.[169] Admittedly, the political and economic situation in Greece during the first years after the adoption of the Evaluation Report in 2009 was precarious, dominated by the economic crisis and political instability caused by the apparent inadequacy of successive governments to cope with it;[170] this has been also mentioned in the first compliance report.[171] The adoption of Law 3870/2010[172] resulted in recommendations (vii) and (viii) being deemed to have been partially implemented as far as local and regional elections were concerned.[173] The situation remained unchanged by the time of the adoption of its second interim compliance report.[174] The extensive amendment of Law 3023/2002 by Law 4304/2014 led to a new interim compliance report, the third and final one. This concluded at last that recommendations (ii), (iv), (v), (vi), (ix), (x), (xi), (xii), (xiii), (xiv), (xv) and (xvi) have been implemented satisfactorily.[175]

At the same time, recommendations (i) and (iii) were considered as only partially implemented;[176] moreover, the implementation of recommendation (vii) continued to be considered as partial only,[177] but the implementation of recommendation (viii) was now considered as satisfactory,[178] as the new regime provided for a dedicated website where all relevant data of candidates to the national or European parliament would be published.[179] The issue that resulted in recommendation (i) being considered as partially implemented was that, although the critical reporting time was increased to six months before the elections, thus being both extended and made precise, the increased time

169 GRECO Eval III, Greece Compliance Report (2012), GRECO Eval III, Greece Interim Compliance Report (2013), GRECO Eval III, Greece Second Interim Compliance Report (2014), GRECO Eval III, Greece Third Interim Compliance Report (2015), GRECO Eval III, Greece Second Compliance Report (2016), and GRECO Eval III, Greece Re-Assessment of Compliance with Recommendation ii (i) 'Transparency of Party-Funding' (2017).

170 From early 2010, when the magnitude of the issues concerning Greece's national debt became apparent, until the election of January 2015, two successive elections had taken place in 2012, of which the first failed to produce a government, and governments by four different parties or coalitions of parties had been formed under three different prime ministers (not counting the provisional prime minister in charge between the two elections).

171 GRECO Eval III, Greece Compliance Report (2012) 11 §55.

172 Officially: 'Election Expenses of Coalitions and Candidates and Control Thereof in Regional and Municipal Elections' ΦΕΚ Α' 138, 2010.

173 GRECO Eval III, Greece Interim Compliance Report (2013) 9 §30.

174 GRECO Eval III, Greece Second Interim Compliance Report (2014) 14 §66.

175 GRECO Eval III, Greece Third Interim Compliance Report (2015) 9 §46, 11 §54, 12 §58, 12 §62, 14 §76, 15 §80, 15 §84, 16 §88, 17 §92, 17 §96, 18 §100, and 19 §104 respectively.

176 Ibid. 8 §42 and 10 §50 respectively.

177 Ibid. 13 §67.

178 Ibid. 14 §72.

179 Ibid. §71. Once more, the poor understanding of the Hellenic Parliament's legislative process by the report's author(s) becomes evident, as the sections of the article, quoted by them here, refer to sections not in the amending but in the amended law, as the quoted Article 19 of Law 4304/2014 contains only two sections numbered as (1) and (2), of which the first amends the title and the second the entire Article 21 of Law 3203/2002.

period concerned only expenses and not donations,[180] while the reason for the same conclusion about recommendation (iii) was that, in spite of new provisions tightening-up of the rules regulating political accounting, no specific measures have been taken to deal with loans being written-off without actually having been paid off.[181]

The situation remained the same by the time of the adoption by GRECO of its second compliance report.[182] In 2017, however, GRECO adopted a re-assessment report of Greece's compliance with recommendation (ii) and more specifically its part about donations to parties and candidates through anonymous coupons.[183] In its third interim report, GRECO had concluded that Greece had successfully dealt with the issue of anonymous coupons, as after the amendment of Law 3023/2002 by Law 4034/2014 their use was abolished:[184] from the moment the new provisions came into effect, the names and tax registration numbers of the buyers of any coupons had to be recorded. In 2017, however, the relevant provisions were amended once more by Article 38 paragraph 3 of Law 4472/2017,[185] reintroducing anonymous coupons of a value of €50 or less. The restrictions placed on the number of anonymous coupons are extensive, and besides those already in place following the amendments by Law 4034/2014 on coupons in general, requiring their stamping by a monitoring committee and the close regulation of their numbers, as well as the return and destruction of any stamped coupons not sold, there is now a ceiling on the total value of the anonymous coupons that can be sold by a party, which cannot exceed €100,000 or 5% of the public aid accrued by the party over the last year, whichever is less (or a maximum of €20,000 in the case of parties not entitled to public aid).

180 Id., p. 8 §43.

181 Id. p. 10 §49.

182 GRECO Eval III, Greece Second Compliance Report (2016) 11 §§54-55.

183 GRECO Eval III, Greece Re-Assessment of Compliance with Recommendation ii (i) 'Transparency of Party-Funding' (2017).

184 Article 7 para 4 of Law 3023/2002 as amended by Article 5 of Law 4034/2014

185 Officially: 'Pension Provisions for the Public Sector and Amendment of Provisions of Law 4387/2016, Implementation Measures for Fiscal Goals and Reforms, Medium-term Financial Strategy Framework 2018-2021 and Other Provisions' ΦΕΚ Α' 138, 2010. It is one of the colloquially called 'memorandum laws', pieces of legislation very wide in their scope and extent, usually adopted to satisfy some requirements imposed on Greece by one of the Memoranda of Understanding concluded with European Union organs and the International Monetary Fund to help Greece deal with its fiscal problems, and most of the times passed through parliament with the use of expedited processes and limited – if any – real debate.

As put forward by the Greek Government, and according to the explanatory report of the draft law, the reintroduction of anonymous coupons aimed at keeping alive the necessary linkage between society and representative institutions, small donations by such means being one of the most common methods of financial support to political parties in Greece; the Greek Government also argued that the reintroduction simplified the operation of small donations and the accounting involved, as well as that a similar situation about very small donations prevails in most European Union countries.[186] What the legislature did not mention was the pragmatic background of the decision, namely that small donations in the form of coupon purchase were vital for the parties' financials, as was evident by the impact their short-lived abolition had on the parties' accounts. Despite the aforementioned restrictions and explanations, GRECO was unimpressed and adopted a re-assessment report, reversing its previous assessment concerning the first part of recommendation (ii),[187] which since the third interim report and up to this point had been considered as satisfactorily implemented.[188] Considering the arguments of the Greek Government, the extensive monitoring of the coupons' issuing and return procedures, the relatively low yearly cap on total donations by anonymous coupons per party (€100,000 or 5% of last year's public aid to the party, whichever is less) and the similar situation in other EU countries (pointed out by the Greek Government, but not examined in any GRECO report), GRECO's reaction seems rather excessive.

At the outset, Greece seems to be the most 'problematic' jurisdiction compared to the two other country specific examples included in this project. Various flaws have been identified in its campaign finance system by GRECO which has been rigorously following up on the implementation of its recommendations by the Greek Government. This seems to confirm the limited public trust attached to the system by the people in Greece – and also globally – as well as the several political corruption cases for which such system has been blamed in recent years, including the conviction or accusation of high-profile Ministers and other members of the Government and the Local

186 GRECO Eval III, Greece Second Compliance Report (2016) 7-8 §39. Indeed, as already mentioned in the previous chapters, there is provision of anonymous donations in the PPERA to the amount of £200, as well as in the FECA to the amount of $50. Another reason, particular to Greece, but not mentioned in the GRECO Reports (and thus assumed not to have been put forward by the Greek Government) is a certain historical sensitivity about and attachment to the anonymity of coupons. During the 20th century and before the establishment of the Third Hellenic Republic in 1974, such coupons had been mainly issued by political parties on the left, who encouraged anonymity, as known supporters of such parties were liable to administrative sanctions such as forced displacement and in certain cases criminal prosecution, see also supra n 39.

187 GRECO Eval III, Greece Re-Assessment of Compliance with Recommendation ii (i) 'Transparency of Party-Funding' (2017) 5-6 §18.

188 GRECO Eval III, Greece Third Interim Compliance Report (2015) 9 §46. There have been warnings, however, about the possible reintroduction of anonymous coupons when the draft amendments that resulted in Article 38 (3) of 4472/2017 became known, GRECO Eval III, Greece Second Compliance Report (2016), pp. 7-8 §§39-41.

Administration for corruption, fraud and other criminal offenses involving the mishandling or embezzlement of public money.

The problem of corruption in Greece seems to be enrooted in the mainstream political culture and is often times dealt with as an existing reality, which decreases campaign finance and other anti-corruption enforcement efficiency. This culture does seem to be disapproved in both the U.S. and the U.K. that have managed to establish a culture based on the principle of eliminating corruption in politics. This is reflected in GRECO's respective Reports as well. A final note: It is the very distrust that the public and the institutions in Greece and globally treat the campaign finance system with that sometimes leads to excessive results. The new Greek legislation introduced to implement GRECO's recommendations was received with doubts by the involved stakeholders, which might result in unreasonably more stringent additional legislation and subsequently more sophisticated ways of circumventing that. One can easily draw parallels with the way the country's international creditors acted in providing financial support to the country during the crisis by imposing draconian, yet often inefficient (sometimes even catastrophic) measures of economic adjustment.

Chapter 6 Comparative Assessment

6.1 Comparative Analysis Background

It has become sort of a truism in the present analysis to emphasize the long and rich history of campaign finance regulation in the U.S., but it is a matter of fact that cannot be disputed. As a result, comparing the analogous regimes of the U.K. and Greece to that of the U.S. is bound to result in more emphasis being placed on the U.S. system due to its more advanced and evolved attributes. That having been said, it is nevertheless worth looking at them from a comparative perspective.

The great disparity between campaign finance regulation in the U.S. and the other two states becomes more evident when reviewing legislation in conjunction with case-law. This is because the great wealth of relevant litigation in the U.S. has not only set the boundaries of a legislative framework but has also actively shaped it through a string of decisions by the SCOTUS, which has on occasion struck various provisions that it has found to be unconstitutional. So, even though some basic principles are found in all three basic pieces of legislation concerning campaign finance currently in force (the FECA for the U.S., the PPERA for the UK and Greece's Law 3023/2002), as for example who is to be considered a permissible donor (to use PPERA's terminology) or restricting the amount of permissible contributions, it is to a great extent due to the jurisprudence of the SCOTUS that there are many more differences than similarities between the FECA on one hand and the other two statutes on the other.

6.2 Major Campaign Finance Norms

In assessing the similarities and differences between the various provisions regarding campaign finance and its regulation, the present analysis will attempt – to the extent possible – to avoid comparing the specific monetary values of various thresholds and limits, not only because the different currencies as well as the different standards of living of the three countries would make any such comparison more complicated and of limited substantive value, but mainly because most of such specific limits are also of restricted temporal validity, either being annually adjustable for inflation[1] or being

1 For example, the spending limits a presidential candidate in the U.S. has to observe in order to be eligible for public funds for the primary and general elections; see Chapter 3 n 138.

dependent on other – often changing – factors;[2] even limits that are not to be adjusted, are often amended (for example the ludicrous limit of 50 pence for independent expenses in the U.K. according to the Representation of the People Act 1983 was increased to – the almost as ludicrous and still highly problematical amount of – £5 after only two years),[3] reducing furthermore their usability as yardsticks. On the contrary, emphasis will be placed on wider concepts and their constitutional background, such as, in the same context, the very existence of such limits, rather than their specific amounts.

6.2.1 Permissible Donors

The concept of the 'permissible donor' (always using PPERA's terminology) is fundamental to campaign finance regulation. One of the most basic and important choices such a regulatory regime has to make, is who is eligible to contribute to election campaigns, and that (bearing also in mind what has been said above about the rather moderate importance of specific limitations) is a much more important question than how much may be contributed. In this area the choices made by the legislature set Greece apart from the U.S. and the U.K. Indeed, while in the latter two countries both natural persons and legal entities can contribute to election campaigns, in the Greek legislative regime only natural persons are entitled to do so.[4] It is an interesting choice, but one may reasonably wonder if what has already been used about a century ago as a method to circumvent similar restrictions placed by the Tillman Act of 1907,[5] namely donations by the directors of corporations who were then reimbursed by increased bonuses, as described in Chapter 3, are going to be prevented; in an age of globalized capitalism, the use of natural persons in the employment of corporations as a conduit for campaign contributions is much easier and allows them, besides the restrictions on the nature of the donors to by-pass any restrictions on their nationality, through the use of the personnel of local subsidiaries and branches. In practice that would mean that restrictions to contribute based on the donor being a natural only person can be circumvented by corporations using their personnel as conduits just as easily as restrictions based on the nationality of the donor can be circumvented by the use of nationals (natural or legal persons) under the control of a foreign donor.

The U.S. and U.K. approach seems more pragmatic, although in the case of the U.S., the continuing abolition of restrictions on the nature of the legal entities allowed to contribute by the case-law of the SCOTUS, as described in Chapter 3, together with the

2 As for example the spending limits of candidates to the national parliament in Greece, which are dependent on the number of members each electoral district gets to elect to the parliament, that number being adjusted after each census according to the relative number of voters of each district; see Chapter 5 n 96.

3 See Chapter 4 n 50.

4 See Chapter 5 n 10.

5 See Chapter 1 n 8.

total absence of any restrictions to the amount of all expenditures by such entities,[6] seem to have shifted the balance against the role of natural persons as contributors. Proof of that is, that amongst the most important cases of the SCOTUS in the field of campaign finance regulation discussed in Chapter 3, only in three of them the litigants opposed to the state (both federal and local) and their representatives were natural persons (*Buckley v. Valeo*,[7] *McConnell v. FEC*,[8] *McCutcheon v. FEC*[9]).

At the outset, this opens up the discussion on the role of the constitutional principle of inclusion in the three concerned jurisdictions. And whilst the U.S. and the U.K. seem to accept that the corporate entities created by natural persons under the such persons' constitutional rights of corporate organization or contractual freedom merit a separate treatment as to their participation in the political process, Greece willingly decides to weigh in more the risk of special corporate interests disproportionately affecting the election process, thus banning their participation to the democratic process as far as funding their preferred parties and/or candidates is concerned. Of course, corruption and inclusion as part of the constitutional background of campaign finance regulation may well co-exist as is the case in the U.S., nevertheless the Greek legislature seems to be consistently concerned about corruption which is emphasized in the relevant legislation. The importance of corruption as a rationale for campaign finance regulation will be further analyzed below in this Chapter.

6.2.2 *Independent Expenditures and Contributions*

The issue of independent expenditures and applicable limits thereof, if any, is another area where there is wide divergence between the approaches of the three countries. In the U.S. there are no restrictions to the amount of money that may be spent by third parties in support of or against a candidate, or by the candidates themselves as a matter of fact. On the other hand, in the U.K. the amount of money allowed to be spent by third parties especially at the constituency level has been historically notoriously low,[10] and has resulted in the European Court of Human Rights finding against the U.K. in the *Bowman* case.[11] Even in the aftermath of that case and the relevant amendment of the legal framework, the limit at the constituency level still remains low, being at the moment set at £500.[12] In Greece, the law does not appear to pay any attention at independent expenditures at all, with no restrictions placed on them; this omission may partly be

6 Also a result of the case-law of the SCOTUS and specifically its decision on the *Buckley v. Valeo* case; see Chapter 3 n 31.
7 Ibid.
8 See Chapter 3 n 92.
9 See Chapter 3 n 108.
10 See Chapter 4 n 50.
11 See Chapter 2 n 28.
12 See Chapter 4 n 71.

explained by how relatively young and underdeveloped campaign finance regulation is overall in Greece, and partly by the virtually nonexistent practice of independent expenditures in Greek politics. Only very recently, during the campaigning period[13] prior to Greek national election of 7th July 2019, there has been some limited independent spending aimed against the election of candidates, who as members of the parliament belonging to the governing coalition at the time had voted in favor of the ratification of the 'Prespes Agreement' between Greece and the Former Yugoslav Republic of Macedonia;[14] it was confined in Northern Greece.[15]

The absence of regulation in the U.S. is justified by the constitutional principle freedom of speech. Third parties must have an unrestricted right to express their views through spending their own funds to support their preferred party or candidate during election campaigns. Again, U.S. federal legislature and judiciary are not moved by any notion of equality whilst the no-restriction approach is not considered to invalidate the legitimacy of the system. Unrestricted spending is considered to be a legitimate means of participating in the public discourse and as such it enhances the trust to the democratic system. The similar absence of regulation in Greece does not seem to have any similar constitutional background. It is rather driven by the reality of such expenditure not really having been incurred to an adequate level in Greek elections.[16] The low limits of third party expenditure in the U.K. seem to respond to another reading of public trust. Third parties being able to spend in an unrestricted way are considered to create great and unacceptable distortions in the electoral process.[17]

What is of more interest is the reason why there are no limits on spending either by third parties or by the candidates in the U.S. The FECA, as originally conceived and put into force, did contain restrictions on both candidates' and independent expenditures, but all were struck down by the SCOTUS in its decision in the *Buckley v. Valeo* case. Ever since, freedom of speech as protected by the First Amendment to the U.S. Constitution[18] has long and consistently been the main legal basis in all litigation challenging campaign finance regulation in the U.S. The great importance attached to it by the jurisprudence of the SCOTUS is quite unlike anything encountered in the U.K. or Greece. Freedom of speech as expressed by campaign financing (contributions and expenditures) has troubled much less the campaign finance legislation and practice of these two countries. The approach of the U.K. legislation is to limit spending by

---

13 See Chapter 5 n 8 as for the duration of the campaigning period.

14 Officially: 'Final Agreement for the Settlement of the Differences as Described in the United Nations Security Council Resolutions 817 (1993) and 845 (1993), the Termination of the Interim Accord of 1995, and the Establishment of a Strategic Partnership between the Parties', ratified by the Greek Parliament on 25 January2019 by Law 4588/2019, ΦΕΚ Α' 9, 2019.

15 A number of anonymous posters appeared overnight in public spaces of cities in Northern Greece.

16 The aforementioned example in Northern Greece being not only exceedingly rare, but also very marginal, as can be evidenced by the anonymity chosen by those behind it.

17 See Chapter 4 n 73.

18 See Chapter 3 n 28 for its text.

political parties (at the national level) and candidates (at the constituency level) as well as by third parties, but effectively to place no restrictions on contributions at either the national or constituency level, other than a reporting obligation over a certain amount.[19] At the same time, the Greek legislation limits both the contributions to candidates and political parties and the expenses by them in the campaigning period, while not regulating - practically ignoring - expenditures by third parties; however, it should be repeated that this choice has nothing to do with any superior constitutional value attributed to independent expenditures, but rather with the - until very recently - practically non-existent relevant practice.

Whereas in the U.K. the relationship of campaign contributions and expenses with the freedom of expression of contributors and spenders has received little attention (and that only in the aftermath of the *Bowman* decision of the European court of Human Rights), and in Greece it does not appear to have be of any concern to the campaign finance regime either at the legislative or the jurisprudential level, in the U.S. it has been at the basis of extensive case-law with advanced and elaborate arguments. It may be recalled how in its *Buckley* decision the SCOTUS adopted two different approaches to the First Amendment value of money.[20] On one hand, the value attributed to contributions was merely as an expression of the volitional impulse of the contributor; on the other hand, expenses were accorded a more 'commodity-like' value that was judged to be of greater importance from a First Amendment point of view. This resulted in limitations on contributions being found constitutional, while limitations on expenses failed to pass muster and were struck, a perspective to which the SCOTUS has consistently adhered ever since.

The main difference between the two different approaches, that of the U.S. on the one hand and that of the U.K. and Greece on the other, is the presence of what could be described as creative control over the use of money. In the first case, contributions, the mere donation is assumed to express the volition of the donor, the amount of money donated serving at most to express the intensity of the donor's feelings towards the recipient.[21] Thus placing limits on contributions involves little restraint on contributors, as they can express in a symbolic way their support while retaining their ability to discuss candidates and issues.[22] In the second case, expenses, money acquires a different and higher First Amendment value, as according to the SCOTUS, it serves an expressive purpose, as it amounts to the spender's speech, since the spender retains control over the final result.[23] The end result of such reasoning is that caps on

19 See Chapter 4 n 29.

20 Monica Youn, 'First Amendment Fault Lines and the *Citizens United* Decision' (2011) 5 Harv. L. & Pol'y Rev. 135.

21 *Buckley v. Valeo*, 424 U.S. 1, 21 (1976).

22 Ibid.

23 Youn (n 18) 142.

expenditures are perceived as heavily burdening free expression and are thus unconstitutional.[24] When the funds of a contribution do end up serving an expressive purpose, this is not the purpose of the contributor but of the spender: the same funds, which have little First Amendment value as a contribution, acquire far greater importance as expenditure.

The tension between the theoretical approaches by the SCOTUS to campaign finance and free expression have already been examined in Chapter 3, as well as how the SCOTUS itself has progressively turned the application of the volitional approach on its head, starting with its decision on *FEC v. National Conservative Political Action Committee*,[25] thus significantly weakening the integrity of the volitional *rationale* approach. However, what is of note is that, regardless of that tension, the fact remains that these are very elaborate and sophisticated arguments, the like of which one does not come across in the jurisprudence of the U.K., much less in that of Greece. Indeed, if one takes into consideration how the decision in the *Bowman* case may be construed to be representative of attitudes across all members of the ECHR,[26] one can speak of a more general lack of arguments of similar sophistication across Europe's legislative and judicial systems. This could serve to underline once again the long and rich history of campaign finance regulation in the U.S., as mentioned at the beginning of the present Chapter, and the more advanced and evolved attributes of its regulatory regime to the field of campaign finance law globally, which has been forged under pressure from continual litigation. It might also serve as an indication of the structural capability of the U.S. federal judiciary to involve itself in a more theoretical, if not philosophical at certain times, approach to legal issues in an effort to reach pragmatic conclusions which their U.K. or Greek peers would not feel comfortable with (or might even find it improper to attempt to), thus restricting themselves on conclusions derived from precedent and/or legislation and their interpretation thereof. But one could also argue that it also underlines the more common sense approach of Europe's regulatory regimes to such a core issue as campaign finance, unfettered from excessively complicated legal argumentation.

6.3 Public and Private Campaign Finance

The three campaign finance systems under discussion are a mixed lot, as far as their sources are concerned. In the U.S. public finance is limited and optional, in Greece public subsidies to political parties are the major source of money in politics, while the

24 Ibid.

25 See Chapter 3 n 55.

26 As for example it has been perceived by U.K.'s Committee on Standards in Public Life, see Chapter 4 n 69.

U.K. paradigm falls somewhere in between. These differences influence the regulatory choices in each jurisdiction, resulting in further differentiations.

6.3.1 *Realities Drive Regulation*

Other than the different constitutional traditions, the different regulatory approaches in each jurisdiction are also linked to the different realities in each national political arena. Of course, constitutional the evolution of constitutional traditions is not independent of the more factual influences on campaign finance, but the main distinguishing characteristic of the latter could be said to be the lack of legal considerations. Significantly different approaches may be observed on how political parties and candidates spend their money for their electoral campaigns and are the main drivers of the relevant regulatory framework in each examined jurisdiction. For example, in Greece the law mostly focuses on public funding, since the 90% of financing stems from public resources, while in the U.K. a mixed system corresponds better to the political reality, since 35% of the parties' resources come from the public while 65% of them are originated from the private sector.[27] Likewise, in the U.S .a mostly private campaign finance regulatory approach corresponds to the huge amounts of money being spent by candidates and political parties in federal elections. Nevertheless, the systems demonstrate certain common elements stemming mostly from the common understanding that financially relevant behaviors may generate illegitimate influence on politics. At the outset, according those realities independent value in the formation of different regulatory norms might sound as a novel approach to campaign finance regulation. However, it seems that such contemporary realities of the economies and political systems at hand may eventually weigh in more than certain historical or legitimacy considerations that might have even been common during the inception phases of each system.

6.3.2 *Public Campaign Finance*

With respect to public funding, a common feature of the three examined jurisdictions is the eligibility criteria for the reception of public financing. The three systems are based on the rates of the electoral success of the parties/candidates in the previous elections, by setting a minimum quantifiable – in votes – limit of political influence above which recipients can be granted with public funding. Different approaches are adopted regarding the periodical disbursement of public finds to political parties. In Greece, the law provides for public funding both at a regular (annual) basis as well as during the

27 See Table 2 in the Appendices.

election period. In the U.K. public funds are only granted on a regular basis, while in the U.S. public funding is only provided in relation to presidential elections; in the latter case, it comes with many subsequent restrictions, leading presidential candidates to avoid it.[28]

6.3.3 *Private Campaign Finance*

The examined jurisdictions provide for almost the same categories of prohibited donors in an effort to limit influence of special interests on politics including those of foreign donors, corporations and anonymous contributions. All three jurisdictions under discussion set a maximum limit on acceptable anonymous donations, the threshold being set at $50 in the U.S. (with limited disclosure requirements up to the amount of $50),[29] at £200 in the U.K.[30] and at €50 in Greece,[31] but only to political parties (anonymous contributions to candidates are outright prohibited) by means of coupons capped at €100,000 or 5% of the public aid accrued by the party over the last year, whichever is less, or a maximum of €20,000 in the case of parties not entitled to public aid.

Contribution limits are also treated differently. While in Greece and in the U.S. legislation provides for specific contribution limits, such limits are absent from U.K. legislation. Expenditure limits are provided for in different forms in all three jurisdictions. Greece and the U.K. set limits both for political parties and candidates, while in the U.S. there are no such limits with the exception of those relevant limitations applicable only to political parties and to presidential candidates who received public funds for their campaigns, as mentioned before.

On transparency, it may be observed that the three countries do not impose reporting and disclosure obligations of the same intensity. Amongst the examined systems, the Greek campaign finance regulation seems to contain the lightest transparency provisions, while both the U.S. and the U.K. – especially the UK – have introduced strict reporting and disclosure obligations for all the significant players in the political arena, not only during, but also beyond the electoral period.

A further comparison of the entirely different approach by the U.S. and the U.K. to the matter of contributions and expenditures limits as well as disclosure requirements in campaign finance regulation is at this point in order. While in the U.S. regime there are strict limits on contributions to candidates, but practically no restrictions on expenditures, both by the candidates as well as by third parties, in the case of the U.K. the exact opposite seems to apply. There are extensive and detailed restrictions on the

28 See Chapter 3 nn 147-149.
29 See Chapter 3 n 261.
30 See Chapter 4 n 211.
31 See Chapter 5 n 185.

amounts that political parties as well as individual candidates can spend, as well the expenses that can be incurred by third parties on their behalf. There are, however, virtually no restrictions on the amounts that can be contributed to either party or individual candidate, other than those of disclosure and publicity. The expenditure limits at the national level were an innovation of the PPERA, since, as it may be recalled,[32] there was no regulation of campaign expenses at the national level before its enactment, and this applied also at the time of the *Bowman* case; this discrepancy made the £5 limit at the constituency level seem highly unsatisfactory, if not outright pharisaic and hypocritical. The absence of restrictions in the amount of donations was considered by the Committee on Standards in Public Life, albeit rather briefly,[33] but it decided against a proposal to institute such limits, considering them impractical and difficult to implement, placing instead emphasis on the disclosure of contributions over a certain amount.[34]

The Committee's faith in disclosure, however, seemed in the immediate aftermath of the PPERA's entry into force to have been somewhat misplaced: despite the Labour party's protests (in power at the time) that donors have gone cold as a result of the PPERA,[35] quite a few millionaire donations have been reported in the period right after the disclosure requirement came into effect.[36] On the other hand, empirical evidence from across the Atlantic seem to imply that the price of corruption, understood as the amount of contribution adequate to create the impression of corruption, can be quite low, as low as $1,000 for members of the U.S. Congress,[37] so the Committee's arguments about the impracticability of contribution limits appear as anything but unfounded. The different approaches in the two legal systems may have been the result of the differences in the normative content of the right to free speech in each one, but are also the outcome of different assessments of what constitutes a legitimate government concern that can excuse imposing restrictions on that right: since equality cannot be typically accepted as such a concern in the U.S., while it is a legitimate aim in the U.K. (and Europe in general, one could deduce from the formulation of the *Bowman v. United Kingdom* decision), these differences become to a certain degree unavoidable.

32 See Chapter 4 n 3.

33 KD Ewing, 'The Disclosure of Political Donations in Britain' in KD Ewing and Samuel Issacharoff (eds), *Party Funding and Campaign Financing in International Perspective* (Hart Publishing 2006) 60.

34 Committee on Standards of Public Life, 'The Funding of Political Parties in the United Kingdom' (Cm 4057-I, 1998) 80.

35 KD Ewing (n 33) 68.

36 Navraj Singh Ghaleigh, 'Expenditure, Donations and Public Funding under the United Kingdom's Political Parties, Elections and Referendums Act 2000 - And Beyond?', in KD Ewing and Samuel Issacharoff (eds), *Party Funding and Campaign Financing in International Perspective* (Hart Publishing 2006) 51.

37 Usha R. Rodriguez, 'The Price of Corruption' (2015) 31 J.L. & Pol. 45. The article uses data from FEC's website to describe how even $1,000 is enough to at least give the impression of corruption (or the appearance thereof, to use the terminology of the SCOTUS).

In fact, the U.S. complete engagement with corruption or its appearance thereof as the only legitimate government concern to impose restrictions on campaign funding is a rather unilateral view of the reality and limits significantly the constitutional toolkit that could have been deployed to put together a functional regulatory framework. And while this seems to be convenient to address the realities of the U.S. economy built around campaign financing, it certainly demonstrates the comparatively more elaborate approach in the U.K. and in Greece (but also broadly in Europe). Equality, as a constitutional principle and legitimate government pursuit, can well co-exist with any anti-corruption rationale behind campaign finance regulation. In fact, establishing a level playing field amongst parties and candidates alike and equalizing the impact which each voter can nominally have in supporting its preferred party or candidate restrict in parallel the opportunity and/or desire of elected officials to exploit office for private gain. And given the various non-monetary support that one can provide during election campaigns, it is fair to believe that freedom of speech does not distort the equilibrium between corruption and equality as described above. Freedom of speech in the democratic process can take various forms but placing it behind rejecting any restrictions seems to defy its very purpose and that of the regulation overall.

6.4 Tackling Political Corruption

Several notions have been developed over time stressing different perspectives of political corruption.[38] The common denominator behind the developed definitions is that there is a malfunction of the exercise of political power, which deviates from its initial aim (i.e. serving the public interest), and ends up being exercised on the premises of personal, private or economic criteria.[39] This conforms to the definition of corruption adopted under Chapter 2, namely the abuse of public office for private gain, which covers both the political power's exercise malfunction and its deviation to serve individual goals other than the public interest.

6.4.1 The Link of Political Corruption to Campaign Finance Violations

In the context of campaign finance regulation the analysis of the notion of political corruption includes two denominators: (i) political corruption therein is not limited to the exercise of public power but covers a broader range of fundraising transactions which

38 An overview of various definitions is presented in Peter Bratsis, 'Corrupt Compared to What? Greece, Capitalist Interests, and the Specular Purity of the State' (2003) The Hellenic Observatory-The European Institute-London School of Economics and Political Science Discussion Paper No. 8, 8-15 http://eprints.lse.ac.uk/5696/1/Corrupt_compared_to_what.pdf last accessed 24 November 2019.

39 Mark Philip, 'Defining Political Corruption' (1997) 45 Political Stud., 436, 440.

may be conducted entirely in the private sector; (ii) it does not necessarily focus on private benefit, but goes further to include the benefit of the entire political party or a specific candidate.[40]

In order to overcome definitional issues between corruption generally, as defined under Chapter 2, and corruption in the more confined context of campaign finance regulation, and to be able to measure the effectiveness of the examined regulatory responses in the three jurisdictions, a *case-by-case* analysis might be more efficient, to also provide an indication of the challenges faced by national regulatory frameworks on specific segments of campaign financing.

6.4.2 Contribution Limits

The first and most obvious case of violations that may lead to political corruption is the direct violation of laws on political financing with contributions going above the prescribed limits. A recently issued report of the Greek Control Committee highlights that, in 2015, Greek political parties systematically violated the regulatory framework, namely by: (i) not performing all the transactions for their expenditure through the declared party bank accounts; (ii) spending the public finance provided to them for research and training purposes to cover their functional needs and (iii) issuing of anonymous coupons;[41] anonymous contributions, in particular, create the suspicion of corruption because of the alleged attempted concealment of the source of funds contributed to the parties, and are therefore regulated in most jurisdictions, including those of the U.S. and the U.K. However, as already analyzed in Chapter 5, anonymous contributions of low amounts in Greece are a matter of great sensitivity and the attempts to abolish them completely, such as that by Law 4034/2014, have caused great criticism and the practice has been allowed once more by Law 4472/2017.[42]

6.4.3 Expenditure Limits

In the U.K. the Electoral Commission fined the Conservative Party for significant failures to respect the limits on campaign expenditure. More specifically, the party did not report with accuracy the campaign expenditure at three by-elections in 2014 and at the 2015 U.K. Parliamentary general election.[43] Such a violation has been considered by the Press

40 Michael Pinto-Duschinsky, 'Financing Politics: A Global View' (2002) 13 J. Democr. 69, 71.

41 Greek Control Committee, 'Annual Report on Financial Control of Political Parties/Coalitions of Parties for the Year 2015' (2018) 2.

42 See Chapter 5 nn 184 and 185.

43 Electoral Commission 'Conservative Party Fined £70,000 Following Investigation into Election Campaign Expenses' (2017) https://www.electoralcommission.org.uk/conservative-party-fined-ps70000-following-investigation-election-campaign-expenses, last accessed 24 November 2019.

as decisive for the outcome of the election on 2015,[44] although such assertions seem a little exaggerated. Victory in the elections achieved by the violation of certain fund expenditure restrictions is the significant benefit attributed to the entire party that links such violation with corruption.

6.4.4 *Unlawful Contributions*

Another violation of campaign finance regulation that may constitute or may result in political corruption is the use of funds stemming from an unlawful transaction by a political party to cover operational or campaign expenses.

6.4.4.1 Unlawful Private Funding

In 2008, the Greek authorities in cooperation with the German ones were investigating the so called 'Siemens scandal'. The case concerned alleged unlawful contributions by officials of German company Siemens to Greek politicians to receive favorite treatment in the assignment of various government contracts by the Greek Government.[45] In the context of the case a principal of the Greek Government of 1999, admitted that he received a large amount of money by Siemens which he then delivered to his – then governing – political party.[46] Here, corruption may be thought to be more 'straight forward'. The circumvention of the Greek law prohibition on corporations to fund election campaigns that allows illegitimate, as such, corporate funds (the funds came from a slush fund of Siemens) to assist a political party to win an election may be seen as the cause of the subsequent abuse of public offices held by members of said party by the adoption of policies friendly to said corporation or even directed by it.

6.4.4.2 Unlawful Public Funding

The use of public money and resources by government executives for partisan political purposes has also been witnessed. A soft form of this type of behavior was observed in the U.S. when Bill Clinton's invited wealthy individuals for coffee in the White House and

44 Ed Howker and Guy Basnett, 'The Inside Story of the Tory Election Scandal' *The Guardian* (London, 23 March 2017) https://www.theguardian.com/news/2017/mar/23/conservative-election-scandal-victory-2015-expenses last accessed 24 November 2019.

45 Penelope Alex Giosa, 'Corruption in Public Procurement: Siemens Greek Bribery Scandal' https://papers.ssrn.com/sol3/papers.cfm?abstract_id=3577112 last accessed on 24 May 2021.

46 Κ.Π. Παπαδιόχος, '«Ομολογία» Θ. Τσουκάτου για Siemens' *Η Καθημερινή* (Athens, 20 June 2008) kathimerini.gr/326195/article/epikairothta/politikh/omologia-8-tsoykatoy-gia-siemens last accessed 24 November 2018.

organized sleepovers in the Lincoln bedroom seeking to increase contributions to his campaign; he was eventually able to secure a victory in the 1996 presidential elections.[47] Another example are the recent allegations of the Press in Greece that the then governing party used public money to draw a social package for citizens in need, as a way to enhance the low poll percentages of its party for the next elections.[48] At a time of great stringency due to the ongoing effects of the recent financial crisis in Greece to use public resources that would have been allocated otherwise to satisfy a specific social group, with little other benefit other than the votes of its members in the subsequent elections,[49] this practice is highly questionable, in spite of legal formalities having been kept. Although not only lawful but to a certain degree a quite legitimate practice in democratic politics, it was its timing and the prevailing great fiscal difficulties that created such a strong impression of corruption that made the legitimacy of the political system suffer; as one may recall from Chapter 2, the perception of corruption is often just as important as actual corruption in matters of legitimacy and public trust.[50]

6.4.4.3 Quid Pro Quo Contributions

The reception of contributions in return for an unauthorized favor or promise in case of success in the elections is also a typical indicator of campaign finance violation resulting in political corruption. This is clearly illustrated in the 'Cash for Honors' case in the U.K. In 2006, investigations commenced concerning the loans granted to the Labour Party by several individuals, in exchange for the promise that they would be bestowed life-peerages, in case the party ultimately won the election.[51] Indeed, this scandal highlighted the limits of using transparency as the only restriction on campaign contributions, because the scandalous behavior in question was perfectly legal according to the strict transparency rules laid down by the PPERA, since it concerned not the donation of money, but the loaning to the Labour Party of vast amounts under

47 CNN, 'Lincoln Bedroom Guest Gave $5.4 Million' (1997) http://edition.cnn.com/ALLPOLITICS/1997/02/26/clinton.lincoln/ last accessed 24 November 2019; John Guare, 'My Night in the Lincoln Bedroom' *The New York Times* (New York, 2 March 1997) https://www.nytimes.com/1997/03/02/opinion/my-night-in-the-lincoln-bedroom.html last accessed 24 November 2019; see also Chapter 3 n 80.

48 Spiegel Online, 'Griechenland - Tsipras Unterstützt Bedürftige mit Milliardenschwerem Sozialpaket' *Spiegel Online* (Hamburg, 14 November 2017) spiegel.de/wirtschaft/soziales/griechenland-alexis-tsipras-unterstuetzt-beduerftige-mit-milliarden-sozialpaket-a-1177898.html last accessed 24 November 2019.

49 The main measure of the social package, which also drew most of the criticism, was the restoration of reduced pensions (in the form of a one-off payment amounting to 100% of the monthly instalment for pensions of €500 or less and a progressively lower percentage for pensions over that value in relation to their size) for the current year only; the fact that this took place during the campaigning period of the 2019 European Parliament election did not help the ruling party's assertion that the measure aimed only at restoring social justice and was unrelated to its campaigning strategy.

50 See Chapter 2 subsection 2.1.4.

51 The Telegraph, 'CPS Cash for Honours Decision Explained' *The Telegraph* (London, 12 April 2008) https://www.telegraph.co.uk/news/uknews/1557970/CPS-cash-for-honours-decision-explained.html last accessed 24 November 2019.

typical commercial terms; indeed, one of the persons involved reported that he was advised by a senior member of the Labour Party not to declare the loan for that reason.[52]

6.5 Regulatory Mechanisms

A comparison of the different regulatory bodies in the three jurisdictions under examination, namely the FEC in the U.S., the Electoral Commission in the U.K. and the Control Committee in Greece, is unavoidable, as the establishment of an institutional vehicle specialized in the regulation of campaign finance and handling the enforcement of such regulation is a condition *sine qua non* for any regulatory regime system to function. Nevertheless, the existence of any such a mechanism is not *per se* sufficient. The integrity of its structural and functional prerogatives from the interference of political interests as well as each body's reach of its actual enforcement capabilities may be considered as the crucial prerequisite for the achievement of the mechanism's ultimate goal, namely the effective enforcement of campaign finance regulation.

Engaging in a comparative assessment of the three mechanisms shall help us further understand their positioning within the respective constitutional frameworks of each examined jurisdiction and draw conclusions about the role specific constitutional principles play in the relevant regulatory frameworks. Measuring effectiveness in the field of campaign finance regulation is a tough riddle to be solved. We shall proceed with setting the evaluative benchmark of the present assessment in several characteristics which indicate the integrity and the proper functioning of the regulatory institutions. More specifically, the regulatory mechanisms in the examined three countries shall be compared based on their structural independence, their flexibility to adopt decisions, their transparency and the extent of their investigatory and coercive powers, all of which are reflective of the constitutional framework of each jurisdiction. The aim of this comparison is to extract meaningful and original conclusions on how the institutional and functional framework of campaign finance should be shaped in order to guarantee effective elimination of political corruption, legitimacy, public trust and particularly transparency.

6.5.1 Independence

The notion of independence refers to the lack of any linkage whatsoever between the regulators with the regulated candidates and/or political parties, so as the former shall

52 Rajeev Syal, 'Labour official told me to keep quiet' *The Times* (London, 20 March 2006) https://www.thetimes.co.uk/article/labour-official-told-me-to-keep-quiet-wbwn83nn6b5 last accessed 11 March 2020.

be free to perform their duties uninfluenced from any pressure or undue influence by the latter. More specifically, independence on campaign finance regulation can be *prima facie* ensured when the representatives of political parties in the executive or legislative branch cannot exercise any influential intervention on the structure and the decisional practice of the regulator. In other words, party members shall be unable to unduly influence directly or indirectly the appointment of the regulators' members and – even more importantly – their decisions in this capacity.

In the U.S., the FEC has been criticized not only for its broad requirements, under which the independence of its members is assessed, but also for its paradoxical relationship with Congress.[53] The influence of the Congress, though indirect and external, has been internalized in the premises of the Commission and has led to the adoption of a more conciliatory approach with regard to the legislature.[54] On the other side of the Atlantic the Atlantic, in the U.K., the introduction of the nominated Electoral Commissioners[55] and the reduction of the timeframe of the Commissioners' absence from the political scene from ten to five years,[56] constitute two features which compromise the Commission's independence as originally conceived. The actual absence from official political duties for a relatively long period is thought to cut off any ties with the exercise of power that would undermine or illegitimately affect their capacity as independent decision makers; nevertheless, a five year absence which amounts to one government full term in the U.K. might not be sufficient to result in cutting the active ties of the Commissioners with the exercise of political power. Finally, with regard to the Greek Control Committee, it has been observed that the considerable portion of its members is appointed by the legislature or present a direct or indirect connection with the legislative power, which has led to criticism[57] and the increase of its members from nine to eleven,[58] the two new members coming from the judiciary, which is now represented by five members.

Overall, this leads to the conclusion that regulators are often not shielded from the influence of the executive and legislative branches and therefore their independence is meaningfully undermined. Indeed, a close to absolute degree of independence requires that the subject of regulation cannot interfere with the regulator's decision making process. Nevertheless, if the former have a say in the latter's appointment then such independence is immediately questioned.

Limited independence, in turn, means limited efficiency and enforcement. One positive feature in the U.K. campaign finance regulation is that the PPERA provides for specific and concrete requirements on evaluating the independence of the

53 See Chapter 3 n 219.
54 See Chapter 3 n 220.
55 PPERA s 3A (1).
56 Ibid. s 3 (4).
57 See Chapter 5 n 135.
58 Law 4571/2018 Article 5 para 1 (ΦΕΚ Α΄ 186, 2018).

Commissioners, compared to the vague and imprecise requirements in the U.S. and Greek systems. Although this feature sets a clear benchmark in establishing the independence of the Electoral Commission, the (very) strong position of the nominated Electoral Commissioners (those proposed by party leaders) goes beyond the scope of enriching the institution with political experience and enhances the probability of institutional bias. Their elimination to non-voting members, with a purely consultative role could be considered as a good compromise in establishing an independent, but also politically experienced regulator. Similar legislative amendments could improve both the structure of the nascent Greek authority and the corresponding authority in the U.S. At the outset, campaign finance regulatory authorities should come with high independence of their voting members from the active political scene, coupled however with the requisite political experience of non-voting members, who might retain active political connections, but on whose experience the body might leverage to issue adequate and pragmatic decisions.

6.5.2 Flexible Decision-Making Procedures

In terms of the flexibility of decision-making process, it shall be observed that only the Greek Control Committee consists specifically of an odd number of members and decisions are taken by simple majority. In the U.K. PPERA's membership fluctuates between nine and ten Commissioners, while in the U.S. the FEC is steadily composed by six voting members. The even number of members in those mechanisms renders the adoption of a decision more difficult and may result in a practically dormant mechanism, where taking action is difficult and inaction is turned into the dominant norm, refuting the very purpose of establishment of these authorities; this is an aspect of the FEC's structure that has drawn considerable criticism.[59]

At the outset, arming a campaign finance regulatory body with a flexible and quick decision-making process increases the ability of the regulator to intervene in order to address as many infringements as possible. However, it should be highlighted that the effectiveness of a flexible decision-making process goes hand in hand with the regulator's independence. The Greek example, for instance, has not been a success story, because the efficiency deriving from the odd number of the Control Committee's members and its simple majority decision making-process cannot on its own guarantee the effectiveness of a mechanism that is institutionally strongly entangled with the legislative branch.

59 See Chapter 3 n 216.

6.5.3 *Transparency, Legitimacy and Public Trust*

Through transparency, public institutions establish the legitimacy of their actions, creating a 'bridge of trust' with people. In the field of campaign finance, trust is even more important, since those regulatory mechanisms constitute the gatekeepers of the most valuable asset of each state, namely its polity. A common characteristic between the examined legal systems is that regulators are highly transparent through the widest exploitation of new technologies. In all the examined jurisdictions, the competent regulatory authorities have created their respective website which is widely accessible to every citizen. On such websites, not only do they ensure the widest publicity of their work and reports on campaign finance, but they also provide significant guidance to the regulated candidates and political parties on how the law of campaign finance is to be interpreted and applied, through published guidelines, decisions and scientific reports. Transparency is indeed an indispensable element for modern campaign finance regulatory authorities, which enhances citizen knowledge and trust that the finances of their representatives and their parties do not remain uncontrolled, and that the citizens can find out themselves who are the individuals or entities that strive to establish undue influence in politics by financing directly or even indirectly candidates and political parties alike. In that sense, securing transparency to the furthest extent does not only have a constitutional value *per se* but also functions as the pre-requisite for securing the legitimacy of the entire campaign finance system and for enhancing the public trust to democracy. Political parties, candidates and elected officials are not above the law; the regulator shall ensure compliance, safeguarding overall the system's integrity and reassuring the constituency that violations will be punished under law.

6.5.4 *Investigatory and Coercive Powers*

While transparency's role may be deemed as rather preventive for the occurrence of future violations, campaign finance regulators need to be armed with extensive detection and suppression measures to tackle violations. The relevant mechanisms must have extensive investigatory powers and the power to impose civil sanctions and fines upon the infringers. In this regard, we saw that U.S. and Greek regulators adopt a more passive attitude, by initiating investigations only when a specific and personal complaint has been filed. Even worse, the Greek Control Committee is restricted to assess the case based only on the material submitted by the political parties. On the other hand, the mandate of the Electoral Commission in the U.K. has been significantly strengthened. The regulator in the U.K. is empowered to initiate *ex officio* investigations and to collect on its own initiative adequate evidence to determine the perpetration or not of violations of the regulatory framework,[60] thus becoming the bright exception amongst the examined legal systems as a regulator possessing a solid investigatory capacity, to conduct a deep examination of any alleged infringement.

However, investigation without the ability to impose coercive measures would remain an empty shell. Punishing campaign finance violations at the civil and administrative level is essential to suppress current infringements and prevent future ones, eventually protecting democracy. In Greece, as already outlined, recent reports reveal the reluctance of the Control Committee to impose fines or administrative sanctions.[61] In 2018, the Greek legislature amended the mandate of this mechanism and deprived totally the Committee from the power to impose fines. Going the opposite way, the Political Parties and Elections Act 2009 has enhanced the powers of the Electoral Commission in the U.K., by extending its scope of examination not only to political parties, but also to individual candidates. Furthermore, the Commission has also the power to impose a wide range of civil sanctions, including fines. Empirical studies have confirmed the success of those powers not only as corrective measures but also as deterrent features for future violations. In the same vein, the FEC also possesses the power to impose similar sanctions, while the criminal aspects of the case are referred to the competent Public Prosecutor.

Overall, tackling effectively political corruption is an issue of many factors, which requires a strong institutional framework embraced with several specific qualities. In general, the examined *fora* can be evaluated as partly successful (the example of the UK, which, as analyzed, has certain strong elements, but where improvement is still required such as in regard to the duration of the Commissioners' required political inactivity) or highly unsuccessful (the examples of Greece and the US). Tackling political corruption requires a strict separation of those mechanisms from the political world coupled with the provision of quick and flexible decision-making processes. Additionally, regulators should be highly transparent in order to boost public trust to the political system and should have the adequate investigatory and compliance powers in order to detect and enforce possible violations or deter politicians from acting in a corruptive way.

Campaign finance reform in terms of enforcement must thus be two pronged: (i) structural and (ii) functional. Self-regulation has been historically challenging. This cannot be expected to differ in politics. By strengthening campaign finance forms and the regulatory authorities enforcing them, politicians must realize that they protect they very democratic system they were elected to serve.

---

60 PPERA s 146.

61 See Chapter 5 n 137.

6.6 GRECO's Perception

Another point of comparative interest concerns how GRECO perceived campaign finance regulation in the three jurisdictions under examination. In this respect, we will not focus so much on the three frameworks' particulars as perceived by GRECO, but rather on the Organization perception of and critique to them, bearing always in mind that – as demonstrated in previous chapters – GRECO appears to have misinterpreted or wrongly evaluated some aspects of the respective regulatory systems.

One of the main US campaign finance issues identified by GRECO is how much candidate-centered the election system in the U.S. is, with candidates, despite belonging to or being affiliated with a particular political party, enjoying wide autonomy and running their campaigns independently of their parties.[62] This creates significant advantage for incumbents over their opponents. When trying to assess this issue, one must always keep in mind that, since individual candidates are left to run their campaigns on their own, with hardly any financial support from their parties, their ability to raise money and of the amounts raised therein is crucial for their election. The advantages incumbents enjoy are not only material (such as the coverage of part of their campaign costs through privileges and resources at their disposal associated with their office), but intangible as well (free publicity as a result of their actions in their official capacity) and ensure, as a rule, their ability to outspend their opponents. This leads to a vicious cycle, where donors, well aware of how unlikely it is for challengers to be elected, offer them limited financial support, thus further diminishing their chances to win the elections.[63] GRECO does not directly address the advantage enjoyed by incumbents over challengers, but hints at it when remarking how low the actual turnover of the Senate and the House of Representatives is (despite their six- and two-year terms respectively), since incumbents seek and generally achieve their re-election.[64]

It is not that incumbents in the U.S. enjoy much more privileges in comparison to incumbents in the U.K. or in Greece. Although the resources at the disposal of a member of the U.S. Senate are certainly greater than those at the disposal of a member of the Greek parliament in terms of nominal value, when one takes into consideration the differences in the relevant 'political markets' and national economies, the disparity appears, in reality, insignificant. What makes a difference, besides the candidate-centered nature of the U.S. election system, is the size and scale of political financing at the federal level; in conjunction with the absence of any limits on independent expenditures, the amount of funds that can be directed towards the election of a candidate as well as the variety of sources are astounding,[65] at least by the standards of

62 See Chapter 3 n 239.

63 Michael Johnston, *Syndromes of Corruption: Wealth, Power, and Democracy* (CUP 2005) 69.

64 GRECO Eval III, U.S.A. Evaluation Report Theme II (2011) 3-4 §12.

65 Ibid. 31 §135.

Greek or even U.K. politics. This means that incumbents, in addition to the privileges of their offices, can take advantage of the vicious cycle described above to divert the flow of money from the campaigns of challengers to their own. What is most striking is, that while GRECO identified both the issue of the candidate-centered nature of the U.S. election system and that of the size and scale of political financing, it failed to connect the dots and identify the problem of the significant advantages enjoyed by incumbents over challengers, in spite of all the indications provided by statistical data.[66] The relevant data are numerous, but perhaps the most impressive is that over the study of almost a quarter century of elections for the House of Representatives, the percentage of incumbents winning over challengers touched in some cases 99% while it never fell below 90%; during the same period almost a quarter of House incumbents faced only nominal opposition or even none at all.[67]

After failing to recognize the issue of the excessive advantages enjoyed by incumbents over challengers at the federal level in the U.S., and besides a remark on the need for electronic filing and thus speedier processing of the required information concerning campaign finance in respect of Senate elections,[68] GRECO's Evaluation Report identified only two significant problems, that are specific to the U.S. and attracted the attention of the Report's author(s). The first is the issue of independent expenditures by organizations organized under section 501(c) of the Internal Revenue Code.[69] The Report took note of the implications of the *Citizens United* case[70] in allowing independent expenditures by organizations that are under limited reporting obligations, as these have to report such expenses only to the IRS, the IRS not forwarding these to the FEC.[71] Furthermore, contributions to organizations under 501(c)(4) are under no disclosure requirements, allowing a contribution to the organization that may eventually be transformed into a contribution by the organization to a candidate or political party to be anonymous, as its original source remains unreported.[72] The other issue raised in GRECO's Evaluation Report is that of the often reported inability of the FEC to take action due to 'deadlocks' in its decision-making process.[73] It is attributed to the partisan composition of the Commission in conjunction with the even number of its

66 Johnston (n 63) 70.

67 Ibid. The numbers for incumbent senators are somewhat lower and the spread wider (75% to 97%), but more than adequately portray the security enjoyed by incumbents. Compare with the percentages of winning of better-financed candidates (Chapter 1 n 86).

68 GRECO Eval III, U.S.A. Evaluation Report Theme II (2011) 32-33 §141.

69 See Chapter 3 n 268. Those organized under 501(c)(4), mainly social welfare organizations such as environmental protection or civil rights groups, those under 501(c)(5), labor unions, and those under 501 (c)(6), business associations.

70 See Chapter 3 n 100.

71 GRECO Eval III, U.S.A. Evaluation Report Theme II (2011) 33-34 §144.

72 Ibid.

73 See Chapter 3 subsection 3.6.3.2.

members.[74] When the FEC is evenly divided, which usually happens in enforcement matters regarding an infringement of the regulatory framework, not only is it unable to take actions of its own, but in case there is also a criminal violation of the FECA it does not refer it to the Department of Justice and the prosecuting authorities.[75] Both issues raised in GRECO's Evaluation Report are valid, but as can also be inferred by the examination of U.S. campaign finance, they are certainly not the only ones. Furthermore, the issue concerning 501(c) organizations is more of a symptom than of a cause, the real cause being the lack of limitations on expenditures.

Bearing in mind GRECO's findings concerning the U.S., it is worth taking a look at its findings in regard of the two other jurisdictions under examination, the U.K. and Greece. In the case of the U.K., the most important issue identified by GRECO was the need for strengthening the Electoral Commission's power, in the fields of both regulation[76] and enforcement.[77] Another issue raised by GRECO concerning the potential future investigation and prosecution by the police of political financing offences is also of importance: there had been reports of the police showing considerable reluctance to carry out an investigation;[78] as serious as the allegation might seem, the recommendation itself about future research was rather mild and suggested a not so great importance, which does not correspond to the actual magnitude of the issue, if true. The rest of the issues concerned the format in which campaign finance information is made available to the public[79] and the need for extending the reporting requirements on loans already in place for political parties to candidates and third parties,[80] as well as for increased transparency at the constituency level.[81] Similar recommendations about the way and format in which campaign finance information is disseminated appear in the evaluations of the U.S. and Greece, and one could venture the guess, that they must be common in most of GRECO's national Reports, as making the wealth of information easily accessible is a recurrent problem of our times. Overall, GRECO's evaluation of U.K.'s regulatory regime is remarkable in only that it managed to identify more issues needing addressing than that of the U.S. (six versus three), despite the former being much more balanced than the latter, as can be inferred by the present analysis, notwithstanding the less serious nature of most issues raised in the case of U.K. regulation.

GRECO's Evaluation Report on Greece raised many more issues, almost double than those raised in the cases of the U.S. and the U.K. combined (sixteen versus nine in total).

74 GRECO Eval III, U.S.A. Evaluation Report Theme II (2011) 36 §151.
75 Ibid.
76 GRECO Eval III, U.K. Evaluation Report Theme II (2007) 25-26 §128.
77 Ibid. 27 §131.
78 Ibid. 27-28 §132.
79 Ibid. 24 §125.
80 Ibid. 24-25 §126.
81 Ibid. 25 §127.

Due to their number, and as they have been already discussed along with the Report's respective recommendations in the relevant section of Chapter 5,[82] they shall not all be repeated here. Notably, the Report failed to take note of two major shortcomings of the Greek Control Committee identified in the present analysis, namely its rather limited powers and the strong direct or indirect connections of a major part of its members with the legislative and executive branches which, considering the example of the evaluation of the U.S. mentioned above, should not come as such a great surprise. After its Evaluation, GRECO followed up rigorously on the implementation of its recommendations by the Greek Government, resulting in no less than five compliance Reports, including three interim ones, and a re-assessment of compliance in the next eight years.[83] Many recommendations were eventually adopted by amending the relevant provisions of the legislative framework, although some of them were considered by GRECO as partially only implemented. What is of interest in our case - and a bit of a surprise - is not so much the Greece's record of compliance which, given the extraordinary circumstances of the period concerned due to a major economic crisis and resulting political instability,[84] could be expected to be far from perfect, but rather GRECO's perception of Greece's campaign finance system and its actions to address the major issues raised in its Evaluation Report in comparison to GRECO's perception of the actions of the other two jurisdictions to implement its recommendations.

In comparison with GRECO's assessment of Greece's compliance with its recommendations, the case of the U.K. is not dissimilar. GRECO seems to have concluded that most of its recommendations were dealt with satisfactorily (some only partially though), but two were not dealt with at all (the recommendations concerning the need for extending the reporting requirements on loans already in place for political parties to candidates and third parties,[85] and the future investigation and prosecution by the police of political financing offences[86]). GRECO's recommendations led to the introduction of the PPERA of 2009, which amended the original PPERA and, amongst others, extended the investigation and enforcement powers of the Electoral Commission, as already discussed; that was not enough for GRECO to assess that its recommendations about the powers of the Commission were fully complied with, as by the time its first Compliance Report was drafted, some secondary legislation was still missing for the amendments to come into force;[87] rather paradoxically, even in the Second Compliance

82 See Chapter 5 nn 155-168.

83 See Chapter 5 n 169.

84 See Chapter 5 n 170.

85 GRECO Eval III, U.K. Compliance Report (2009) 5 §25, and GRECO Eval III, U.K. Second Compliance Report (2012) 6 §30.

86 GRECO Eval III, U.K. Compliance Report (2009) 8 §42, and GRECO Eval III, U.K. Second Compliance Report (2012) 7 §41.

87 GRECO Eval III, U.K. Compliance Report (2009) 7 §§ 37-38.

Report, which assessed the recommendations about the powers of the Commission as satisfactorily addressed,[88] there seemed to be some form of reservation about the amendments of the PPERA, the Report noting that: 'GRECO is no position to assess the new powers of the Electoral Commission.'[89]

GRECO's treatment of the U.K. and (much more) of Greece stands in sharp contrast to that it reserved for the U.S. and its actions – or rather lack of them – to comply with GRECO's recommendations. The term 'generously' may well be used to describe how these have been received by GRECO as, although the relevant initiatives were many, as GRECO's Compliance Report admits, they have resulted in nothing really tangible;[90] nevertheless, the Organization assessed all three of its recommendations as satisfactorily dealt with.[91] Two years later, and although the U.S. had still nothing tangible to show, GRECO stood by its assessment that its three recommendations had been dealt with in a satisfactorily.[92] To be fair, there have indeed been some relevant legislative attempts. In the case of the recommendation concerning the need for electronic filing and speedier processing of the required information during Senate elections, no less than five different bills (three in the Senate and two in the House of Representatives) were introduced to that effect;[93] nothing came out of them.[94] *Mutatis mutandis*, the same happened in respect of the issue with 501(c) organizations, where six different bills (four in the Senate and two in the House of Representatives) were introduced;[95] the outcome remained the same: nil.[96] But in the most important issue, that of the FEC's even number of members and the resulting 'deadlocks', the only actions taken were some, mostly informal, discussions;[97] still, GRECO's compliance Report concluded that this issue has also been satisfactorily dealt with.[98] One may reasonably wonders whether GRECO has fallen victim to its own high regard of the U.S. political finance system,[99] a regard that the present analysis does not support.

Not only were different standards applied in the Compliance Reports about the three jurisdictions, but similar problems appeared in the Evaluation Reports themselves, which ought to have provided a concrete assessment of each framework's ability to tackle corruption. Comparative data could also have been used in this regard. At the outset,

---

88 GRECO Eval III, U.K. Second Compliance Report (2012) 6 §36.
89 Ibid. 6 §35.
90 GRECO Eval III, U.S.A. Compliance Report (2014) 14-17 §§ 47-60.
91 Ibid. and more specifically §§ 51, 55 and 60.
92 GRECO Eval III, U.S.A. Second Compliance Report (2016) 12 §41.
93 GRECO Eval III, U.S.A. Compliance Report (2014) 14 § 49.
94 Ibid. 14 § 50.
95 Ibid. 15 § 53.
96 Ibid.
97 Ibid. 16-17 § 58.
98 Ibid. 17 § 60.
99 Evidence of GRECO's high opinion of the U.S. political finance system can be found for example in GRECO Eval III, U.S.A. Evaluation Report Theme II (2011) 29 §130, 33 §142, 38 §158, and GRECO Eval III, U.S.A. Second Compliance Report (2016) 12 §41.

the evaluations seem to show much tolerance to or inordinate absence of criticism of important problematic aspects of some systems, while serious criticism was leveled at other issues, often of clearly secondary importance, with the same issue sometimes receiving completely different treatment depending on the jurisdiction involved.

A clear example, which emerged in Chapter 5, was the issue of donations by means of anonymous coupons to Greek political parties.[100] GRECO initial position towards anonymous coupons, as well as its reaction to their reintroduction after a brief abolishment, seemed rather extreme, especially considering (i) the extensive monitoring of the coupons' issuing and return procedures; (ii) the relatively low yearly cap on total donations by anonymous coupons per party (€100,000 or 5% of last year's public aid to the party, whichever is less); and (iii) the similar situation in other EU countries, not to mention the status of anonymous donations in the U.S.[101] and the U.K.,[102] where no aggregate limits exist. It must be mentioned that in the last two cases, anonymous donations failed to draw any reaction by GRECO, other than that of noting the current state of affairs in this area of regulation. If one takes into account that small donations are the prime means of involving the majority of population (and not just a few major donors) with campaign finance, and applies the reasoning of a very interesting decision of the German Constitutional Court,[103] GRECO's reaction does not appear only excessive, but outright undemocratic in its essence. One has also to add to the critique of the GRECO evaluations their erroneous substantive understanding of the particulars of certain regulatory regimes it sought to examine, especially in cases like that of Greece, where – in sharp contrast to U.S. and U.K. legislation – the legislative original language barrier constitutes an additional hindrance. In the case of Greece, at least four different instances have already been noted where the authors of GRECO's Reports have misunderstood the real meaning of provisions of the legal framework they were evaluating.[104]

Overall, it seems that GRECO's evaluations of the examined jurisdictions cannot offer much to a substantive comparative analysis of the three jurisdictions at hand, because of the different perspective the Group's Committee is adopting in each of the relevant Reports, even when addressing identical campaign finance norms. What is of value, though, is the very comparative analysis of such different perspectives which demonstrates in summary three things: (i) a potential biased positioning vis-à-vis each

100 See Chapter 5 nn 183-187.

101 See Chapter 3 n 261.

102 See Chapter 4 n 211.

103 85 BVerfGE 264, 287 (1992). The Court decided against the constitutionality of unrestricted public subsidies to political parties, finding them undemocratic as, according to the Court, political parties should depend on the approval and support of the voters not only politically, but economically (and organizationally) as well, and public funds should not absolve parties from failing to secure sufficient such support. The reasoning of this decision is even more important in the case of Greece, the legal system of which bears many resemblances to that of Germany.

104 See Chapter 5 nn 151, 154, 164 and 179.

campaign finance system based on stereotypes about each concerned jurisdiction; (ii) a lack of systematic analysis that would include, at least a deeper understanding of the constitutional framework within which each system operates; (iii) an inability to engage in a structured assessment of the efficiency of the relevant regulatory frameworks, which is what the entire project initially aimed at and was really about.

Chapter 7 Towards Campaign Finance Reform

7.1 Introduction

To the degree that political corruption (or its appearance thereof) undermines the legitimacy of political systems, campaign finance regulation becomes essential also for effective governance. Nevertheless, controlling electoral campaign finance affects certain aspects of the democratic process entwined with some of its core values and principles, such as the freedom of expression, legitimacy, public trust, inclusion and transparency. Thus it becomes an immensely complicated regulatory field, whereby every measure has to be constantly assessed and balanced against its purpose and any conflicting rights.[1]

Furthermore, experience has shown that stopping completely illegitimate funds from seeping into the political arena through its cracks is an almost Sisyphean task. Money seems to always be able to find its way into modern politics, exploiting any gaps in legislation or enforcement, and taking advantage of the high financial demands of modern political campaigning. Campaign finance regulation is a dynamic field, where new measures are constantly needed to complement or replace previous ones that have been effectively challenged or bypassed. In this respect, the line between current campaign finance regulation and its required reform can become more difficult to draw, because the inherent natural dynamism of such regulation makes it seem more than a constantly changing process rather than a status quo.

Nonetheless, and notwithstanding the specific meaning that campaign finance reform has acquired within the context of the discourse in the U.S. as the movement aiming at reducing the effect of money in political campaigning, it should not be regarded as a concept constrained within U.S. limits, nor is it less important within the political systems of other democratic societies. The search for the optimal regulatory regime is an endless task, where perfection may be well impossible to achieve, however a better understanding of the common challenges faced in conjunction with the goal of achieving better functioning democracies is what stakeholders need to be looking at. In this respect, this study aims at going beyond the rather narrower limits adopted by the

1 Magnus Öhman and Hani Zainulbhai, *Political Finance Regulation: The Global Experience* (International Foundation for Electoral Systems 2009) 13-14.

– admittedly – comparatively longer and more extensive experience of U.S. campaign finance regulation.[2]

This study's main objective has been to identify the main principles and objectives of campaign finance regulation. As seen, such specific objectives of campaign finance regulation vary depending on the specific historical, cultural and legal background of each system. Nevertheless, reflecting on the different rationales and constitutional principles already discussed in Chapter 2, it stands to reason to try to reach some more generally applicable conclusions of universal validity that relate to the constitutional framework behind campaign finance regulation and more particularly with regard to the following constitutional principles that may function as the regulation's rationales: (the fight against) corruption, equality, freedom of speech (and of expression, more widely), legitimacy, transparency, and inclusion.

7.2 Campaign Finance Constitutional Principles in Review

7.2.1 *Towards Conclusions of Universal Constitutional Value*

Considering that human behavior is consistently replicated in a cross-jurisdictional manner, campaign finance reform needs to follow global trends, thus close monitoring the international regulatory tendencies should have a positive impact on the implementation and revision of local regulation. Of course, nationally specific realities are similarly important when designing campaign finance regulatory structures. Certainly, given the complexity and innate imperfection of campaign finance regulation, no model amongst the three examined (U.S., U.K., Greece) could possibly be assessed as being the best, or even greatly superior; nevertheless, hopefully some conclusions of universal applicability and value can be reached. These conclusions may affect more than one area under consideration, so that strict boundaries aligning each conclusion with each specific aspect of campaign finance regulation are not of much use in this final assessment. Therefore, after commenting on the principles discussed in Chapter 2 focusing on the jurisdiction each of them has gained more importance for regulatory purposes, there will be also some important and valuable conclusions pertaining to the greater process of campaign finance regulation.

2 The objectives of campaign finance regulation could be summed up from a U.S. point of view as: (i) eliminating legalized bribery; (ii) preventing extortionate raising of contributions by elected officials; (iii) dampening interest group activity; (iv) furthering the principle of political equality and (v) protecting elected officials from time-consuming fund-raising activities, see David A. Strauss, 'What is the Goal of Campaign Finance Reform' (2011) 1995 Univ. Chic. Leg. Forum 141, 141.

7.2.2 Political Corruption

The most cited rationale behind campaign finance regulation (and, to recall SCOTUS' case law, the only legitimate government concern to restrict freedom of speech[3]) is the prevention of corruption. Bearing this very statement in mind, it would also seem that it is also the only rationale on which all three examined systems agree totally and unequivocally; as such, it is bound be the focus of greater attention. The wide range of corrupting means linked to campaign finance and to political life in general, demonstrates the high degree of adaptability and efficiency that each campaign finance regulatory system should possess to block any illegitimate influence of money on politics. Tackling political corruption in the field of campaign finance is a tough riddle to solve and requires a careful and meticulous assessment of the various interests at stake, trying to strike a balance between them and avoiding emphasizing one to the detriment of another (as for example in the U.S., where emphasis on freedom of speech trumps almost any other concern, including the prevention of corruption). Most importantly, any measures introduced in this direction should always be proportional in order not to place significant barriers in the exercise of the fundamental right of individuals to participate in the political life (freedom of association and expression).[4]

For the purposes of the present study corruption has been defined as the abuse of public office for private gain.[5] However, one has to bear in mind that each of the three legal and regulatory systems under examination has a different perception of the concept of corruption. Furthermore, the conception of corruption by each system is not only more or less dissimilar, but is often intertwined with other broad concepts and principles, the attitude toward which may also differ and cause further divergence or convergence; as much as this is the case in the three examined states, it is also a factor of universal applicability to be borne in mind when assessing political corruption and its handling worldwide. The differences in this respect are also another reason to adopt the syndromes of corruption approach expounded in Chapter 2,[6] as such an approach can better account for qualitative differences than a single universal standard. A good example of the differences in the content of the term 'corruption' attributed to it by each jurisdiction, is the way the regulatory regime in the U.S. is concerned only and strictly with what it refers to as *quid pro quo* corruption,[7] considering the huge amounts of money spent in political campaigning quite legal and morally acceptable; quite opposite is the approach adopted in the U.K., the corrupting influence of money

3 See Chapter 2 n 2.

4 Organization for Security and Co-operation in Europe, *Handbook for the Observation of Campaign Finance* (Organization for Security and Co-operation in Europe–Office for Democratic Institutions and Human Rights 2015) 35.

5 See Chapter 2.1.1.1.

6 See Chapter 2.1.1.2.

7 See Chapter 3, mainly 3.5.1.

in political campaigning being attributed to its detrimental effects on equality.[8] This example also underlines the importance of examining relevant principles such as equality, because even if they fall outside the scope of campaign finance regulation as in the U.S., they nonetheless contribute in shaping the framework by defining its limits.

7.2.3 Equality

The U.K. legal system is much more sympathetic to issues of equality in campaign finance, to the detriment of the freedom of expression as it is understood in the U.S. The *Bowman* case in the pre-PPERA regime, which highlighted the absurd and rather derisory limits placed on independent expenditures (£5 at the time),[9] serves as an excellent example of the - perhaps excessive - value placed by the U.K. legislature on keeping money out of politics by establishing a level playing field amongst political candidates and parties, even though the wider framework within which such limits were placed was fragmented and ineffective.[10] These limits, and the higher - but still rather low - ones placed on independent expenses by the PPERA following the recommendations of the Committee on Standards in Public Life,[11] in conjunction with other measures such as the Short/Cranborne schemes, the Policy Development Grant, free access to public buildings for holding meetings during campaigning periods and limited free use of the postal system, free airtime and the ban on political advertising in broadcast media,[12] served the purpose of limiting the role of money in politics by restricting the financial needs of political parties and candidates.

The judiciary's acceptance of the legislature's approach to the role of money in politics and the importance attached to leveling the playing field is demonstrated by the proceedings of the *Animal Defenders International* case before the House of Lords. In its decision, Lord Bingham specifically mentioned the leveling of the playing field as highly desirable, as a further protection of the freedom of expression from the power of the purse of well-endowed interests.[13]

Both the *Bowman* and the *Animal Defenders International* cases reached the European Court of Human Rights, their outcome, however, was different. In *Bowman*, the Court found in favor of the applicant; in *Animal Defenders International* the applicant's claim was rejected. As already discussed in Chapter 4, it was the derisory low limit of £5 that was found disproportionate by the Court in the *Bowman* case. Equality within the context of campaign finance regulation was recognized as a

8 See Chapter 4 n 73.
9 See Chapter 4.2.3.
10 See Chapter 4 nn 2 and 3.
11 See Chapter 4 nn 65 and 70.
12 All measures independent of the PPERA and already discussed in Chapter 4.2.2.
13 *R v. Secretary of State For Culture, Media and Sports* [2008] UKHL 15§28.

legitimate government aim[14] and the Committee on Standards in Public Life in its Fifth Report found that there were 'clear indications' that the European Court of Human Rights would be sympathetic to the 'level playing field' argument.[15]

As already discussed in Chapter 4, in the *Animal Defenders International* case, the European Court of Human Rights found in favor of the U.K. government, admittedly by the slimmest of majorities (9 to 8), deciding that the restrictions imposed on the applicant were necessary for the prevention of the undermining of the democratic process,[16] noting the Court's fear of the 'risk of wealthy bodies with agendas being fronted by social advocacy groups created for that precise purpose.'[17] It further remarked that possible financial caps on advertising, as argued by the applicant, '*could be circumvented by those wealthy bodies creating a large number of similar interest groups, thereby accumulating advertising time.*'[18]

On a side note, the Court's approach to the issue of freedom of expression in both cases seems to indicate that, despite U.K.'s legal system – in contrast with most other European legal systems – being a common-law system, the U.K.'s perception of the role of money in politics and the orientation of its campaign finance regulatory regime is in agreement with what is considered to be the norm in those European legal systems, including the Greek one. Indeed, in this respect, and despite both being common-law systems, the divide between the U.S. and the U.K. appears insurmountable, not helped at all by the peculiar sense of exceptionalism that seems to pervade many aspects of U.S. jurisprudence more generally, and not only in the field of campaign finance regulation.

As mentioned above, the U.K.'s approach to the relationship of political financing with issues of equality is in agreement with what is accepted in Greece. As already discussed in Chapter 4, the Greek paradigm is uniquely poor amongst the three jurisdictions under consideration in case-law concerning campaign finance regulation. However, the campaign finance regime can safely be said to promote equality, as can be inferred by the interaction of its legal norms with the specific characteristics of the political landscape, mainly the great dependence of political parties on public funding with the extensive provision of public funds to almost all political parties, except for the ones who fail to cross a very limited threshold in elections.[19]

Although the U.K. approach appears to err on the side of equality at the expense of other rights, most notably that of freedom of speech, at least according to the decisions of the ECHR, it cannot but be seen as moving in the right direction. Equality enhances not only the integrity of the political system, but also helps increase its legitimacy, this being another example of how intertwined all these principles are in campaign finance

14 See Chapter 4 n 58.
15 See Chapter 4 n 69.
16 Animal Defenders International *v. the United Kingdom*, ECHR 2013-II 203, 237.
17 Ibid. 238.
18 Ibid.
19 See Chapter 5.4.1 for details.

regulation. It is a factor to be taken very seriously into consideration in this extremely complicated setting. The fact that there have been attempts in the jurisprudence of the SCOTUS to introduce equality into its reasoning, albeit disguised as something else,[20] can only underline its great importance, even for a legal system that seems to pay hardly any attention to it.

7.2.4 *Freedom of Speech*

It has already been discussed in Chapter 3 how the U.S. legal system emphasizes freedom of expression and freedom of speech over any other concern. Based on a – very extensive – interpretative analysis of the First Amendment to the U.S. Constitution,[21] the SCOTUS has developed a rather sophisticated doctrine of what it perceives as permissible regulation in the field of campaign finance. A much-quoted *dictum* from its decision on the *FEC v. National Conservative Political Action Committee* case[22] case is the basis of a very restrictive list of acceptable government interests of actually only one item, which according to the court may justify the regulation of campaign finance: that is the prevention of corruption or the appearance of corruption.[23] Every other conflicting right and interest has to yield to the paramount importance of the freedom of speech, while at the same time, according to the landmark decision of *Buckley v. Valeo*, equality and leveling the playing field as a measure to ensure it in politics is specifically excluded from the list of legitimate and compelling government interests as being '*wholly foreign to the First Amendment*'.[24] Of course, aphorisms centered around such vague notions as 'corruption' (or, even more, 'the appearance of corruption') are open to interpretation, and this is why the term 'doctrine' has been chosen: it does not mean simply a static position of the U.S. Supreme Court on the matter, but rather its evolution through numerous decisions and interpretation attempts by drafters of majority, dissenting and concurring opinions, in a struggle to express their understanding of those notions and shift the court's jurisprudence to the direction of their understanding.

The evolution of the U.S. Supreme Court's position on campaign finance in relation to free speech is intricately connected with the great value common-law legal systems as that of the U.S. place on precedent, also known as the principle of *stare decisis*.[25] Put simply, that means to stand by things already decided.[26] As the *Buckley v. Valeo* decision has set

---

20 See Chapter 3.2.5.

21 See Chapter 3 n 24 for the text of the First Amendment.

22 See Chapter 2 n 2.

23 Ibid.

24 See Chapter 2 n 3.

25 From the Latin maxim '*Stare decisis and non quieta movere*', meaning to stand by decisions and not disturb the undisturbed, Ronal Collins and David Skover, *When Money Speaks: The McCutcheon Decision, Campaign Finance Laws and the First Amendment* (Top Five Books LLC 2014), 83.

26 Ibid.

the wider framework of campaign finance regulation, including the contribution-expenditure dichotomy,[27] all following relevant cases had to take it into account as a source of law, even though *stare decisis* is not absolutely binding on the SCOTUS (or any supreme court for that matter), as it formulates its own precedent and is not bound by precedents set by other courts of law. Furthermore, this kind of precedent, also called 'horizontal precedent',[28] besides being not absolutely binding, has also been argued to be sometimes not only expedient, but also proper to be disregarded, as for example it has been based on an erroneous reading of the Constitution.[29] Of course, this would require the Supreme Court to admit erring, which it may – understandably – be very reluctant to do.

Although freedom of speech is the main principle affecting the regulation (or more precisely the deregulation) of campaign finance in the U.S., it is also a factor to be taken into consideration in the U.K. In fact, both major cases about campaign finance before a court of law in the U.K. (and later on in the ECHR) concerned mainly the restriction of the right to freedom of expression by the regulatory regime: the *Bowman* case[30] was about restrictions on independent expenditures, while the *Animal Defenders International* case[31] was about restrictions on political advertising. And although in both instances the court's decision seemed to emphasize other principles more than freedom of speech, the issue was examined, as can be demonstrated especially by the proceedings in the latter case before the House of Lords.[32] In Greece, the issue of freedom of speech has not been raised; although the fact that the law does not pay any attention to independent expenses may well be attributed to the very limited practice,[33] there seem to be few restrictions in this respect, while the caps placed on expenditure by political parties and candidates have never been challenged.

As far as freedom of speech is concerned, the U.S. paradigm should be viewed as an abnormality, where the almost absolute and virtually unqualified primacy given to it has led to a very narrow regulatory regime, with a trend towards further deregulation. The obsession of the entire system with protecting this specific freedom, to the detriment of other rights at play within the context of campaign finance, could be viewed as a unique example of a rather one-dimensional approach to the very complex issue of campaign finance regulation, which the very elaborate reasoning applied in U.S. case-law cannot obfuscate. The approach adopted by the U.K., on the other hand, seems much more

27 Monica Youn, 'First Amendment Fault Lines and the *Citizens United* Decision' (2011) 5 Harv. L. & Pol'y Rev. 135.

28 As distinguished from 'vertical precedent', precedent set by the decision of superior courts; for the distinction between vertical and horizontal precedent see Keenan D. Kmiec, 'The Origin and Current Meanings of Judicial Activism' (2004) 92 Calif. L. Rev. 1441, 1466-1467.

29 Ibid. 1467-1468.

30 See Chapter 4.2.3 for its details.

31 See Chapter 4.2.4 for its details.

32 See Chapter 4 n 73.

33 See Chapter 6.2.2.

reasonable, even if at times somewhat restrictive; and as demonstrated by the proceedings before the ECHR in both aforementioned cases, *Bowman* case and *Animal Defenders International*, not far from what is considered acceptable in most European countries.

7.2.5 Legitimacy

Legitimacy has been already described as an important rationale of campaign finance regulation. It is the reason why the SCOTUS has concluded that the only legitimate government interest it recognizes in campaign finance regulation comprises of the prevention not only of corruption, but also the appearance thereof. If legitimacy was not an issue, the appearance of corruption would not have mattered, at least from a legal point of view. In campaign finance regulation therefore, fighting against corruption is intertwined with seeking legitimacy.

The changing content of the meaning of corruption has already been analyzed while discussing the SCOTUS' approach to campaign finance regulation above. Judging by the wide reactions and the increasingly more popular demand for campaign finance reform in the U.S., it would appear that the shifting position of the Supreme Court towards deregulation, as described in its jurisprudence (and its evolution) examined in Chapter 3, has been deficient in establishing the system's legitimacy. The still unchallenged importance of fund-raising for political parties and the political system in general can be illustrated by the fact that Nancy Pelosi, currently (since January 2019) the Speaker of the U.S. House of Representatives, has remained practically unchallenged in her role as the leader of the Representatives belonging to the Democratic Party, despite having led them to four consecutive electoral defeats;[34] although the presidential system of the U.S. helps in diffusing responsibility for defeat, the most probable reason is her being the most effective Democratic fund-raiser the House has ever seen.[35] This assertion does not imply that the means used by Nancy Pelosi to raise funds are illegitimate, nor that continued electoral failure should necessarily and always be followed by the replacement of leadership; it shows, however, both the importance of fund-raising and the way it sidelines other important interests of the political parties. If actual electoral success or failure do not appear as important to a political party as the amount of funds to be raised, one does not have to possess a vivid imagination to conclude that neither the legitimacy of the political system is going to be ranked any higher.

The case of Greece is not helpful as far as legitimacy is concerned; the extensive legitimacy issues faced by its political system in the aftermath of its almost decade long financial crisis do not allow any reliable conclusions to be drawn. However, and perhaps

34 Frances McCall Rosenbluth and Ian Shapiro, *Responsible Parties: Saving Democracy from Itself* (Yale University Press 2018) 114-115.

35 Ibid.

because of the less restrictive approach to campaign finance regulation by its judiciary, legitimacy seems to be an objective achieved more easily in the U.K. regulatory regime. Indeed, its entire inception and operation is much more conducive not only to securing legitimacy, but also to further other objectives such as equality and inclusion. In this respect, and judging mainly by the results, the U.K. system seems a better source of inspiration than the respective U.S. one; and if one also took into account the general idea of exceptionalism that pervades U.S. jurisprudence, the not altogether arbitrary conclusion might be reached that the U.S. paradigm serves best as an example to be avoided rather than to be imitated. This is something to be kept in mind for later on, when some issues concerning GRECO will be addressed.

7.2.6 Transparency

The twin role of transparency has already been discussed in Chapter 2: On one hand it is in itself a useful tool to fight corruption and enhance public trust, without unduly restricting freedom of speech;[36] on the other hand, it helps monitor regulatory compliance with the applicable framework.[37] The role of transparency becomes even more prominent, if one takes into consideration how great a challenge it presents to formulate an effective campaign finance regulatory regime. According to the Money, Politics and Transparency Project created by Transparency International (hereafter TI Survey), regulating campaign finance is rather ineffective at a global level. According to said research project, no matter the number or the sophistication of the provided restrictions, in most countries of the world, political parties and candidates circumvent the prohibitions of the legislation. They manage to do that either by benefiting from loops in the existing framework or by relying on the insufficient enforcement by the authority afforded with the power to monitor the application of campaign finance laws in that jurisdiction.[38]

The examination and analysis of the three *fora* showed that the sharpest differences between them can be found in the field of private campaign finance, demonstrating the variety of regulatory means used by the legislature in trying to combat the illegitimate influence of private money in politics. While the Greek system has rather strict but modest provisions for contributions and virtually none as far as expenditures are concerned, the U.K. system focuses on campaign expenditure while the U.S. system regulates almost exclusively the amount of permissible contributions. According to the

36 But see Chapter 5.3.2 on how disclosure requirements have been seen as disturbing a very sensitive issue in Greek politics, even if only from a historical point of view.

37 OSCE (n 4) 20.

38 Money, Politics and Transparency Project, 'Contribution and Expenditure Restrictions' (2014) http://moneypoliticstransparency.org/sections/2/ last accessed 28 November 2019.

TI Survey, the latter approach seems to present greater effectiveness.[39] This conclusion seems logical, because strict limitations on the resources of the political parties constrain their economic leeway. Limitations on expenditure are thought to be more easily maneuvered, because if political parties are already in the possession of large sums of money, they will more easily find creative ways of spending while staying under the radar of the regulatory authority. This is why transparency is so important irrespectively on what way each system decides to take on the restrictions to impose. One may think of transparency as the necessary additive without which the regulatory recipe of campaign finance is highly unlikely to succeed.

In addition, political corruption benefits from the lack of transparency about the economic resources of political parties and candidates. It must be recalled that transparency is a core factor in eliminating corruption and restoring the trust of the public to the political system. Based on the results of *the TI survey,* it is a general trend that almost in all countries there are at least some reporting and disclosure obligations. However, in practice, 87% of the researched countries face significant omissions in the disclosure submissions of political parties and candidates before the competent authorities. The same stands true with regards to public disclosure, where only 3.7% of the examined countries make all reported data available in machine-readable format and less than 25% provide information in standardized, comparable formats.[40]

On that basis, transparency should be guaranteed in three directions: (i) extensive reporting and publicity obligations should be imposed on both political parties and candidates, on an ongoing periodical basis and not only during the electoral period. The relevant reports should include all contributions (public or private) as well as accurate expenditure figures; (ii) inclusion of adequate donor information so that political remain easily identifiable; (iii) expenditure incurred by third parties on behalf of parties and candidates should be equally treated as donations and not be exempted from the reporting and disclosure obligations.[41]

---

39 Ibid.

40 Money, Politics and Transparency Project, 'Reporting Requirements to the Oversight Entity' (2014) http:/ moneypoliticstransparency.org/sections/3/1/ last accessed 28 November 2019.

41 Transparency International, 'Recommendations on Political Financing for Open Government Partnership National Action Plans' (13 August 2018) https://www.transparency.org/whatwedo/publication/ recommendations_on_political_financing_for_open_government_partnership last accessed 28 November 2019; Transparency International, 'Policy Position No 1/2009: Standards on Political Funding and Favors' (2009) issuu.com/transparencyinternational/docs/2009_1_standardsfunding_en? mode=window&printButtonEnabled=false&shareButtonEnabled=false&searchButtonEnabled= false&backgroundColor=%23222222 last accessed 28 November 2019.

7.2.7 *Inclusion*

Inclusion is one the ideals that every society should aspire to; it is even more important for the operation of modern representative democracies. Its relevance to campaign finance regulation and its function as the latter's rationale thereof may be described as follows: Limited regulation of campaign contributions and expenditures means that there is more money going around, it is thus possible for segments of society that feel themselves excluded to find more easily the financial resources needed for them to seek representation in electoral contests; at the same time the greater availability of funds to mainstream political parties may allow them to recruit political personnel from less privileged backgrounds, as already argued in Chapter 2.

Of course, this is – as always – dependent on other parameters as well. In the U.S., for example, where regulation is generally loose due to the lack of any restrictions on expenditures, politics at the federal level do not appear to have been affected in any of these two possible positive ways. This may though well be the result of other factors at play: the majoritarian voting system tends to crush all political parties but the two major ones, while the inherent weakness of party leaderships[42] precludes any attempt by them to impose candidates from less privileged backgrounds, offering members of local elites considerable advantage to be nominated to run for the Senate or the House of Representatives;[43] as for presidential candidates, Bernie Sanders, coming from a less than privileged background,[44] was in recent years perhaps the one notable exception that reaffirmed the rule, and anyway he failed to win his party's primaries to be nominated to run for president in 2015 and seemed to be losing them too in 2020, before he withdrew his candidacy.

Bearing the U.S. case as described above in mind, one cannot but be troubled about the relative value, if not the merit, of this aspect of inclusion as a rationale to shape campaign finance regulation. If one does not take the external factors such as the majoritarian system into consideration, inclusion would seem as completely irrelevant. The cases of the U.K. and Greece do not appear helpful either. The U.K. may have a majoritarian voting system not dissimilar to that of the U.S., but that is where similarities end: the need of the government to secure the House of Commons' confidence and strong regional political forces mean that smaller political parties are

42 A result of the Founding Fathers' distrust of political parties, see McCall Rosenbluth & Shapiro (n 24) 119-122. Indeed, the weakness of the two major parties' leadership can be demonstrated by the fact that their chairpersons (at the moment Ronna Romney McDaniel for the Republicans and Tom Perez for the Democrats) are widely unknown.

43 Traditional constituency-based selection procedures tend to produce wealthy middle-aged white male candidates, ibid. 89.

44 Nicole Gaudiano, '6 Things to Know about Bernie Sanders', *USA Today* (McLean Virginia, 28 April 2015) https://web.archive.org/web/20150727170730/http://onpolitics.usatoday.com/2015/04/28/6-things-to-know-about-bernie-sanders/ last accessed 12 May 2020.

not smothered as in the U.S. but still, although parties' leaderships are powerful, they have had difficulties promoting candidates from minorities, or even women.[45] Greece, on the other hand, has a proportional representation political system and parties' leaderships that are very strong, even stronger than those of the parties in the U.K. However, the operation of political elites who trace their origins in the upper social and financial classes in the country result in few candidates from less privileged backgrounds making it to the top of the political ladder.

One might conclude that inclusion should not be made a central issue of campaign finance, especially if attempting to achieve inclusion would lead to less regulation. That does not mean that inclusion is not pertinent to campaign finance. We should recall the analogy between inclusion and public trust made in Chapter 2. A political landscape that appears less dominated by special interests in conjunction with greater availability of funding does indeed promote the inclusion of all voters' groups that feel themselves sidelined from mainstream politics, inducing some of them in running for office. Inclusion, as most things in campaign finance regulation, works both ways. And while it may appear as a truism by now, this only reinforces one of the main conclusions: the need to strike a careful balance, in this case not between conflicting interests, but between conflicting aspects of (or approaches to) the same principle.

7.2.8 Striking a Balance: The Role of the Judiciary

It should be borne in mind that it is the judiciary's prerogative in applying constitutional norms that plays such a prominent role in striking a balance between the conflicting rights in the complex area of campaign finance regulation. This means that the orientation of the jurisprudence of each state's Supreme Court and, consequently, of its legislation, is dependent on that court's perception of basic rights and freedoms in question. As a result, different approaches to the various conflicting rights at the supreme constitutional level can considerably alter the legal framework of campaign finance regulation. The examination of the regulatory framework of the U.S., the U.K. and Greece in Chapters 3, 4 and 5 respectively has already highlighted the considerable differences in perception resulting from a different balancing of important constitutional rights and, often, their overall acceptance thereof as part of the relevant applicable to campaign finance regulation constitutional framework.

Considering the central role the judiciary plays in campaign finance regulation, which cannot be understated, that should hardly appear as odd. Not only is the judiciary responsible for applying the legal provisions pertaining to campaign finance regulation, but as the final arbitrator on the matter of the compatibility of said provisions with the wider constitutional and legal framework, it can effectively circumscribe any legislative

45 McCall Rosenbluth & Shapiro (n 24) 89-90.

initiative of campaign finance reform. The classic example in this respect is the *Buckley v. Valeo* decision of the U.S. Supreme Court,[46] which, as already discussed in Chapter 3, struck down all spending restrictions imposed on federal candidates by the 1974 Amendment to the FECA,[47] thus breaking asunder the contributions-expenses nexus envisioned by the legislators; the fallout of that decision still defines – at least partly – the context of campaign finance regulation in the U.S.

When a provision of campaign finance regulation is successfully challenged before a supreme court, this in principle results in the annulment or amendment of the said provision by the legislature itself, in order to conform to the court's decision. This has been repeatedly the case in the U.S., where, continuing with our last example, the *Buckley v. Valeo* decision led to the amendment of the FECA.[48] Cases like *Buckley v. Valeo* are by nature political and the justices of the Supreme Court are forced to make political decisions, but are required to ground them on the Constitution; in such cases doctrine can be less a legal guide than a political tool.[49] This is why the content of concepts such as 'corruption' tends to vary and change over a series of decisions, as the Supreme Court attempts to shift its position on the matter, something quite unsurprising given the social and political changes in the meantime, without appearing to overturn its own precedent. This is something to remember, when discussing freedom of speech and the SCOTUS.

Even in the U.K., where the most recent successful challenge of campaign finance regulation in the *Bowman* case[50] resulted from proceedings not before its own judiciary, but rather before an international tribunal (the European Court of Human Rights), an amendment of the relevant provision but also a wider reform of the legislation considerably influenced by that decision were quick to follow in the form of the PPERA, which was granted royal assent about two and a half years after the European Court of Human Rights rendered its decision.

Therefore, even if somewhat indirectly, contemporary case-law is one of the main parameters (if not the main one) affecting the formulation of a campaign finance policy and the relevant regulatory regime. The central role played by the judiciary should also be kept in mind when discussing other major principles of campaign finance regulation, such as equality and – especially in the case of the U.S. – freedom of speech. And the fight against political corruption should be always taken into account as the background against which all those principles are examined and assessed.

46 See Chapter 3 n 31.
47 See Chapter 3 n 23.
48 See Chapter 3 n 33.
49 Robert E. Mutch, *Buying the Vote: A History of Campaign Finance Reform* (OUP 2014) 190.
50 See Chapter 2 n 28.

7.3 CAMPAIGN FINANCE REGULATION: A ROADMAP FOR FUTURE REGULATION

By examining the basic constitutional principles shaping campaign finance regulation, this study provided an overview of the constitutional concerns faced by each jurisdiction when introducing campaign finance legislation. But what comes next? The analysis in the previous chapters demonstrated certain strengths and weaknesses of the different regulatory approaches. These are further elaborated below to demonstrate what the future regulator can rely on when addressing certain aspects of the regulation that could form part of a broader campaign finance reform.

7.3.1 Public Campaign Finance: Helping or Underlining the System?

According to the TI Survey, already mentioned above, there are also considerable challenges in regulating public campaign finance: although the three examined jurisdictions have introduced (at least to some extent) regulation on public campaign finance, the application of those mechanisms has been in practice undermined.[51] For example, the relevant system in the U.S. has scored moderately in that survey, because it dissuades candidates in the presidential elections to accept public funding by imposing limitations on their expenditure.[52] Another important issue which can be indirectly correlated with public campaign finance is the fact that, although most of the countries in the world have adopted prohibitions on the abuse of state resources for campaign finance purposes, the rate of violations linked to public resources remains a strong indicator of political corruption.[53]

The challenges in regulating public campaign finance are therefore twofold: (i) creating an efficient and equitable system which will support political parties and politicians not only in theory (as the aforementioned example of public funding for presidential candidates in the U.S.) but in practice as well and (ii) ensuring that state resources (monetary or non-monetary) are not abused by such parties and political personnel for electoral purposes.

With respect to the former, among the several options to determine eligibility criteria for public funding,[54] it may be assessed that the criterion of previous electoral success coupled with a provision of some minimum funding for newly established political

---

51 Money, Politics and Transparency, 'The Money, Politics, and Transparency Campaign Finance Indicators' (2014) 27-28 http://assets.sunlightfoundation.com.s3.amazonaws.com/mpt/MPT-Campaign-Finance-Indicators-Key-Findings.pdf last accessed 28 November 2019.

52 Money, Politics and Transparency, 'United States of America' (2014) http://moneypoliticstransparency.org/countries/US/ last accessed 28 November 2019; see also Chapter 3.3.1.

53 'The Money, Politics, and Transparency Campaign Finance Indicators' (n 51) 28-30.

54 Organization for Economic Co-operation and Development, *Financing Democracy: Funding of Election Campaigns and the Risk of Policy Capture* (2016) Organization for Economic Co-operation and Development Public Governance Reviews, 41.

parties, balances the interests of rewarding popular acceptance reflected in the election results with supporting new voices in the political arena. This is thought to establish a relative level playing field between all participating collectively organized actors in the political game, in an implementation also of the constitutional principle of equality.

The second challenge goes directly to the heart of political corruption. Abusing state resources to secure election or reelection is a casebook example of political corruption. The temptation is exceptionally strong for the political party in power, as many activities of government officials are difficult to categorize and thus it is easy to abuse the system. In that respect, the core aim of the legislators should be to clearly define the limits between party-related and public activities, and to introduce even an explicit ban on the use of state resources for electoral purposes.[55] Of course, even an outright prohibition is not sufficient if not accompanied by additional preventive and enforcement measures. To that direction, the creation of a robust legislative framework which will encompass constant controls on the economics of political parties, beyond the election period, should be a first priority.[56] Furthermore, the neutralization of the public administration from political influence should be pursued.[57] Ensuring the integrity of public servants and imposing obligations on neutrality when exercising government duties shall act as a deterrent to such abuses while ensuring transparency. Finally, during the election period, the law should require the disbursement of public funds only for specific purposes related to the exercise of governmental authority.[58] In this vein in Greece, Article 28 of Law 2190/1994[59] is a good example of sensible regulation, providing that during the election period civil servants cannot be appointed, promoted, transferred or affected in any other way until after the election, in order to safeguard their impartiality and enhance transparency at the pre-election level; certain exceptions concerning new appointments are allowed to face urgent and unforeseen needs, but in this case they have to be approved by the Council of State, the country's supreme administrative court.[60]

---

55 Matthew Jenkins, Transparency International, 'Best Practices on Preventing the Abuse of Public Resources' (Transparency International 2017) 5 https://www.transparency.org/files/content/corruptionqas/Best_practices_on_preventing_the_abuse_of_state_resources_2017.pdf last accessed 28 November 2019.

56 Ibid. 1.

57 Magnus Ohman , *Political Finance Oversight Handbook* (International Foundation for Electoral Systems 2013) 154-158 https://www.ifes.org/sites/default/files/tide_political_finance_oversight_handbook_0.pdf last accessed 28 November 2019.

58 This is illustrated in the example of the Greek system, where the provision of public funds is embedded to a clearly identified purpose.

59 Officially: 'Creation of an Independent Authority for Personnel Selection and Other Provisions' (ΦΕΚ Α' 28, 1994).

60 Ibid.

7.3.2 *The Role of Control Mechanisms*

One of the main deficiencies noted in various campaign finance regulatory regimes was the lack of efficient control mechanisms. A good example was the regime established by the Federal Corrupt Practices Act (FCPA) of 1910 (amended in 1911 and 1925); the lack of efficient enforcement provisions was one of the main reasons behind the famous remark of President Lyndon Johnson that it was more a loophole than law.[61] A similar deficiency had been noted regarding the pre-PPERA regime in the U.K.[62] Both the current FEC and the Electoral Commission rely on strong regulatory bodies with wide responsibilities and supervisory powers, dedicated to enforcing campaign finance limits and restrictions. The current campaign finance regulatory regime in Greece, established by Law 3023/2002,[63] also confers an important role to the Control Committee, even if the latter does not have the same clout as its U.S. and U.K. counterparts.

7.3.2.1 Legal Foundation

The efficient operation of enforcement mechanisms depends on many factors. One of the main prerequisites for the efficiency of a regulatory body is a solid legal foundation. In this respect, the three mechanisms under consideration appear to have been without blemish, as no serious challenge has been leveled against them, with the sole exception of two not so important hitches concerning FEC's composition: The first when the FEC's appointment scheme was found unconstitutional in the *Buckley v. Valeo* decision and appropriately modified by Congress;[64] and the second concerning the participation of the Secretary of the Senate and the Clerk of the House of Representatives as two *ex officio* non-voting members with the Commission, which was also deemed unconstitutional after the United States Court of Appeals for the District of Columbia Circuit's decision in the *FEC v. NRA Political Victory Fund* case as violating the principle of separation of powers;[65] it must be reminded that although the case did reach the SCOTUS, it was dismissed on technical grounds.[66] In none of the three cases under consideration the legal foundation of their enforcement mechanisms appears as wanting, and they could all supply a valuable example for states with less developed institutions.

61 See Chapter 1 n 10.
62 See Chapter 4 n 11.
63 See Chapter 5 n 1.
64 See Chapter 3 n 41.
65 See Chapter 3 n 179.
66 Ibid.

7.3.2.2 Independence

Another important factor for the efficiency of a regulatory body is its independence. When examining the three Commissions in Chapter 6, it was revealed that a common complaint against all three was the perception that they were not adequately independent. FEC's functional independence appears as limited by Congress, which cannot only not only veto FEC's proposed regulations, but also control its budget.[67] Additionally, the strong links of its members with the two major parties lead to the FEC's strong politicization.[68] The independence of the PPERA's Electoral Commission is clearly more solid, with a stated preference towards the appointment of members without political experience[69] and numerous requirements for prospective commissioners;[70] yet there is still concern, especially after the reduction of the Commissioners' mandated period of absence from the political scene from 10 to 5 years and the introduction of Commissioners nominated by the political parties, contrary to the suggestions of the Committee on Standards in Public Life.[71] The Control Committee in Greece faces also considerable criticism regarding the independence of its members, despite its statutorily declared independence;[72] a considerable number of its members are directly or indirectly appointed by the legislature and the executive and three of them, including the chairman, are members of the Parliament, as detailed in Chapter 5.5.1, seriously eroding any distinction between the regulators and the subjects of the regulation.[73] It would thus appear that of all three commissions are found to be lacking in matters of independence, although PPERA's Electoral Commission seems to fare better than the other two.

7.3.2.3 Commitment

It takes more than an adequate institutional framework for a regulatory body to fulfill its mandate; it also takes commitment. The commitment to tackle corruption in campaign finance may be adversely affected by deficiencies in the legislation and the compromised independence of each commission's members. In this respect, both the FEC's and the Control Committee's records seem wanting, at least in comparison with that of the Electoral Commission. Especially the record of the FEC is disappointing, particularly

---

67 See Chapter 3 n 219.

68 See Chapter 3 n 229.

69 See Chapter 4 n 12. One wonders if this preference may not also have a somewhat negative influence on the Commission's appointed members' abilities to navigate through the labyrinth of party politics. This deficiency may well be the one of main reasons behind the introduction of nominated Electoral Commissioners.

70 Ibid.

71 See Chapter 4 n 190.

72 Article 3A (1) of Law 3213/2003, as introduced by Article 225 of Law 4281/2014, officially: 'Measures for the Support and Development of the Greek Economy, on Organizational Issues of the Ministries of Finance and Labor, Social Security and Welfare, and Other Provisions' (ΦΕΚ Α' 160, 2014).

73 See Chapter 5 nn 109 and 112.

bearing in mind its long existence of 45 years. Not only does it often appear reluctant to investigate serious complaints, going after petty infractions instead, but its activities are often restrained by the politicization of its members. Its composition of an even number of Commissioners, which are almost always evenly split in line with their affiliation to one of the two major parties, means that in cases one of those parties considers important to its interests, its bloc can deadlock any decision.[74] Although this would appear to be a mainly structural problem, the inability of the Commission to overcome this inherent weakness after 45 years seems to hint of lack of commitment to overcome partisanship; especially if one takes at face value claims that the even number of Commissioners was intentional and aimed at fostering consensus and bi-partisan cooperation.[75] The Greek Control Committee, although not hampered by a similar structural weakness, has also appeared reluctant to impose sanctions within its powers[76] and opted for confining itself in simply monitoring infractions, considerably weakening the deterrent value of its function. There have been few complaints about the lack of eagerness on the part of the U.K. Electoral Commission to exercise its powers and enforce campaign finance regulation as laid down by the PPERA, even though the Commission has on occasion expressed its intention to avoid imposing formal sanctions reserving its power to do so in the future in order to ensure future compliance.[77]

7.3.2.4 Transparency

There are, of course, positive aspects in the functioning of each of the three enforcement mechanisms under examination. FEC's role in promoting transparency in campaign finance cannot be overstated. The function of the U.K. Electoral Commission, which was in any event the least troublesome of the three, also promotes transparency and has proved a more than adequate deterrent of serious legislation infractions, while its wide remit offers to its regulatory activities a more in-depth understanding of the intricacies of campaign finance. This could also be thought to apply to the remit of the Greek Control Committee, which might though be overly broad. Besides being tasked with monitoring the enforcement of campaign finance regulation, it also has extensive monitoring tasks in the wider public sector consisting in the oversight of material assets of members of the executive, the judiciary, the civil service as well as the law enforcement and security agencies in order to combat corruption; these tasks consume a not inconsiderable amount of the Committee's time and resources, fragmenting its efforts and diminishing its ability to go deeper into campaign finance regulation issues. The most important of the Committee's roles, as far as campaign finance is concerned,

---

74 Harvard Law Review, 'Eliminating the FEC: The Best Hope for Campaign Finance Regulation?' (2018) 131 Harv. Law Rev. 1421,1431-1432.

75 See Chapter 3 n 226.

76 See Chapter 5 n 136.

77 See Chapter 4 n 185.

relates to its oversight of the disbursement of public subsidies to the political parties in a campaign finance system heavily reliant on public funding; even without taking advantage of its enforcement powers to their full extent, the Committee's positive impact on deterrence should not, as such, be understated.

7.3.3 *Lessons to be Learnt*

What are the lessons in the field of enforcement that could be drawn from the record of the regulatory bodies of the three countries under examination with regard to the prerequisites for successfully combating corruption by campaign finance regulation? First, a solid legal foundation is required; one could include within it the absence of such structural impediments as the body's composition of an even number of members;[78] providing for an odd number of members in administrative organs is a widely and well-known practice aiming at reducing the possibility of deadlocks and resulting inactivity. Second, institutional and functional independence: the mechanism should be constituted by members with as limited links to party politics as possible, and endowed with adequate funds and resources to carry its functions properly, without undue restraints on its funding by the legislature, which is after all the main subject of campaign finance regulation; in this respect it should be added that the appearance of independence may be as important as the actual independence of a regulatory body when considering its legitimacy. Third a broad enough scope of competence to enable a broader and more in-depth understanding of the intricacies of campaign finance, without any exceptions that would cause the fragmentation of the regulatory framework; not too broad, however, as to affect the body's focus on regulation. These are mostly objective factors; the subjective factor should not be underrated, however. The actual commitment of any regulatory commission to fulfill its mandate is fundamental to achieving positive results.

7.3.4 *Regulatory System Orientation and Typology*

The categorization of each national campaign finance systems under Chapter 6 in one of the campaign finance categories identified under the typology adopted in Chapter 2 demonstrated the differences between public and private campaign finance. What can this typology mean for future regulation?

Recipients of such funding can be either political parties or individual candidates. Ensuring adequate funding through either or both of those finance models to parties and candidates is crucial in reducing the need of and dependence on illegitimate funds

78 Which still plagues FEC's function.

by them, thus removing a possible incentive for corruption. At the same time, preventing the flow of funds (and other resources) to parties and candidates for illegitimate purposes, without unduly burdening their ability to finance their activities, is one of the critical objectives of each campaign finance regulatory regime; achieving a balance thereon is the major objective.

All of the three systems examined are mixed, in the sense that they combine to some degree elements of both public and private finance, and the balance within each system between each source of funds varies greatly. This is also a somehow global trend since there are very few systems denying altogether either public or private campaign financing of political parties and candidates. According the distinction established in Chapter 2, the three systems belong to each one of the three different categories: The U.S. has adopted a private campaign finance systems with certain public campaign finance elements, the U.K. a true 'mixed' system with a relative balance between public and private campaign finance norms, and Greece a public campaign finance systems with certain private campaign finance elements.

What is certain is that it is almost impossible (and certainly in most cases entirely undesirable) to have a campaign finance system that is entirely focused on either private or public funds or resources. Even in the U.S., where at the federal level only presidential candidates may be entitled to public funding, the relevant normative background does exist,[79] notwithstanding the fact that in recent election campaigns candidates of the major parties have declined such funding for reasons of convenience.[80]

On the other side of the spectrum, in Greece, which follows a trend of many European countries that provide public subsidies to political parties, there is considerable leeway for legitimate private financing, even though the major flux of funds stems from public resources. Not only is a completely public finance system undesirable, it may also prove to be unconstitutional: As already mentioned in Chapter 6, the German Constitutional Court has decided against the constitutionality of unrestricted public subsidies to political parties, finding them undemocratic, as according to the Court's reasoning, political parties should depend on the approval and support of the voters not only politically, but economically (and organizationally) as well; public funds should not absolve parties from failing to secure sufficient such support.[81] The U.K. has steered a course in between the two extremes, as neither tax incentives to contributors (a characteristic of systems oriented towards private funding), nor direct state subsidies (a hallmark of public funding systems) have garnered much support there.[82]

79 See Chapter 3 n 136.
80 See Chapter 3 nn 147-149.
81 See Chapter 6 n 103.
82 Navraj Singh Ghaleigh, 'Expenditure, Donations and Public Funding under the United Kingdom's Political Parties, Elections and Referendums Act 2000 - And Beyond?', in KD Ewing and Samuel Issacharoff (eds), *Party Funding and Campaign Financing in International Perspective* (Hart Publishing 2006) 53.

It has already been mentioned that a regulatory regime focusing on limiting campaign expenditure rather than campaign contributions is often considered more efficient than a system of the opposite orientation.[83] This should not be interpreted as a main reason for condemning the U.S. model in relation to other regimes, especially since, in an analogous way to the relationship between public and private funding, the relationship between restrictions on contributions and restrictions on expenditures should combine elements of both in order to achieve the optimal result. This is not the case with the U.S. system, even if that was so originally. As may be recalled from chapter 3, the 1974 amendment to the FECA, which was less of an amendment than a revision of a the law,[84] and still forms the core of the U.S. campaign finance regulatory regime, initially included extensive provisions for restricting expenses both by third parties and by the federal candidates, but the SCOTUS struck down these restrictions as unconstitutional in the *Buckley v. Valeo* decision.[85] Therefore, the weakness of U.S. campaign finance regulation lies not on a lack of emphasis placed on limitation of expenses, but rather on the absence of such limitations altogether (except in the case of presidential candidates having accepted public funding).

On the other hand, in the U.K. system there are no limits as to the amount of permissible contributions; restrictions relate only to the mandatory disclosure of the identity of permissible donors in conjunction with disclosure obligations. Even though this would appear to make the system a bit imbalanced, the matter was examined by the Committee on Standards in Public Life that decided against it;[86] in retrospect, this choice does not appear to have adversely affected the system's internal cohesion in a way that the ramifications of the *Buckley v. Valeo* decision have affected the integrity of the FECA.

7.3.5 GRECO: The Need for More Systematic Review

It has already been stated in Chapter 2 that GRECO's assessments are a most valuable tool in the present research. Although not part of the research question itself, its importance not only as a source of data but – perhaps more importantly – as a systematic approach to the study of political financing in a range of countries cannot be underrated; these assessments are indicative of issues of political corruption and the reaction to them by means of campaign finance regulations, as well as the perception of these issues by a competent supranational organization, and we have seen already when discussing legitimacy how the perception of corruption can in some cases be almost as importance as its substance. Previous Chapters examined GRECO's assessments of the

83 Supra n 28.
84 Mutch (n 6) 30.
85 See Chapter 3 n 33.
86 See Chapter 6 nn 33 and 34.

three campaign finance systems with regard to the transparency of party funding and with reference to the Recommendation of the Committee of Ministers to member states on common rules against corruption in the funding of political parties and electoral campaigns. GRECO's evaluations, as they are formally called, provided a concrete comparative systematic analysis of campaign finance regulation in the three jurisdictions in relation to ability to tackle corruption.

The problems examined in Chapter 6.6 should not diminish the noteworthy achievements of GRECO's in this field; to the contrary, such weaknesses can offer some valuable insight into the challenges of measuring the efficacy of regulatory attempts to combat corruption in political campaign finance, while upholding other constitutional principles of the respective frameworks. At the outset, a valuable lesson to be learned[87] is that much has to be done in the direction of the harmonization of assessment methods and criteria. Although, as stated in Chapter 2, it is fortunate that all three countries under examination are members of GRECO for the purposes of the present study, one has to wonder whether the inclusion of the U.S. is helpful to the systemic integrity of the GRECO system. The inclusion of a system that has so many differences with the other legal systems within the Council of Europe, as previously noted, may help increase inconsistencies, and thus undermine GRECO's credibility. Trying to integrate a state alien to the underlying foundation of GRECO, the Council of Europe, into its system might have an adverse impact on the Council's role as a regional mechanism. Perhaps GRECO has overreached itself and it should consider addressing the issue sooner than later.

All these underline the contemporary need of a global review of campaign fiancé regulatory regimes that would keep capitalize on the existing knowledge and through systematic review of different jurisdictions offer national regulators with the necessary tools to achieve campaign finance reform within the constitutional framework of their jurisdictions.

7.3.5.1 Towards a New Universal System

The solution to the problem of the harmonization of assessment methods and criteria might be the adoption of a more global approach to the various regulatory attempts to combat corruption in political campaign finance. What global scholarship and jurisprudence seem to be in need of is a truly universal system of reference, with the adequate theoretical and organizational background and the necessary resources to carry out its role on a truly global scale, yet with an agenda specific enough so as not to be sidetracked by regional interests or sovereign priorities. Perhaps such a mechanism could be established within the framework of the United Nations, although its funding

87 Besides the obvious one of the need of increased diligence by the GRECO Reports' authors as well as the governments of the states concerned.

then would be far from secure, while one would think that countries such as the U.S. would immediately acquire a dominant role for that very reason;[88] there appears not to be an easy or obvious solution. Nevertheless, circumstances have not been more mature for this global dialogue to – at least – commence.

7.3.6 *A Constant Need for Improvement*

As mentioned above, money seems to always manage to find its way into modern politics. This statement is both less and more than a truism. Less, because, despite the great amount of empirical data that support such a conclusion, there are still attempts to create the 'perfect' campaign finance regulatory system. More, because it should be a constant reminder that such a system should not remain static, but should constantly evolve and improve, at both the legislative and the enforcement levels. Considering the long history of campaign politics, the three regimes examined are rather young and immature. U.K.'s PPERA and Greece's Law 3023/2002 are hardly twenty years old, the first having replaced an antiquated and fragmented[89] legal framework, the latter being enacted shortly after two successive previous pieces of legislation.[90] FECA is more than twice that old, but despite its comparatively longer lifespan and the rich and long background of campaign finance regulation attempts in the U.S., it appears to be perhaps the less effective overall, measured against its objectives and reach. If these three different paradigms are to serve as a guide for what applies to campaign finance regulation globally in western-type democracies, it would appear that much remains to be done.

The need to tread softly on important aspects of the democratic process, such as the freedom of expression, is an important characteristic of campaign finance regulation. It is also the reason why it is utopian to believe we can achieve the complete isolation of politics from the influence of the purse of wealthy interest groups. Although not a strictly zero-sum game, the act of balancing the goals of campaign finance regulation with other freedoms means that heavy-handed regulatory measures are most probably going to affect adversely such freedoms, while granting these freedoms an absolute character, as is the case in the U.S. with freedom of expression, will seriously undermine any regulatory attempts. As the European Court of Human Rights has many times stressed when called to apply the standards of the ECHR in a particular case, states enjoy a margin of appreciation when called to strike a balance between

88 Amanda Shendruck, Laura Hillard and Diana Roy, 'Funding the United Nations: What Impact Do U.S. Contributions Have on UN agencies and Programs?', *Council on Foreign Relations* (New York, 24 April 2020) https://www.cfr.org/article/funding-united-nations-what-impact-do-us-contributions-have-un-agencies-and-programs last accessed 12 May 2020.

89 See Chapter 4 nn 1-2.

90 See Chapter 5 n 3.

conflicting rights.[91] The same could be said to apply when trying to establish a more universal standard for campaign finance regulation. Certainly, each state's approach to the problem is dependent on factors tailored to the constitutional priorities and realities surrounding that state.[92] But there are certain limits, which should not be exceeded, if we want the regulatory regime to be efficient. The obsession of the SCOTUS with the First Amendment and its complete rejection of the principle of equality go beyond those limits, regardless of whether the reasons behind this are political or strictly jurisprudential.

Attempting to simply copy the solutions successfully applied within a regime to largely similar problems within a different system has the risk of upsetting the existing balance of rights and freedoms and any corresponding national constitutional interpretations. It is therefore wise to carefully examine possible ramifications well in advance and seek to adapt them to local conditions as much as possible. The seminal work done by the Committee on Standards in Public Life, especially with respect to the integration of the findings of the European Court of Human Rights in the *Bowman* decision, as discussed in Chapter 4, is an excellent example. Although the Committee did not appear entirely convinced by the Court's reasoning,[93] it took the matter in hand, understanding the need to reach a compromise between the current - at that time - approach to independent expenses in the U.K. and the need to comply with the findings of the Court's decision;[94] it thus proceeded with proposing the finally adopted limit of £500.[95] This is one valuable lesson to be kept in mind. Generalizations about the nature and the causes of political corruption, as well as the methods to tackle political corruption, are one of the main drawbacks of tools such as the Corruption Perception Index of Transparency International, the questionable accuracy of which has already been pointed out in Chapter 2.[96]

What this study has shown is that the efficiency of the whole hinges on the smooth relationship and integrity of its parts. FECA's original scheme, as formulated in its 1974 Amendment, called for the limitation of both contributions and expenses; so much time has passed since the *Buckley v. Valeo* decision and the efficacy of the Act still appears compromised by the shattering of that scheme's integrity. Another lesson to be drawn:

---

91 See Chapter 4 n 61.

92 Here one could recall the issue of anonymous coupons and its historical sensitivity which, assuming it was brought to GRECO's attention, was completely ignored, see Chapter 5 n 186.

93 Committee on Standards in Public Life, *The Funding of Political Parties in the United Kingdom* (Cm 4057-I, 1998), 129, noting the risk: 'If one third party can come into a constituency and spend much more than £100, say up to £1,000, in seeking to secure the defeat of a candidate, then a second third party or a third or fourth could do likewise. Cumulatively they could spend a significant proportion of the candidate's own spending limit of around £8,000, and, as was argued, in *Bowman*, could force that candidate to devote part of his or her limited resources to rebutting the attacks made by the third parties.'

94 Ibid.

95 Ibid. 129.

96 See Chapter 2 nn 13-15.

the need for legislation capable to combat corruption, yet in line with the constitution and current jurisprudence.

The importance of close cooperation between all three branches of government is also fundamental; an ultimate balance is necessary. The legislature is of course responsible for laying down the legal framework, but as being the main subject of the regulation, it may often find itself facing an obvious conflict of interest. The executive is often involved in the appointment of the regulators and can be in a position to shift the legal framework by means of delegated legislation;[97] especially if the regulatory body does not have exclusive responsibility in this matter, while it is also responsible for law enforcement in general. The judiciary is responsible for judging serious infractions and overseeing the integration of campaign finance regulation within the wider legal system, while it may also participate in the composition of regulatory bodies (as is the case with the Greek Control Committee). The complex interactions between all three branches tend to complicate even further campaign finance regulation. These interactions can be hampered by conflicting interests, diverting points of view on important issues, or even simply by red tape. Therefore, there is plenty of room for improvement, in order to facilitate better cooperation between these branches to the advantage of the efficiency of campaign finance regulation in particular and of the rule of law in general. If one of the branches of government appears reluctant or deficient in carrying out its responsibilities within the system, it should fall to the other two to point out the problem and create the adequate pressure for a fast resolution of the deadlock.

Campaign finance as a field of regulation is complex in itself, without taking into account the intricacies of coordinating the activities of the various agencies and institutions drawn into it. The problem is that wealthy interests are not usually hindered by such limitations. They can, and often do, take advantage of anything that can let them slip into politics and bring their purse to bear. *Lacunae* of the legal framework, gaps at the enforcement level, ingenious manipulation of the laws and the judicial system are some of the methods used to siphon money into electoral campaigning legally, despite the intentions of regulators. The challenge of soft money in U.S. campaigning, already discussed in Chapter 3, comes immediately to mind as an example, even though one has to recall that it came as a result of FEC's own advisory opinions.[98] Furthermore, the reaction of wealthy interests to the dynamic evolution of the regulatory regime tends to be less constrained by institutional inertia. This edge just underscores the need for constant improvement in all areas.

Campaign finance regulation is, as already mentioned, still relatively immature. It should focus on keeping abreast corruption in election campaign finance and, to the

97 Also known as regulatory law in U.S. parlance.

98 Richard Briffault, Expenditure, 'Soft Money, Congress and the Supreme Court' in KD Ewing and Samuel Issacharoff (eds), *Party Funding and Campaign Financing in International Perspective* (Hart Publishing 2006) 192.

extent possible, closing the gap that usually exists between the time a financing practice becomes intolerable and the time it is actually banned. Studying the developments in a variety of democratic societies is a way to obtain insight into wider issues of campaign finance regulation. Drawing lessons of more universal applicability is not easy. The number of such lessons may be small, but that only increases their value. One can only hope that the present study has proved somehow helpful in this respect and may eventually facilitate a better understanding of campaign finance regulation not only in the three states examined, but also at a more universal context.

List of Cases

European Court of Human Rights

Bowman v. the United Kingdom ECHR 1998-I 175

Animal Defenders International v. the United Kingdom, ECHR 2013-II 203

Supreme Court of the United States

Austin, Michigan Secretary of State, et al. v. Michigan Chamber of Commerce, 494 U.S. 652 (1990)

Burwell, Secretary of Health and Human Services, et al. v. Hobby Lobby Stores, Inc., et al., 573 U.S. ___ (2014), docket no 13-354

Buckley, et al. v. Valeo, Secretary of the U.S. Senate, et al., 424 U.S. 1 (1976)

California Medical Association v. Federal Election Commission 453 U.S. 182 (1981)

Citizens Against Rent Control/Coalition for Fair Housing v. City of Berkeley, California, 454 U.S. 290 (1981)

Citizens United v. Federal Election Commission, 558 U.S. 310 (2010)

Colorado Republican Federal Campaign Committee v. Federal Election Commission, 518 U.S. 604 (1978)

Federal Election Commission v. Massachusetts Citizens for Life, Inc., 479 U.S. 238 (1986)

Federal Election Commission v. National Conservative Political Action Committee, 470 U.S. 496-497 (1985)

Federal Election Commission v. National Rifle Association Political Victory Fund, 513 U.S. 88 (1994)

Federal Election Commission v. Wisconsin Right to Life, Inc., 551 U.S. 449 (2007)

First National Bank of Boston, et al. v. Bellotti, Attorney General of Massachusetts, 435 U.S. 765 (1978)

McConnell, v. Federal Election Commission, 540 U.S. 93 (2003)

McCutcheon, et al. v. Federal Election Commission, 572 U.S. ___ (2014), docket no 12-536

Meyer, Colorado Secretary of State, et al. v. Grant, et al., 486 U.S. 414 (1988)

Newberry, et al., v. United States, 256 U.S. 232 (1921)

Randall, et al. v. Sorrell, Attorney General of Vermont, et al., 548 U.S. 230 (2006)

Santa Clara County v. Southern Pacific R. Company, 118 U.S. 394 (1886)

United States Courts of Appeal

Buckley, et al. v. Valeo, Secretary of the U.S. Senate, et al., 519 F.2d 821 (D.C. Cir. 1975)

Federal Election Commission v. Massachusetts Citizens for Life, Inc., 769 F.2d 13 (1st Cir. 1985)

Federal Election Commission v. National Rifle Association Political Victory Fund, 6 F.3d 821 (D.C. Cir. 1993)

Michigan Chamber of Commerce v. Austin, Michigan Secretary of State, et al., 856 F.2d 783 (6th Cir. 1988)

United States of America v. S. Steve Sourapas and Crest Beverage Company, 515 F.2d 295 (9th Cir. 1975)

Massachusetts Supreme Judicial Court

First National Bank of Boston, et al. v. Attorney General, et al., 359 N.E.2d 1262 (Mass. 1977)

House of Lords

Animal Defenders International, Regina (on the Application of) v. Secretary of State For Culture, Media and Sports [2008] UKHL 15

Court of Appeal (England and Wales)

Vote Leave Ltd v. The Electoral Commission [2019]

Central Criminal Court of England and Wales

Regina v. Tronoh Mines Ltd [1951] 1 All ER 697

Central London County Court – Mayor's and City of London

Darren Grimes v. The Electoral Commission [2019

Supreme Court of Canada

Harper v. Canada, 1 SCR 827, 2004 SCC 33

Federal Constitutional Court [Bundesverfassungsgericht]

85 BVerfGE 264

Council of State [Συμβούλιον της Επικρατείας]

Decision [Απόφαση] 518/2015

Data Protection Authority [Αρχή Προστασίας Προσωπικών Δεδομένων]

Advisory Opinion [Γνωμοδότηση] 1/2018

www.ingramcontent.com/pod-product-compliance
Ingram Content Group UK Ltd.
Pitfield, Milton Keynes, MK11 3LW, UK
UKHW051310180926
15262UKWH00005B/25